Pagan Channel Islands

Pagan Channel Islands

Europe's Hidden Heritage

S.V. Peddle

Robert Hale · London

Robert Hale Limited
Clerkenwell House
Clerkenwell Green
London EC1R 0HT

Printed in Singapore

Contents

Preface

This is not a guidebook to the stone monuments of the Channel Islands, nor is it a study of their archaeology. It is not even a book about contemporary paganism or Wicca on the Channel Islands.

It started out by trying to answer two simple, but very puzzling, questions: why were the ancient monuments built, and why are they known locally as *Pouquelayes* – a Norman–French word that means Puck stones or fairy stones? What possible link could there be between these solid and permanent lumps of rock, and the elusive fantasy world of fairies, pixies and mischievous sprites?

The answers to those questions have proved fascinating, and have linked the legacy and traditions of the Channel Islands with the world of fairy tales, legends, early religions and ancient earth rituals. Much of this wonderful heritage has been forgotten in recent centuries. But, as we show, it only requires a little imagination and respect for the landscape and ancient tradition to bring the monsters, fairies and ghosts of our legendary past to life, and allow us to relive the magical originals of all art and religion.

Welcome to the miraculous domain of the Channel Islands.

S.V. Peddle
October 2006

Illustrations

Line drawings

Credits

Sandra & Vince Peddle: 1–53.
Fig. 1–3: Jacquie Rutter.

Part I:
The Living Mystery of the Stones

1 The Neolithic Underworld

'If you look around Jersey you will see some very old and strange rocks sticking out of the ground.' This striking sentence, taken from a local educational website, vividly sums up the experience of discovering for the first time the numerous prehistoric remains which sit so naturally in the landscape of the Channel Islands.

Around 3,000–5,000 years ago, an ancient people covered the islands with these stone monuments. We do not know why they built them. We only know they must have gone to a lot of trouble to do so.

They left us basically two kinds: dolmens, stone chambers sometimes roofed and covered with a mound, and menhirs, single standing stones.

Of course, stone structures like these can be found all over the British Isles and Europe. But what makes the Channel Islands special is the huge number of monuments that were once concentrated on their small landmass. According to an account written in 1685, there were 'half a hundred' of them on Jersey alone. This makes the Channel Islands a microcosm of an ancient culture that once spread across the Western world.

Unfortunately, most of these monuments have since disappeared, and it is easy to see why. For a builder looking for scarce material, a standing stone is a free gift; too tempting not to dig out or blow up. To a farmer, it is an infuriating obstruction; many an ancient monument was probably smashed to pieces by an enraged farmer trying to plough a field. In fact, as recently as 1982, a serious attempt was made to destroy the greatest remaining menhir in Jersey, La Blanche Dame. The destruction was halted, but not before the ancient monument was left in a half-ruined state.

In addition to the economic pressures on these stones, there is the hostile attitude of the church. The Bible seems quite clear on the subject: you should 'make no idols or graven images; neither shall you set up any image of stone in your land'. The Council of Tours in 567 ordered priests to bar from their churches anyone who 'offered worship to stones set up on end'. Later the Protestant church, a strong influence on the Channel Islands, was especially determined to eradicate as much as it could of what it saw as the islands' pagan past. Many Christians would have destroyed these relics of pagan piety as a moral duty.

In view of this multiple attack, to say nothing of their great age, it is a miracle that any dolmens or menhirs have survived at all. The fact that so many are left is thanks to a few enlightened individuals, such as John De Havilland, who saved Guernsey's wonderful Dehus dolmen from being reduced to builder's rubble by buying up the land on which it stood.

However, it is possible that a number of dolmens and menhirs have survived because of something more mystical: the influence of folklore. Even a thousand years of Christianity has not completely erased the influence of Channel Island folklore, or what is sometimes known as 'popular superstition' or 'old wives' tales'.

Much Channel Islands folklore was collected and published in the nineteenth and twentieth centuries. It makes fascinating reading. For one thing, it contains many old stories warning of the evil consequences of destroying or even tampering with a dolmen or menhir. Penalties include horrible deaths from illness, murder, drowning, freak accidents and – on one occasion – a landslide.

The terrible fate of Guernsey's stone-breaking businessman, Mr Hocart, is typical. After he destroyed a large menhir on his property, his house burned down twice, then he lost two trading ships and their entire cargo at sea. Bankrupt, he sailed away from Guernsey in search of a new home, and was killed when part of the rigging of a ship crashed on his head. The message of the story is clear: don't tamper with menhirs.

Even in the twentieth century, it was still believed that the evil spirits of the underworld inhabited these monuments, and could do evil to those that desecrated them. This explains why many locals felt uneasy when L'Islet dolmen was uncovered in 1912, an unease that seemed justified when an unusual number of robberies, assaults and deaths took place in the vicinity. All of these misfortunes were attributed to a curse from the spirit of the underworld which had inhabited the dolmen and was angry at being disturbed.

Tales like these were given extra credence by the famous story in the 1920s of the curse of Tutankhamun. According to the newspapers of the time, everyone involved in opening the pharaoh's tomb suffered a hideous misfortune, such as financial ruin or sudden and untimely death. The most famous victim of the curse was Lord Carnarvon, a financial backer of the project, who died seven weeks after the opening. At the moment of his death, it was said, his dog howled and died, and the lights of Cairo all went out. Such stories were believed even by literate and educated people and seemed to express a deeply held abhorrence of interfering with such ancient sacred sites and the secrets they held, secrets that the modern world no longer understood but really ought to respect.

Of course the stories of Tutankhamun's curse were exaggerated by the press and have since been discredited. It is all too easy to dismiss folklore in the same way, as ignorant and misguided superstition to be laughed at or consigned to the outer fringes of Western culture. Yet stories like that of Mr Hocart were not made up by journalists. They are old legends, deeply rooted in our background, the cultural property of the people of the Channel Islands. Any 'superstitious' content preserves an inherited memory of a time when these dolmens were held in great awe and regarded as holy stones.

In fact, it could be argued that these old tales represent a link, however tenuous, with the society of the ancient builders themselves. This is not as unlikely as it sounds. It has been argued before that the folklore of the Channel Islands has survived better than anywhere else, mostly because of their small size. As one researcher in 1971 was informed, rather ominously, no person is unknown here, and no event is ever forgotten.

On the other hand, it might seem silly to say that these simple folk stories could possibly stretch back thousands of years to the time of the dolmens. Absurd it might appear, yet Channel Islands legends contain themes and images that can be found in mythologies across the world. There are unmistakeable parallels between many Channel Islands stories and ancient Greek, Egyptian, Norse and Middle Eastern mythology. Even more significantly, these same common themes can be traced back further to what we know of the earliest religions and rituals – including, as it happens, the religion of the dolmen builders themselves.

Like the ancient stones, Channel Island folklore is a microcosm of the great mythologies that once flourished in the West.

We are not alone making this link between folklore and ancient religion. The German anthropologist Cles Redon once said that memories of ancient belief and fertility rites once practised at ancestral tombs still survive in strange popular customs. The Guernsey archaeologist V.C. Collum made a similar point, suggesting that the tradition of the megalithic cult could be found in folklore and superstitious practices.

We know that the dolmen builders arrived on the island around 4,000 BC, settled for a while and then vanished, leaving some inscrutable but fascinating evidence behind them in the form of stone monuments and various scattered artefacts such as basic tools and pottery.

They were called the Neolithic or New Stone Age people, but they looked nothing like the stereotype of the hairy, primitive, woman-bashing Stone Age caveman. These 'New' Stone Age people did not live in caves, but in substantial, well-built settlements. They were successful farmers, and developed crops such as wheat, barley and beans. They were artistic and skilled with their hands; their craftwork included basketry, mat making, spinning and weaving. Their pottery was decorated, burnished and well fired. They made tools to high standards and practiced international trade. In short, the Neolithics were a civilized people.

A visit to a site like La Hougue Bie in Jersey makes this clear. La Hougue Bie is probably the biggest and most impressive single Neolithic structure in the whole of Western Europe. The people who could build a monument like this were not brutish, grunting, wild-haired cavemen. They were advanced enough to accomplish feats of engineering, calculation, teamwork and long term planning on an impressive scale.

But now an even bigger mystery emerges. Why did they go to all that trouble to build La Hougue Bie at all? What strange obsession drove them to make the extreme effort needed, with such basic tools, to carve the huge stones out of the living rock, and construct trolleys on wooden wheels and pulley systems to move them, and finally to co-operate as a community to transport these huge stones to the chosen building site?

The mystery deepens with our scanty knowledge of the Neolithics' physical appearance. It seems that they were not fair-skinned Anglo-Saxons or blond Celts. They are depicted as being rather small, with dark eyes and hair, aquiline features and a 'brunette' complexion, which suggests that they were not European at all. They may have originated from the East – or even as far away as Africa. One prominent Egyptologist directly linked the Neolithic dolmens to the pyramids of Egypt, tracing a line of monuments from North Africa to Crete, Spain and Portugal, and through to Brittany and the Channel Islands. (It is interesting that the famous Egyptian curse of Tutankhamun can be compared with similar curses from Channel Islands monuments.)

Sadly, modern carbon dating has placed a large question mark over assertions like these. There is, apparently, no clear chronological or demographic line between the Ancient Levant and Neolithic Europe. Yet the astonishing similarities between dolmens and Egyptian pyramids should not be dismissed out of hand. Both were built as burial chambers. In Brittany there are even two dolmens that appear to be rough pyramid structures: the Cairn du Barnenez, consists of two stepped pyramids, and the Gavrinis Cairn has been compared to an Egyptian pyramid in shape as well as size.

Like the pyramids of Egypt, the dolmens in the Channel Islands were more than simple graves. In fact, as one excavator has pointed out, the chamber mound of a dolmen is not really a grave at all. It is actually erected *over* the buried dead body, just like an Egyptian pyramid, and would have served a variety of sacred functions, perhaps connected to the dead person.

But this link with Ancient Egypt has another, perhaps more uncomfortable association. Ancient Egypt, with its tombs for dead kings and great dignitaries, is known to have been a necropolis, a land of the dead. It was a culture in which the dead were as important as the living and could be found everywhere, in architecture, art and ritual, and even the details of everyday life. If the dolmens of Brittany, Normandy and the Channel Islands are the western counterparts of Egyptian or Minoan tombs, it would argue that the Neolithics practised a similar death cult on these islands.

Despite our wonder at the achievements of the dolmen builders, we might feel some unease at the idea that they were motivated by a morbid obsession with death. It almost seems that life in Neolithic society was like living in a large cemetery.

Whatever the cultural link between the Channel Islands and Egypt, they had one important thing in common: they were farming communities. They shared a closeness to the land that fed them – a closeness that we have lost. Humanity's early link to the soil, a domain in which life and death are almost indistinguishable, might explain why, to take their minds away from the daily needs of survival, they took immense pains to build great permanent shrines, partly to appease and maybe also to defy, the inescapable presence of death. Whether they built dolmens or pyramids, the universal human need that created these monuments was the same, as we shall see.

The very first farmers were groundbreakers – literally and metaphorically. When human beings learned to till the earth for food, it was a huge breakthrough in human progress. Farming was the first 'civilized' act that distinguished us from animals, which can only hunt, scavenge or forage, merely taking what is already there.

Admittedly, when we humans were hunter-gatherers, we did more than merely kill and consume our prey. We turned its skins into clothing. We learned to make weapons from trees, and tools from stones. We learned to utilize, creatively, what was already there, rather than just eat it.

But when we started to cultivate the earth, we did something completely new. We began to *create* a food supply. We entered into a unique partnership with the earth, developed a personal relationship with the forces of nature and took a hand in our own destiny. As such, farming could be called a religious act.

To early farmers, the very earth was sacred. It was the universal provider – and sometimes the withholder – of the basic means of existence, the source of everything that lived and breathed. Even today, in our God-fearing tradition, we sometimes speak affectionately of 'Mother Earth'. Maternity is the origin of all human life, so it follows that the earth, the source of all life, would once have been regarded as the mother of all creation.

These early farming societies, living in direct contact with the giver of all life, revered this great earth mother. This is perhaps one of the most profound and important differences between the dolmen builders and the societies that succeeded them; they worshipped a female goddess, rather than a male god. As a result, the dolmens and menhirs that they built, their own versions of churches and statues if you like, would have expressed a feminine vision of the divine. This applies especially to the dolmens, which were rooted within the very fabric of Mother Earth.

To the Neolithic minds, the shape of the land, such as hills, valleys, or rivers, were parts of the body of the great earth mother. They were not prudish about this. For example, if they saw a natural rounded hill, they saw it as the earth mother's breast. If a river or spring ran near the hill, this represented the mother's nourishing milk. In fact, their dolmens expressed the most delicate, private female shapes of all. The opening of a dolmen symbolized nothing less than the vagina of the Great Goddess, leading to the inner chamber, which was her womb. More than one commentator has also compared the outer earth mound to the shape of a pregnant woman.

The dolmens, therefore, are feminine structures and express the femininity of the earth in a very intimate way. These early farmers, using only hands and simple tools, had a great deal of physical contact with Mother Earth, and the planting of the seed in her body would have seemed a very intrusive, even sexual act. The dolmen celebrated this close relationship. The inner chamber of the dolmen, the womb, was buried inside the earth itself, the domain of transformation, the origin of all growth; the place where the concealed seed grew into life-giving crops.

The miracle of the growing buried seed must have bewildered the very first farmers. What exactly was going on down in the ground after the seed was sown? Just what strange power existed in that dark region of mud and soil, which caused a tiny undistinguished seed to grow into flowering beauty and food? Even in today's scientific age we barely understand the miracle of growth. In Neolithic times, it would have been seen as a microcosm of the mystery of life and the universe itself. It also confirmed that the concealed, dark underground realm was the domain of the Great Goddess and contained the true source and mystery of her procreative omnipotence. The 'underworld', as it was later to be called, was originally the Goddess's sacred domain: the realm of feminine procreation, the primordial womb.

That is why, in mythic tradition, barrows or dolmens were magical places. They were doorways to the realm of the Goddess, a natural grotto representing an entrance to the underworld.[1] But there was another side to this magical place – a more frightening side. The underground realm was also, of course, a place of death; the site where dead bodies were buried and decayed. It was a domain of fear, of darkness and destruction, yet it was also the source of all life, as manifested in the germinating seed, the glory of spring and the wealth of a good harvest.

The dolmen mound was a place of death and rebirth, the womb from which the dead are reborn. It was sacred, regarded with fear and respect, and never approached without trepidation. To inhabit this mysterious, infernal region, the dim and cryptic domain of death, was a true mark of the goddess's immortality and divinity. Only the chosen few could enter her underworld.

The narrow, constricted entrance to the large public dolmens would have ensured that those entering the sacred domain did so stooping, in an attitude of respect. The modern visitor to La Hougue Bie is obliged to bend double at the low entrance channel, and to remain uncomfortably bending for quite a long way before reaching the central chamber, much as one would do today when approaching royalty. Indeed, it is probably safer, though no more comfortable, to crawl through this conduit on one's hands and knees. This long, effortful route is humbling and undignified, has all the hazards of a rite of passage, and is probably intended to represent the blindly claustrophobic struggle of being born (or reborn).

But it is worth it. Having reached the dark central chamber of the dolmen, one can stand upright and claim to have reached the underworld, the womb of the earth, the centre of the mystery of all growth, and an early symbol of our own hopes of rebirth after death. It is perhaps appropriate that the visitor should enter and leave this domain stooping in an attitude of humility, a word which comes from *humus* meaning earth, also implying a closeness to this chthonic realm of the goddess.

But the early farmers and dolmen builders did not have a perfect relationship with the earth and the Great Goddess. They could not grow crops all year round. They had to face the grim reality of wintertime, when the fertility of the land failed and nothing would grow at all. No matter how hard they worked, they could not prevent this annual loss of nature's bounty, the dead parts of the year which would refuse to yield any food. To them this was the dark side of the goddess. She could be generous and giving – but she could be harsh and cruel, inflicting freezing winters and barren land on her people. At times like these she was the death goddess, harbinger of misery and destruction, and the early farmers learned to fear her.

It is impossible to exaggerate the harsh reality of this loss of fertility to a people whose very existence depended on the produce of the earth, or to understand their desperation and even terror at the thought that the fruitfulness of the land might never return.

So the early farmers built dolmens, which celebrated the miracle of the sprouting seed and expressed their enduring hope that nature's productivity would never end. At the site of these dolmens, they paid their obeisance to the goddess in the form of elaborate ceremonies, in the hope that she would take pity on humanity, send favourable weather and release the earth's fertility in the New Year.

Note
1 Collum, p.38

2 The Cauldron of Birth and Death

In contrast to the roundly female dolmen, a menhir looks very male; an erect, phallic structure, perhaps a precursor of the vertical steeple or minaret. Despite this, it is common for single menhirs to be identified as female. In the Channel Islands a common name for menhirs, as well as other megalithic remains, seems to have been *dames* (ladies). The name also survives in names such as Notre Dame des Pas and La Rue à la Dame in Jersey, both of which, as L'Amy points out, had megalithic remains in the vicinity. We have already mentioned Jersey's largest surviving menhir: La Dame Blanche (Norman French for 'the white lady').

Les Dames Blanches, to give them their French title, are a familiar presence in the folklore of neighbouring Normandy. Here they are ghostly old ladies, wandering spirits of the night and definitely not nice to meet. They lurk near streams, bridges, and ravines, where they accost travellers and torment them, before finally tossing them into ditches. They linger outside homes, weeping and wailing whenever a family member is about to die, which makes them rather unwelcome visitors at any time. In this respect, they are similar to the Irish Banshees, female spirits who also linger around households, howling at the approach of death. Their counterpart is also the *Rusalka*, a water spirit of Slavic lore said to be the spirit of a dead female; and the Sirens of Greek mythology – *femmes fatales* all who either portend or actually lead men to their deaths.

The name *Blanche Dame* was also used for other standing stones in the St Clement's area of Jersey, an area where the wandering white lady herself was once frequently seen. The writer Victor Hugo experienced several sightings, including one on a hill (which might have been Mont

Ube) and another on his way home at midnight. He was actually woken up one night at 3 a.m. by a bell ringing, and saw what he described as phosphorescent trails on the bedroom wall. He says that he felt the presence of La Dame Blianche in his room.

The goddess of death, as we have already suggested, is the goddess of winter that cruel, cold time of year in which the fertility of the earth is dead and similar extinction threatens the early farming community.

But by far the most obviously feminine menhirs in the whole of the Channel Islands can be found in Guernsey. These are two ancient standing stones, both of them carved in the shape of an old woman. One of them, La Gran'mère du Castel or Câtel Gran'mère stands in the cemetery of the church of St Marie du Castro. The other has a row of curls on her head (or it might be a headdress) and displays bare breasts. She stands at the gate of St Martin's Church and her full title, La Gran'mère du Chimquière, means 'the grandmother of the cemetery', because that is where she used to stand.

The Gran'mère dolmen at St Martin's Church, Guernsey. A Neolithic crone fertility goddess. Even today she is crowned with flowers whenever a wedding is held in the church

The Gran'mère dolmen in the grave-yard at Castel Church, Guernsey. The shape of this Neolithic crone goddess looks very similar to the modern gravestone

The goddess of winter is nearly always personified as an old woman, or crone, because of winter's association with infertility, loss of beauty and the season's (or life's) end. The crone is the Old One who rules the time of winter. (In the Isle of Man, the Caillagh ny Groamagh, known as 'gloomy old woman', is a winter and storm spirit.) Perhaps it is no coincidence that these carved Guernsey menhirs, the old grandmothers, have long associations with church graveyards. This seems appropriate for a death goddess.

So *La Dame Blanche* represents cold, darkness and death. In the winter months she brings freezing cold, blizzards and ice. She acts as destroyer, bringing the frost that strikes down the tiniest signs of spring growth, kills the first shoots of plants and the early lambs. (In some Norse traditions and popular fairy tales, La Dame Blanche is also known as the Snow Queen.)

Of course, the goddess did not represent only winter and death. There was a spring goddess, portrayed as a young girl, and a summer goddess – usually the plump or pregnant mother. Often these three goddesses – maiden, mother and crone – were portrayed together as one, and known as the triple goddess. However, it is the old crone goddess that tends to feature in Channel Islands folklore.

La Dame is, of course, an appropriate Neolithic goddess, or goddess of the stones. A stone symbolizes static existence; the very opposite of spring's dynamic regeneration. The immobility of stone expresses the petrifying effect of frost, which whitens everything in sight and freezes all life and movement, bringing on the appearance of death. Much folklore makes mention of people 'turned to stone', presumably imprisoned by the forces of winter and waiting for the renewal and rebirth of spring.

In other ways too, a winter goddess is an appropriate deity for the Channel Islands. Despite our idyllic scenery and mild climate, we still endure the dark, cold and seemingly interminable winters of the northern hemisphere. Farming in this climate has never been easy. This could explain why our ancestors were obsessed with winter and why their surviving monuments mainly portray the goddess as harbinger of death and misfortune.

Channel Islands folklore is full of the presence of the Neolithic winter goddess. There are many recorded sightings of a mysterious white woman who can appear without warning on dark lanes and walks beside her victim. Although she is less malign than the Normandy Dame Blanche, it is apparently impossible to come too close or touch her; she is as fleeting as moonlight. One famous Blianche Dame in Trinity, Jersey, has been described as 'shimmering' and dressed in white. Because of her wintry presence, this particular lane is 'always cold'.

In Guernsey, a megalith called La Laöngue Rocque at Les Paysans, said to be in the shape of an old woman, is believed to come to life and wander around on moonlit nights. When the folklorist De Garis recorded this story, no one in Guernsey dared to visit the monument after dark for fear of confronting the white lady. A similar ghostly woman in Guernsey, carrying a distinctive lantern as bright as moonlight, has been described as 'zigzagging' down the road, a devious course rather like the wandering path of the moon.

Wintry weather, particularly snow, is also associated with an old woman in Guernsey folklore: the old lady up in the sky (*la Gran'mère*) who is shedding her rags. Hence the Guernesiais term for snowflakes, *des chiques* (meaning 'rags'). Children used to chant a rhyme when the snow fell: '*I' tcheir des chiques a bouan marchi, ma gran' mère a l'derrière perchi.* According to De Garis, this old lady was a pagan goddess who was responsible for cold weather.

Even the summer can be blighted by the sort of unseasonable weather that spoils a farmer's crops. The people of Guernsey used to have an interesting name for a destructive summer whirlwind: the Heroquiaze. It was named after Herod's wife, the much maligned mother of Salome who caused John the Baptist to be beheaded. Any sudden gusts of wind whirling round the harvest fields would cause the reapers to exclaim: *'Ch'est la fille d'Herode qui chaque ses cotillaons.'* (Herod's girl is shaking her petticoats.)

Because of her association with the gruesome story of John the Baptist's ritual beheading, Herodias is perhaps an appropriate figure for a death Goddess. (Strictly speaking it was her sexy daughter Salome who ordered John's ritual death, but the older Herodias is a more suitable crone figure.) She was known as the queen of the witches and would lead the dances at Catioroc and Rocquaine. For that reason it was considered unwise to dance at harvest time, for fear of rousing the death goddess into dancing with you. A dancing Herodias could raise a tempest that would not only spoil a harvest but also cause shipwrecks and disasters at sea.

Apart from the wintry weather of the *Gran'mère* in the sky and the Heroquiaze, the death goddess makes other appearances in Channel Islands folklore, often as a malign and frightening figure. Louise Lane-Clarke wrote in a tone of prim disapproval of Sark's lingering belief in the ancient goddess and her works, especially the 'simple people' who feared the midnight spells of many a withered crone. [1]

There is a grim story from Jersey about a 14-year-old boy called Edouard G, who deliberately insulted a woman, known paradoxically as 'the Black Lady', by calling out her name disrespectfully in the street. The woman, who had a reputation as a sorceress, answered the boy's insolence with this stark promise: 'It will be a fine day, my boy, before you eat bread.'

The dire prophecy came true. From that day, Edouard was unable to eat bread. He grew thin and sickly and lost all his strength and animal spirits. He continued like this for four years and only recovered when the Black Lady died.

This is a seasonal story. The Black Lady is the winter goddess, representing the end of the fertile season and the beginning of the dark months. The boy's sickness symbolizes the earth's infertility in wintertime, during which it loses its strength and 'animal spirits'. The bread which no longer nourishes the boy is the growing grain, the bread of life, the basis of all farming and cultivation. The four years that the boy lives under the curse correspond to the four months of winter, during which the grain cannot flourish. The 'fine day' that the lady predicts is, of course, the eventual return of spring and the return of fertility to the land. A very similar parallel story concerns a girl who quarrelled with a local woman believed to be a witch. Like the boy Edouard, this girl was condemned by the insulted sorceress to eat no bread and so, 'deprived of the staff of life', she faded away to a shadow.

Despite their happy endings, these cautionary tales are a reminder that the Great Goddess demands obeisance and respect in return for the bounty she offers us all. If she is slighted in any way, all prosperity and life will fail.

There are many similar stories warning of the consequences of not respecting the goddess, or failing to make offerings to her when she asks. Guernsey has produced a number of tales of a certain Marie Pipet, the 'matriarch of a family', who was an inveterate beggar and woe betide anyone who refused her alms.[2] Those foolish enough to deny her requests would suffer a variety of curses, including butter that would not churn, food that would not cook, corn that failed to grind and cows that refused to eat. All of these misfortunes symbolize the disaster of a bad harvest.

Fishing is a source of income as important on the Channel Islands as farming. Many folklore stories tell of fishermen's prosperity being ruined by the activity of an old woman or crone who has not been sufficiently respected. She could cause fishing lines to tangle up in seaweed, she could empty lobster pots, and cause shipwrecks by raising storms. To avoid such a fate, these stories advise, it is advisable to 'treat all old women with a marked respect.[3] The Jersey story of the Thirteenth Fish sets out a rather grim scenario: any fisherman who passes the witches' meeting place without paying tribute will have his boat dashed to pieces on the rocks, resulting in his death.

As we see from this and other stories, the Channel Islands goddess, the Dame Blianche, is given a very unpleasant name in many folk tales; she is described as a 'witch'. Certainly the old hag of fairy tale, a cackling harridan and worker of evil magic, is reminiscent of the crone of winter, the old woman whose dire powers are associated with evil and the blighting of good fortune.

In a book on the Channel Islands first published in 1904, Edith Carey suggests that witchcraft is a survival of the ancient worship of the goddess of the underworld and the festivals of seed time and harvest. L'Amy in his anthology of Jersey folklore had little doubt that it was on the old matriarchal rituals that the witch cult of the Channel Islands was based. Hickman, in his scholarly survey of Guernsey Neolithic tombs, also seemed fairly certain that witchcraft was a mixture of ancient customs and beliefs.

It has even been suggested by many folklorists that the origin of the witch's flying broom is a fertility dance in which branches or trunks of wood were thrown high in order to encourage the crops to grow. Perhaps the broom is an acknowledgement of the woman's domestic sphere. There used to be an expression in Guernsey: *en faire des mánches dé berousaïsses* ('to make broom handles out of someone'), meaning to tease someone. The musician Andrew Lawrence King suggests that this refers to an ancient fertility dance involving a broom handle. Another expression, *sautair pardéssus le ragot d'g'neis* ('to jump over the broom') meant to get married – another event with obvious fertility implications.

In 1968 folklorist Stephen Dewer came to Guernsey to research current witchcraft, and found a surprising amount of it still being practised, particularly in what he called the 'quieter' parts of the island, untouched by tourism. He had no doubt that it represented the survival of earlier customs and beliefs, driven underground by a new religion. He summed up witchcraft, quite lucidly, as the desire to impose misfortune on your neighbour. This, basically, seems to be the only legacy of the goddess that has come down to us; that of the vengeful winter goddess imposing sterility and death on the land, and misfortune to mankind.

But this might not have been how the Neolithics saw her. Although she represented winter – and of course the Neolithic farmers dreaded winter – she does not only represent age and decay; she is not always a sinister figure. She also stands for accumulated experience and wisdom. (The word 'witch' basically means 'wise one', related to the words 'wit' and 'wisdom'.) She is both destroyer and healer; the grandmother and the eternal womb of rebirth.

The two ancient carved menhirs in Guernsey – the stone grandmothers – give some idea how the crone goddess might have been seen by the Neolithics who created her. She is not a frightening or destructive figure. In fact the stone crone at St Martin's is still sometimes seen as a fertility goddess, even to this day. People leave offerings of flowers or fruit in the two cups hollowed into the stone at her feet, in the hope of good fortune. Brides put garlands around her neck to bring them prosperity in their new lives. Apparently there was once a local belief that if you knew how to perform certain rites at the correct time of the year, you could witness this stone lady moving, as if this frozen goddess would emerge into life with the melting of winter's frosts and the coming of spring.

In another Guernsey legend, said to date from the eighth century, the crone goddess is mentioned as a healer, able to raise the dead. In a story set in the lost forest of Vazon, a young girl suffers a serious head injury. Immediately the call goes out for the local crone to heal her: the woman's name is surprisingly similar to that of the Christian mother of Christ: 'Send for Marie!' the cry sprang from many mouths: 'Send for Marie, the wise woman!' [4]

We never meet Marie, but we know that she is an object of fear and even revulsion in the community, despite her powers. One of the characters in the story reflects on the woman Marie's squalid abode, 'where human skulls, skeletons, bones of birds and beasts, dried skins, and other ghastly objects had been so grouped as to add to the superstitious feeling inspired by the repulsive appearance of the crone herself.'

Clearly this woman's domain is associated with the world of the dead in all its aspects, human and animal. This is confirmed by another healing woman in the story, who makes this strange and ominous comment about the absent Marie: 'Marie said with her last breath,' she muttered to herself, 'that ere the oaks were green again the sweetest maidens in the island would be in her embrace.'

This again associates the local crone with the world of the dead – more specifically the death of the season, the winter time before 'the oaks are green again'.

The old crone Marie is also believed to be dead, so it is a younger healer Judith, a mother, who does the healing. She is aided in her work by her beautiful young daughter, Hilda. So here, in the story, we clearly have the maiden, mother and crone involved in the process of healing and rebirth: the triple goddess.

And there is a circular link between this triple goddess and the crone menhir that we mentioned earlier, which is still crowned during the spring festivals. In the Vazon story, the young maiden Hilda is crowned queen of the spring dance within the stone circle where the dancing takes place. (It is her rival for the crown that suffers an accidental – and symbolic – blow to the head.) When this accident happens, the young girl takes off her crown 'and placed it on one of the stones of the circle, by which she stood contemplating the scene'. The young girl stands next to the crowned stone, until she is asked to help in the gathering of healing herbs. Having found the herbs and passed them to her mother, she 'resumed her position by the stone'. Clearly the crowned stone and the young girl of the new spring are interchangeable.

We know that the ancient Greeks worshipped a young spring goddess called Kore. But even her story is closely associated with death; she is abducted while frolicking innocently in the fields, and dragged down to the underworld by Pluto (Greek god of the underworld). Her mother, Demeter, the goddess of the grain, lays the land waste in her grief and people begin to starve. Eventually, in order to save mankind, it is arranged that Kore should be returned from the dead, providing she has not eaten anything while there. Unfortunately Kore swallowed a few seeds of pomegranate and so she has to return there each autumn and be restored to her mother every spring.

It is possible that the title of Kore is still used today in Brittany and the British Isles, where the root word *ker* appears in the names of Neolithic sites such as Kar as in Karnac or Carnac, and nearby Kermario, Kerlescan, Kercado, and so on. In the British Isles the name is linked to ancient sites including Cornwall (called Kernow in Cornish), Cardiff, Carlisle, Caernarfon, Caermarthen and many others.

Many commentators suggest that the 'ker/car' in these names means 'stone' or 'rock', an appropriate Neolithic title. But our Vazon story makes a clear connection between the young girl and the stone, so perhaps ker/car is linked with Kore after all. It is also possible that she appears, in older guise, in another of the Channel Islands' folk traditions.

Vazon is the site of an even more famous story from folklore. According to the legend, a ghostly sow and her piglets have been seen haunting the sands there at the full moon, searching the beach for acorns. A large forest once stood at this coastal site, before it was submerged by a tidal wave in 709.

This is not the only sow in Guernsey folklore. There have been other mysterious sightings of sows and piglets across Guernsey. According to the BBC Guernsey website, they would actually enter people's homes. 'They are said to have walked in through the front door and out the back door of a house if alms to the poor hadn't been paid as they should. As soon as the alms were paid, the visits by the pigs stopped.' This behaviour sounds very similar to that of the Black Lady or Marie Pipet and her sometimes persistent, begging visits. Again, it seems, dire consequences will follow if you do not offer the Goddess her due respect.

It may seem disrespectful to compare the Great Goddess to a sow. Unlikely as it may seem, however, the sow is a common goddess figure. She is known as Keridwen, the Great White Sow, which is an almost universal symbol of the Great Mother. Keridwen has the same root *ker* meaning 'Kore' or 'stone', but like the Dame Blianche, Keridwen is the goddess of winter. She has power over rain, fog and mist, and silver is her colour – the colour of the moon.

To us, the sow's corpulence is a source of mild disgust or perhaps amusement. But to a farmer a fat sow represents prosperity, the condition of being well fed. Her ample body is a living expression of the benefits of Mother Earth's munificence. As well as her great appetite, the sow is also noted to be a creature of great fecundity and productivity. She can give birth to a large litter of offspring and suckle them through her large, many-teated breast. The sight of piglets suckling at the sow is an oddly comforting sight and a primeval archetype of universal motherhood. It follows that the ample sow has an equally plentiful womb, which could explain why, in many images of the goddess, Keridwen is traditionally shown stirring a large cauldron.

The witches' cauldron is a traditional source of fear and disgust. All sorts of vile, disgusting ingredients are thrown into it. The image of a witch cackling over a smoking pot is familiar from the three witches in Shakespeare's *Macbeth*, who fill their cauldron with all sorts of unspeakable objects:

> Eye of newt and toe of frog
> Wool of bat and tongue of dog.

Yet the cauldron was not always an object of revulsion. It once represented the womb of the Great Goddess, from which all things are born and reborn again and, by extension, it expressed the bounty of the earth. Keridwen's cauldron is an ancient feminine symbol of renewal, rebirth, transformation and inexhaustible plenty. In ancient myth and legend, the crone is often seen with her great black cauldron stirring up brews for magical transformation or bringing the dead back to life.

The Neolithics built the witch, Keridwen, or the crone, into their landscape. This is the dolmen, with its vaginal entrance to the huge womb, the vast cauldron, which represented death as well as rebirth. This domain of the great earth mother, as old as the earth itself, was the cauldron or womb we would all pass through, and from which we would eventually attain immortality.

As we have said, the goddess did not give of her bounty unconditionally. She demanded respect. She was offended if she was ignored and the consequences of that could be catastrophic. It was essential to thank her for her bounty and it was even more essential to make it clear that you wanted this bounty to continue. That is why, as we have said, the Neolithic people performed regular seasonal rituals, or little dramas, to appease the goddess and ensure the return of the spring.

These rituals were not empty observances or unintelligible mumbo-jumbo. It was genuinely believed, in early societies, that any action carried out by human beings would be copied in nature. They worked closely with nature and the goddess, and were convinced that this was true. So, if a group or clan enacted something that they wanted to happen, such as a warm spring or a good harvest, then it would happen in reality.

This is called homeopathic or imitative magic – the idea that you can make things occur simply by acting them out. For example, farmers might throw tree branches in the air to encourage the crops to grow tall, light fires to rekindle the sun, or perform elaborate 'falling' dances to evoke wind or rain. By the same token, you had to be careful *not* to perform certain acts at the wrong time in case they brought about an undesired outcome. In Guernsey, as we have said, it was considered unwise to dance at harvest time, because that would start up strong winds, the curse of Herodias. For the same reason, Channel Islands fishermen never whistled in a boat on a windy day. On the other hand, if a boat became stranded or becalmed, a soft whistle would result in favourable winds.

There are many other superstitions and traditions in Channel Islands folklore that can be traced back to the ancient fertility rituals that the Neolithic farmers performed to ensure a prosperous year. Many of them still centre on the same ancient megalithic sites. For example, there is a small boulder in a field named La Houmière in Guernsey, known as the Guernsey weather stone. It is believed to bring on the rain if disturbed, an event most unwelcome at haymaking time. In another ritual, according to Lempriere, all the newly cut hay in the neighbourhood had to be paraded in the presence of this stone, to prevent bad weather spoiling the uncut crop. Clearly this is a survival of an ancient rite to appease the Blanche Dame, and ensure the continued fertility of the crop. This menhir is also called a *pierre sainte*, a Christianized menhir, because of the cross-shaped fissures that have been carved on its face, presumably to make this example of surviving menhir lore acceptable to the church.

Another modern fertility custom is associated with an ancient well called the Fontaine du Rouge Pré, in Vale in Guernsey. Before any water could be taken from this well, 'a canful had to be emptied at the foot of a whitethorn [hawthorn] bush'. If the grass around this thorn bush was cut, parched or damaged in any way, a storm of wind and rain would immediately follow, no matter how fine the weather had been.[5] To avoid the sort of weather that could endanger crops and ruin a good harvest, a little imitative magic was required, hence this little offering of water to keep the grass flourishing.

In a strange custom in Jersey, gardeners thought it beneficial to sow seeds to an accompaniment of oaths and curses. These expletives, offensive to modern ears, might have been a survival of sacred incantations or spells to the goddess, probably prayers for a favourable harvest.

In Guernsey, if a person particularly wanted the weather to be fine on a certain day, he or she would say: I' *faudra mognaiar ses p'tits bouas'*. ('We will have to manipulate the little sticks.') This referred to a secret ritual in which sticks were thrown into the air to land in a certain pattern on the ground. Marie De Gras says that the full ritual of the sticks is now probably lost and that no one will even admit to remembering it. However, she mentions an eighteenth-century sorcerer who was imprisoned for practising a very similar ritual. Clearly this prophetic ritual, similar to rune casting, evoked strong official disapproval. [6]

In fact, this rite sounds very similar to the ancient Greek practice of casting stones to ensure a good harvest. In Troezen, Greece, there was a 'curious festival of stone throwing' in honour of the fertility goddess, and according to Frazer, this was a common way of ensuring good crops across the world. It certainly sounds similar to Guernsey stick-throwing and its causal relationship to favourable weather. It is not easy to work out exactly what the action meant. Perhaps it imitated the falling of seasonable rain, or the act of scattering the seed.

All of these simple, harmless-sounding ceremonies actually represent the earliest stirrings of the magic arts. The basic idea behind a lot of magic is the Neolithic idea of imitation: that you can make any event happen in nature simply by impersonating it, or performing a series of actions that expresses it. Subsequent religions, especially Christianity, have tended to denounce magic as an evil art.

However, many of the more innocent, party-like customs in the Channel Islands also seem to have a fertility background to them. In a spring ceremony very similar to the modern 'trick or treat', it used to be the custom for children in Guernsey to go from house to house in search of tips, chanting: *'Oguinani, oguinani,* open thy purse and shut it again.' The meaning of that obscure greeting, *oguinani*, becomes clearer when compared to a Brittany chant, similarly used by children, which opens with the chorus: *'Oghin an eit, oghin an eit!'* (the wheat is springing up, the wheat is springing up.)

Notes
1 *Channel Islands Anthology*, pp. 54–5.
2 De Garis, pp. 266–7.
3 Wolley, pp. 7–8.
4 These quotes are taken from *The Project Gutenberg* eBook of *The Forest of Vazon*.
5 L'Army, p. 103.
6 *Folklore of Guernsey*, p. 94.

3 The Moon and the Magic of Time

The seasonal rituals performed by the Neolithic farmers, some of which have survived as popular superstition, may seem like primitive nonsense to many of us. However, they had an eminently practical outcome. Marking each season with a ritual became a means of measuring time.

Learning to measure time was essential for the long-term survival of our species. The early farmers could not avoid the winter, but if they knew when it was coming and – just as importantly – how long it would last, they had a better chance of surviving it. The dolmens and menhirs assisted the farmers in their attempt to measure time, which makes them an early form of clock or calendar.

But one thing seems rather puzzling: we can be sure that the Neolithics could not count in the way that we understand today. Even the Romans' counting system was slipshod and clumsy in the extreme. It is hard to understand how the Neolithic stone calendars actually worked if they were unable to count and measure hours or days.

It seems very likely that the earliest method of measuring time originated from observing the motions of the moon, which was an object of wonder and fascination to early humanity. It is the heavenly body closest to the earth. It is less remote and anonymous than the stars and not as ferocious as the sun; it is both easily recognizable and comprehensible. More importantly, the moon is an interesting object; it keeps changing its shape. It grows from a slender new moon into a well-rounded full moon, then wanes away into another crescent shape, and then disappears, before being born again as the new moon.

The waxing and waning of the moon would have seemed like a model of human destiny. Like the moon, we all grew from weak babyhood to full adult strength, and, like the moon, decline and inevitably die. The moon, however, did not die forever; after a brief death she was always reborn in the form of a new moon. Such clear evidence of immortality, the certainty that rebirth always followed after death, could have been the origin of humanity's hopes of personal resurrection.

It did not take people long to realize that the moon's shape changed with predictable regularity. It never failed to grow, reach maturity, fade, die and be reborn. It is these fixed cycles of the moon that gave early humanity the first model of measuring time beyond the basic span of a single day and night; indeed the word *mensua*, meaning 'measurement', comes from *mensis*, meaning 'moon'.

When it became clear that each moon cycle lasted as long as the reproductive cycle of the woman (hence menstrual cycle, from the same root again as *mensis*), the immortal moon was personified, just like the all-nurturing Mother Earth, as a divine woman: the Great Goddess. Names were given to her phases of growth and decline. The new crescent moon was called the maiden, the full moon the pregnant mother, and the declining moon was the old woman or crone. She was three in one – maiden, mother and crone – and was known as the triple goddess.

Using the moon to measure time was not a straightforward task. There was more to it than just observing her phases of waxing and waning. It was necessary to track her elaborate, meandering movements across and around the sky, and this would have been quite a challenge. The moon is a wanderer, fickle and inconstant, as Shakespeare was later to say; there seems to be no pattern or reason to her movements. Yet there is evidence in the surviving alignments of recumbent and standing stones across Europe that Neolithic people were well able to keep track of the wandering moon in the farthest limits of her movements over long periods of time.

This might have been one of the functions of the menhirs: tracking the motions of the moon. The white stones of the Channel Islands would have expressed the moon's radiance and followed her meandering inconstant movements; a roving which seems uncannily similar to the elusive and misleading motions of the night-time figures of the Blianches Dames themselves.

There is plenty of evidence that early agriculture was dictated by the cycles of the moon, which was believed to influence the growth of crops. As the moon grew and died, so did everything else living. So any planting was done during a waxing moon, while harvesting or tree felling should only be done when the moon was on the wane. Significantly, the earliest existing calendar, or agricultural manual, from 800 BC, is lunar based, and advises farmers to regulate their activities by the phases of the moon.

There is plenty of evidence that the megaliths across Europe were originally built as moon observatories. In 1974 the archaeologist Alexander Thom suggested that Stonehenge was originally an observatory for studying the movements of the moon. In fact, the ancient stone circle in the Orkneys is still known as the 'Temple of the Moon' and the vast stone alignments of Carnac in Brittany have been identified as a lunar observatory. Gavrinis, also in Brittany, is aligned to the sun at the winter solstice, but the main orientation of the passage is towards an extreme position of the rising moon.

Although the entrance to Jersey's La Hougue Bie is set towards the rising equinoctial sun, as every visitor to the site is told, the whole structure is built to the same orientation as another Jersey dolmen: the Neolithic tomb at Faldouet set some 19 degrees south of east. The reason for this alignment is clear to anyone who climbs the big capstone at the time of the September full moon. The moon can be seen rising from the sea below, directly in line with the opening passage of the grave.

Among surviving moon megaliths in Scotland, the function of the recumbent stone altar south-west of the monument was to observe the course of the moon. This is the part of La Hougue Bie, opposite the location of the sunrise, which corresponds with the inner area, the womb within a womb, the exclusive *sanctum sanctorum*, or holy of holies, of the structure. Although no longer used as a direct observatory of her movements, perhaps this dark area, this realm of death, was still dedicated to the moon.

For the Neolithics, time measurement, guided by the moon, would have been a magic art, as sacred as the seasonal rituals, as miraculous as the growing crops. Predicting the seasons, as we have said, is a way of controlling them; of assuming goddess-like power to prevent misfortune. The guidance of the moon, telling farmers when to plant certain crops in order to realize maximum yield, was another way of keeping winter at bay.

These select few who became proficient at the tricky task of tracking the moon's wandering path would have been sages, in charge of a deep and important mystery. Farmers would have consulted these wise people who, from years of observing the moon's course, could answer such questions as: 'How soon will winter come?' or 'When should I sow this particular crop?' The ability to predict coming misfortune (winter) or its opposite (spring) would ultimately develop into the wider-ranging magical arts of divination and prophecy, perhaps as seen in the ceremony of the sticks.

We may never know to what extent the Channel Islands dolmens were centres of prophecy, like the oracular temples of ancient Greece. However, it is appropriate that those ancient stones of the Channel Islands, so instrumental in tracking and influencing the fortunes of the community, should eventually have been given the title Fata or 'Fate'. The notion of fate is central to all divination and fortune telling and it is interesting to think that the practice may have begun among these Neolithic white stones.

> One kind of these the Italians Fata name;
> The French call Fèe; we Sybils, and the same
> Others White Dames. [1]

The moon continued to be a divine presence in Channel Islands culture until after the Second World War.

The writer Sidney Bisson, while researching a book about Jersey in the 1950s, spoke to a local farmer and discovered, to his astonishment, that the moon's divine status had hardly changed since the time of the Neolithics. According to this man, farmers still believed that crops grew better at the time of a waxing moon, and root crops flourished only when the moon was on the wane. Certain other crops were only sown at a full moon, and this was also the regarded as the best time to slaughter pigs. Later, the folklorist De Garis discovered similar beliefs thriving in Guernsey in the 1970s. To many Guernsey farmers, all seeds had to be sown during a waxing moon, and any cutting or harvesting was undertaken when the moon was waning.

It was also believed that the moon could affect the weather. Whenever the new moon fell on a Saturday, bad weather was sure to follow. If the weather changed at the time of a new or full moon, then that change, whether it was good or bad, would last for a fortnight. There can be little doubt that these traditions were based on the ancient belief that the moon directly influenced the wealth and fertility of the earth.

Indeed, veneration for this 'fair lady' (as the moon was called in

Guernsey) and her effect on growth and decay seemed to extend into most other areas of society. According to De Garis, all children in Guernsey were taught to venerate the full moon. Girls were required to curtsy to it and boys had to bow to it three times. Did this three-times homage once express the presence of the triple goddess? In households across the island, great care was taken to cut a child's hair on a waxing moon and nails on a waning moon; a practice that the child was expected to continue into later life, and pass on to his or her children.

At the time of the new moon, adults would often perform private rituals in order to ensure good fortune. For example, it was regarded as bad luck to look at a new moon through a window or through trees (a belief that can be traced back to the ancient matriarchy of Minoan Crete). Instead, you should always look at it over your right shoulder and tap your pocket with your hand. This would ensure that you had plenty of money for the duration of what was called the moon's reign. Clearly the all-giving moon still had a regal title in Guernsey until very recently.

In all these strange old sayings and practices, perhaps, we hear the distant echo of the sages of the Neolithic dolmens, pronouncing their wisdom and offering advice, as they measured the moon's progress from their barrows and henges, which were circular in shape like the moon and were centres of her mystery: the domain of the moon goddess on earth.

Because the moon was often seen reflected on calm seas or inland lakes, these were believed to be the earth-based dominion of the moon goddess, a belief confirmed by the fact that the motion of the moon had a regular, seasonal effect on the tides. Water nourished and fertilized the earth, enabling it to produce food and sustain human life; it was a key element in the goddess's procreative powers. Gradually water, in the form of sea, lakes, rivers and especially wells, was seen as a divine element in itself.

According to some historians, the most ancient wells were originally constructed, not only to provide a source of water, but as a means of bringing the moon down to the earth, in the form of its reflection, and assisting with astronomical observations and measuring time. They would have had a similar status to menhirs, and this accounts for why they are still called holy wells. The old saying 'Truth lies at the bottom of the well' has probably come down to us from those ancient times.

We have already mentioned the importance of a well in Guernsey, the Fontaine du Rouge Pré, which could help guarantee favourable weather and good crops. Until recently Sark's wells were its main source of fresh water, and therefore its sole means of survival. One local writer called them 'the water of life' and added that 'the well holds the very spirit of poetry'. [2]

They were used until recently as sources of divination. There was a well in Guernsey that was used as a means for women to discover the identity of the man they were to marry. If a girl peered down the well of the St George estate on nine consecutive mornings at dawn she would see the face of her future husband gazing up at her on the ninth morning. What is astonishing is that the local priest would take this testimony seriously and apparently many a young man was forced into a reluctant marriage on the testimony of the well, which it was thought was ruled by St George himself.

Linked to the worship of the Great Goddess of the moon is a reverence for the cow. The cow is a source of liquid nourishment believed to have unique life-giving properties. Milk is the first food given by a mother to a newborn child, so the cow, as dispenser of this maternal nourishment, was a figurehead for the mother goddess, especially as milk is coloured white, like the moon.

The cow has always been a universal symbol of the Great Mother among agricultural peoples. To the ancient pastoralists, this most motherly of animals, with her abundant white nourishment – an analogy of mother's milk – was the moon goddess's creature on earth. Her horns were the same shape as the crescent moon, a shape which inspired the mythical cornucopia, symbol of nature's plenty. (In Greek mythology, the cornucopia is a horn which refills perpetually with food and drink. It symbolizes prosperity and the wealth of the earth.)

Some of the most famous goddesses in mythology are cows. The Greek Goddess Hera's names include white-armed Hera, a title of the moon goddess, and, more significantly, cow-eyed Hera. The Egyptian goddess Hathor embodied the source of maternal bounty and she was known as a cow goddess.

The cow is also a central figure in Channel Islands farming communities. Its uniquely rich milk has long been a source of wealth to the islanders, especially on Jersey, where the cow has achieved almost sacred status. It is protected by law; no gene input may interfere with the purity of the Jersey cow. It is not only in Hindu tradition that the cow is regarded as holy.

Many legends in Jersey feature the cow; a good example is the story of the Sick Cows. A farmer who could not afford the loss of any of his cattle had three sick cows. They were the best of his herd, and in spite of all his efforts, they gradually became worse.

In desperation, he consulted a white wizard who lived in the neighbourhood, and was given the following instructions: 'Kneel down in front of your cows on three successive evenings and make use of this incantation. On the morning of the fourth day, the cows will be cured.'

What the incantation was is not recorded, but the farmer followed the wizard's instructions, and when he entered the stable on the fourth morning he found that the cows had completely recovered from their ailment.

Significant again in this vanished rite is the number three, (as in the three sick cows and the three nights the farmer performed his rituals). Like the act of bowing three times to the moon, this sacred number would have been essential to any ancient rituals invoking the fertilizing power of the triple goddess of the moon. In this case, it restored the fertility to his cows.

According to Joan Stevens, the Jersey cow probably originated in or near Mesopotamia thousands of years before Christ, when domestication of the cow first began. The Jersey is thought to be descended from the old horned auroch and its cultivation as a source of food marked the beginning of more settled farming, as opposed to the old hunter-gatherer nomadic way of life. Neolithic man, with his cattle, could well have reached Jersey via the Mediterranean, which suggests that the Jersey cow has the same origin as the cow of ancient myth, the Greek Hera and Egyptian Hathor.

It is appropriate that the modern Jersey cow, a beautiful and oddly feminine creature, world-class cream producer and vital source of prosperity, should symbolize the island of Jersey today, especially as it is, in Joan Stevens' words, the most ultra-feminine of creatures.

Notes
1 *Hicrarchie, viii*, p. 507 in *Brewer's Dictionary of Phrase & Fable*.
2 Clark, L., p. 49.

4 Blood Rites

There is a darker side to the history of our ancient monuments. The nineteenth-century writer J. Stead could hardly contain his disgust and horror when he visited the dolmen at Jersey's La Coupe. He regarded the monument as a relic of barbarity. It was, he claimed, a warning to mankind of the 'cruel orgies that were therein celebrated: the blood … offered as a libation'. He had no doubt that all the island's dolmens were once used for human sacrifice and expressed this view with gruesome frankness: *'Here man poured out the life stream of his fellow, a solemn act of devotion.'*[1]

Stead was not alone in his belief. The writer, Blanche B. Elliot, visiting Jersey's Le Couperon, commented on the wildness of the scenery around the lonely dolmen and found herself responding to what she called a curious mystery which still clung to the island: a mysticism that was not friendly but 'wild and cruel' and reminiscent of a barbaric past.[2] For years, the dolmens or *pouquelayes* were regarded as Druids' altars; the word 'altar' alone implies an association with human sacrifice. Samuel Bonamy, Bailiff of Guernsey, wrote a guide to the island in 1749, describing the megaliths as pagan altars, places where, he suggested, the ancient inhabitants used to offer sacrifices to the god of the sea. Daniel Defoe described Jersey's ancient stones as 'the altars on which sacrifices, often human, were immolated'.[3] Another nineteenth-century visitor called them 'foul altars, which formerly ran with blood'. To many Jersey people, the so-called Tables des Marthes, a large slab of red granite near Corbière, was long regarded as a sacrificial altar. Even the name was thought to mean (incorrectly as it turned out) 'table of the martyrs'.

The unpleasant idea that the Channel Islands dolmens might have been sites of slaughter partly explains why an entire Jersey dolmen was

Jersey's La Coupe or Couperon dolmen. Stead called it a warning of past 'cruel orgies'

A Christianized menhir at St Michael's Church *above left* and St Saviour's Church *above right*, both on Guernsey. A similar Christianized menhir, known as the Guernsey weather stone, was until recently the centre of Neolithic fertility rituals

dismantled and shipped off to Henley-on-Thames in 1788 as a gift to a departing general. A poem commissioned by the Vingtaine to mark the removal of the fine Mont de Ville Pouquelaye on Fort Regent justifies this vandalism:

> This Dolmen with stone and altar lays
> Where, as sacrifice, did human blood,
> For Caprice's gods, run as a flood.[4]

To establish whether these claims are justified, we need to look more closely at the builders' deep sense of closeness to the earth, a closeness so profound that they personified the earth as mother, the all-giving, all-nurturing Great Goddess. This earth, their deity, was the source of all their food, but as we have already said, she did not feed them all year round. Every winter she failed them. At this terrible time the earth changed from a nurturing mother into a callous, even murderous, 'dark' goddess, capable of letting her worshippers starve to death. People

43

would perform elaborate and desperate rituals to mitigate winter's curse, in an attempt to regain the goddess's good will. One of them would have been the sympathetic re-enactment, in some form or other, of nature's death. Hardly surprisingly in a matriarchal culture, they were imitating – and probably carrying out – the death of a man.

This was not an act of mindless violence. It was not a case of powerful women murdering helpless men for fun. Men were important in Neolithic society. Even a culture that worships a goddess still needs men to make babies. Without a man's fertilizing capacity, no woman can give birth, and no community, however flourishing and prosperous, can survive. The early farmers certainly knew this, and would have applied this human function to the world around them. They assumed that the great earth mother herself – and consequently the land – needed a husband or male consort to become fertile.

Although a man is necessary for fertilizing the woman, he is not a divine creature. His role in childbirth is brief. He does not feed and carry the child inside his own body for months, nor does he suffer in bringing it into the world. Woman, and woman alone, is the true procreator of life. Men are mere mortals, creatures of a day, and that means they cannot escape death.

Similarly, the goddess's consort was mortal and he too died. In fact, it was the consort's death that caused the failure of the earth's fertility every year. Every time the consort died, the goddess grieved for him, abandoning the earth, and consequently all life departed from the land and it was laid waste. This was the reason for winter.

But how could the farmers ever think that committing a ritual murder would help bring winter to an end? The answer is that the killing was another imitative act, inspired again by the moon.

To early humanity, the moon was the embodiment of eternal life. Her decline and death, followed by her unfailing rebirth, demonstrated that death was not the end of life, but an inseparable part of the ongoing, eternal process of life. Humankind wanted to incorporate this unity and immortality into their own lives. Under the aegis of the moon, and perhaps under her gentle light, they would re-enact a human death to imitate the 'death' of the earth's fertility. In this act of sympathetic magic, they believed they were guaranteeing the resurrection of nature and the return of fertility to the land.

Of course, an act of ritual bloodshed is deeply offensive to us and we might wonder how such an apparently civilized people as the

Neolithics could bring themselves to perform such a brutal act. But we must remember that life was harsh for them; their goddess could be cruel and destructive. Perhaps the intense privations they suffered every year forced them to commit extreme acts.

Besides, from a Neolithic viewpoint, farming was full of deeds of violence, sometimes of the most hideous sort. To them, the earth was the Great Goddess incarnate. To plough the land was to wound her body and the cutting and grinding of the wheat in harvest was an act of cruel desecration of her works. The offering of a mere human being would have been a small act of atonement for the defilement of the person of the divine Great Goddess herself.

As well as this, blood-letting was a reality for every woman at the end of her body's 'month'. A woman's personal 'death' period of menstruation, when her body's fertility drained away in a libation of blood, meant that the spilling of gore was a disagreeable but natural part of the cycle of creation. It was perfectly right and proper to imitate it in their rituals.

So these dolmens, which tracked the movements of the moon on earth and marked the cycles of a woman's blood, might also have functioned as tombs and memorials to the sacrificed consort.

Perhaps this is the reason why the tombs are not stuffed with human remains like a modern graveyard; the consort's body would not have been interred there permanently, but regularly replaced. The dolmen was the place where the consort was buried, and the place from where the new consort emerged. The hollow chamber was both tomb and womb.

Maybe this explains why some surviving burials, such as that at Mont Grantez in Jersey, show bodies lying in crouched positions, which Hawkes describes as common Neolithic practice. This was not a space-saving device. The crouched posture of the corpse would have represented the foetal position, expressing the hope of rebirth after death. Clearly those buried bones were expected to walk again.

However, as if to contradict that, there are disturbing signs that bodies in some of the Channel Islands dolmens were deliberately mutilated after death. In some burials, the victim's feet and hands have been severed, loose bones distributed amongst the burial chambers, and skulls and finger bones have been sorted into almost random piles. In Jersey a group of standing stones in St Ouen's bay has been called the Ossuary from the mass of jumbled and crushed human remains found there, representing at least twenty individuals. Once it was thought that

The Ossuary in St Ouen's Bay, Jersey. A mass of jumbled and cleaned human bones was found there, similar to those discovered in early Egyptian tombs

the grave had been vandalized by robbers; now it is believed that this was more or less the state in which the Neolithics themselves left it. The condition of the bones suggests that they had undergone excarnation, which means they were cleaned of all flesh, usually by prolonged exposure to the air, or being offered to predators, before they were buried. A recent discovery of cleaned bones at a Neolithic site in Stoney Middleton, Derbyshire, has confirmed that excarnation might well have been a normal Neolithic burial custom.

Such wholesale dismemberment might suggest a vindictive contempt for the dead. Any individual identity, the slightest hope of rebirth, would surely be obliterated in such a collective and random confusion of anonymous bones. On the other hand, it could be argued that such careful preparation before burial shows a deep respect for the bones, however bizarre and inappropriate it may seem to us today. Perhaps the Neolithics wanted to produce their own permanent memorial to the dead, through the robust longevity of human bones. By cleaning from them all remnants of flesh and everything else perishable, they were able to offer to the earth something both pure and immortal: the essence of life, substantial yet as incorruptible as the soul. Maybe the impulse of the dolmen builders was to cheat the dissolution of death as surely as the ancient Egyptians preserved their dead by mummifying their bodies.

In fact, the Egyptians might be able to teach us something here, because they used to dismember their dead in much the same way in predynastic times, and even intermittently down to the Sixth Dynasty. At a dig at Naqada, shocked excavators found bones that had been separated into scattered groups: ribs and leg bones lying in heaps in different parts of the tomb.

Fortunately the ancient Egyptians, unlike the Neolithics, left some writing behind them to explain, at least in part, what they were up to. In the pyramid texts there are prayers to the dismembered body within: 'Awake, O King, raise yourself, receive your head, gather your bones together, shake off your dust and sit upon your iron throne.' [5]

Spencer suggests that this must refer to the myth of Osiris, consort to Isis, the Egyptian goddess of the grain. In the Egyptian myth, the body of Osiris is cut up after his ritual death and scattered far and wide, an event paralleled in the broken and strewn bodies found in Egyptian tombs. Basically, Osiris was a John Barleycorn (a modern corn dolly), buried during seedtime to rise with the corn. This means that, with his broken, strewn body, he represents the scattered seed.

This helps makes sense of the burial practices of the dolmen builders. It links with their belief in the sacred nature of stone. Stones gestate inside Mother Earth; they are her very bones. The Neolithics associated stone with rebirth through the White Lady, their goddess of the death of the year. To them the stone was frozen life, petrified by the frost of winter and waiting for the thawing renewal of spring. If stone was nascent growth, like the seed, then the scattering of bones was the scattering and burying of the seeds of the body, from which the body would be reborn.

This link between stone and life reminds us of Kore, goddess of the scattered and buried seed, who lived in the underworld during the winter and rose again in the spring. Her nature and even her name seem to be linked to the emergent sacred stone, as well as the buried bones, that make up the Neolithic dolmens.

There is an echo of this belief in the ancient Greek myth of the flood. Deucalion and Pyrrha ask Zeus how they might repopulate the earth after the flood has wiped out all humanity. Zeus advises them to 'throw the bones of your mother behind you'. They understand bones to mean stones – i.e. the bones of the Mother Goddess – so they scatter handfuls of stones over the earth and human kind is reborn.

We have mentioned a festival of stone throwing in Troezen, performed to ensure a good harvest, and linked it to the old custom of throwing sticks in Guernsey to guarantee good weather. Perhaps this old local game of scattering sticks was an echo, however faint, of the ritually scattered bones in the dolmens.

The goddess's consort represented the yearly decay and revival of vegetable life and was personified as a king, a priest, or even a god, who died every year and rose again from the dead. He symbolized the fertility of the land. This meant that the earth was only productive when the consort was healthy and virile.

Because the consort died regularly and returned from the dead, he effectively inhabited both worlds; he could switch from one to the other.

This made him a link between this world and the next, an intercessor between humanity and the goddess.

Eventually the semi–human, semi-divine consort became the basis of a whole religion and mythology. The ancient Greeks called him Adonis, to the Egyptians, as we have seen, he was Osiris, in Asia Minor he was known as Attis, and in the East his name was Tammuz. The mythical life stories of these consort figures, which evolved from the seasonal rituals that marked the year, are very similar. They all die violently, and their violent deaths express the cutting down of the crop and the burial of the seed. They are also born in violent circumstances, and this unity expresses the cyclical nature of vegetation life and the rites of sacrifice that attended it. For the seed to flourish it must be buried; for the crop to grow, it must be cut down. Robert Graves once suggested that a hero was originally a sacred consort who had been sacrificed to the Greek earth goddess Hera.

There might even be a named Channel Islands consort to compare with Adonis or Osiris, but he is no hero; he is rather elusive and sometimes mischievous, but is a clear presence in our landscape, particularly the ancient stone dolmens and menhirs. In Norman French, (the original language of the Channel Islands) a dolmen or menhir is called a *pouquelaye*, which literally translates as 'puck stone'. In Jersaiase, the word for menhir or standing stone is *blianche-pièrre*, or 'white stone'. In a Jersaiase dictionary, the word 'puck', along with the English alternative 'Peter', is translated as *Pierre Pouque*, or 'puck stone'.

Pierre, Peter, Puck; in this context the names are all related to stone, the sacred material used to construct the dolmens and menhirs. This suggests that the Channel Islands consort, the male counterpart of Dame Blanche, is none other than the impish, playful Puck.

Puck or Pouque is not only the title of the god of the stones. It is the local word for the fairies, or little people, of the Channel Islands. It has long been believed that they were the original builders of the dolmens and menhirs. This belief is reflected in many of the names of the monuments, such as Le Trou de Faîtiaux ('the Hole of the Little People'), La Roche de Fée, ('the Fairy Rock') and Le Creux des Fées ('Fairy Cross'), all in Guernsey. In Jersey's capital, St Helier, there is a street called La Pouquelaye, named after a long-vanished dolmen known locally as a fairy palace. In 1912, an old man warned an excavation team working on a dolmen at St Ouen's, Jersey, not to disturb the fairies. The dolmen in question was also known locally as La Creux des Faîtiaux ('the Cavern of the Little People').

Le Creux des Fées dolmen, Guernsey. An archetypal fairy mound

Even a book written exclusively for children, *Fairy Tales of the Channel Islands*, links the fairies directly to the ancient dolmens. It tells the story of an unnamed and now long lost dolmen in Jersey, which was once the home of the fairies and pixies and describes a bower near to the dolmen, where the fairies used to hold their weddings.

It is now generally accepted that 'fairies' were not tiny winged figures like J.M. Barrie's Tinkerbell. Anthropologists have long argued that the fairies were really the Neolithic people – probably a race memory of the Neolithics, conquered and suppressed by later invaders. We have already suggested that they lived in a matriarchal society, an idea echoed in the tradition that fairies were ruled by a 'fairy queen'. The description of this subjugated peoples as a diminutive race, smaller in stature than modern Western man, also sounds very similar to descriptions of the Neolithic people. There is additional evidence from folklore that the fairies were agriculturalists; their desire to be useful, their love of order, their power over the crops, all show how important they once were in peasant economies.

Fleeing the invaders, these Neolithic peoples were literally driven underground, where they remained, lurking in woods and mounds, doing casual service for gifts of food, but distrustful of their conquerors. They made up for their inferior strength and stature by art and the power which the superstition of the enemy invested in them, and they were credited with an intimate and secret knowledge of the country which had always been theirs; a knowledge hidden from the more sophisticated, but less intuitive invaders.

Puck was a fairy character, made famous by Shakespeare in his play *A Midsummer Night's Dream*. Here he is a mischievous, sylph-like creature, a 'merry wanderer of the night', a spectre as free as air, who can go where he likes. According to Shakespeare, one of his roguish traits is 'misleading night wanderers, laughing at their harm'.

Like the Dame Blanche, Puck brings confusion and misery to travellers at night. He is said to haunt places of death or crime with howling, just like the Dame Blanche and, like the Dame Blanche again, he has even been associated, in some parts of the British Isles, with wells.

But Puck is no mere winged Tinkerbell of fairy story. Like the Dame Blanche he is our Blanche Pierre, god of winter and death. He is present in our landscape, through the megaliths, as the god of the rock – that wintry medium of frozen life. He is the god and figurehead of our

Neolithic ancestors, who worshipped his spirit in the stone monuments they built.

It is possible that Puck himself, the spirit of the rock, was actually seen by a Guernsey farmer in September 1922. There was a large dolmen on this farmer's land. Early one morning, the man saw a stranger with a great beard sitting on one of the dolmen's capstones. The stranger never spoke, but offered the farmer a drink. The farmer accepted it, upon which the stranger bowed and left. The farmer did not understand the nature of the ritual he had participated in, but was convinced of its momentous, even sacred nature. 'It was,' he always said, 'a sign.'

Puck has entered Western culture as the Pierrot, another version of the Pierre or Neolithic god of the stone. Pierrot is a melancholy moon clown who, according to his story, began life as a naked, white snow child. His familiar guise is with a white costume and white face; white denoting stone, the frost of Neolithic winter and the paleness of the moon passing over the white stones. Moon man Pierrot became famous later as the white-faced circus clown, as well as the comical crescent-moon faced Punch. All of them are jesters and tricksters, like Puck.

And perhaps Puck is also present in that mysterious folk song of love and death, a song once very popular in the Channel Islands, as in France, *Au Clair de la Lune* ('By the Light of the Moon'):

> *Au clair de la lune, mon ami Pierrot*
> *Prête-moi ta plume pour écrire un mot*
> *Ma chandelle est morte, je n'ai plus de feu*
> *Ouvre-moi ta porte, pour l'amour de Dieu.*
> (I'm standing by the moonlight, my dear friend Pierrot
> Please give me a pencil, I need to write a note
> My candle is dying, I have no more flame
> Open up your door for me, for the love of God

The link between the moon and death expresses an ancient folk memory of the ancient rituals of the dolmen builders.

Notes
1 *A Picture of Jersey*, p. 159.
2 *Jersey: An Isle of Romance*, pp. 75–6.

3   Daniel Defoe, *A Tour through the Whole of Great Britain*, 1st edn, quoted in *Eye on the Past Yearbook*, 1992.

4   Quoted by the *Jersey Evening Post*, 29.1.05.

5   Spencer, pp. 40–1.

5 Festivals for the Dead

Puck has his own festival, called Samhain, traditionally held on the eve of the first of November. Samhain is even called Pooky Night – Puck's Night – in some parts of Ireland.

Samhain marks the beginning of winter, the time when the old god dies and the crone goddess mourns for him. To the early farmers, it was the very end of the fertile year, when the last of the crops was brought in. Anything remaining in the fields after this day belonged to Puck; it was considered *puka*, and not fit to eat. This identifies Puck as the winter consort, inflicting waste after the harvest, killing the fertility of the land and everything that grows in it.

So Samhain signifies the end of the old year and the beginning of the new. This is why the feast date, 31 October, was traditionally known as New Year's Eve. It is now the date of Halloween, a night of ghosts and witches. It is the time when the dead are supposed to wander the earth with all the freedom and licence of the living.

It is appropriate that Halloween, a festival which marks the arrival of winter, should celebrate the dead. At this dead time of year, deceased ancestors were traditionally invited to join the land of the living in their festivities, to be reunited with their loved ones and offer their mystic wisdom in performing divinations and prophecies. On this day, this cusp of the turning year, past, present and future were perceived as one.

Nevertheless, there were dangers involved in communing with the dead. You needed to make sure that you were not visited by the vengeful spirits of dead enemies. You also had to avoid being cursed by the dark goddess and her trickster consort Puck, which might well happen if you did not show sufficient respect on this, his special night. For that reason it was usual to place offerings of food outside your house, to conciliate the numberless dead spirits and guarantee future good fortune. Just as Marie Pipet or the crone goddess Keridwen always demanded tributes and hospitality, so did these wandering spirits of winter.

Today's popular Halloween custom of 'trick or treat', although believed to be an American import, can be traced to these ancient European customs of appeasing the dead. The children who call on households on Halloween night with the choice between good and bad luck (trick or treat, give me a sweet or I'll do something nasty to you), personify the old spirits of the winter, who demanded reward in exchange for good fortune.

Today's 'sweets' would originally have been sweet cakes, baked in honey. These were not merely nice to eat. They were a significant part of winter rituals because they represented the product of the grain, carefully preserved in honey to last throughout the winter.

It is believed that honey cakes were ritually eaten as part of the secret rites at the feminine Eleusian mysteries in ancient Greece. Honey, in fact, was a sacred substance in many ancient societies, because of its ability to preserve food, and thus halt the effect of time. It contained the essence of immortality and was a gift of the goddess.

For a while the Church, worried by Halloween's pagan associations with death, tried to change it into a Christian festival of prayer for departed souls. Even the sweet cakes were Christianized and called 'soul cakes', offered in return for prayers for the souls of saints. Now, in the twenty-first century, it seems to have given up all claims to the festival. Halloween is still the witches' sabbath, the time of Keridwen the crone goddess of winter, stirring her cauldron of life, death and rebirth to await reincarnation.

Very close to Halloween in the modern calendar is Guy Fawkes (or Bonfire) Night, celebrated on 5 November. It is widely assumed that it commemorates the gunpowder plot of 1605, a famous event in English history when Catholic insurgents tried to blow up the Houses of Parliament. But Bonfire Night, like trick or treating, is older than recorded history. It is a Samhain fire festival marking the turning of the year and, like Samhain, really belongs to New Year celebrations. In fact, until quite recently, in the Channel Islands it used to be held on New Year's Day. Even after the date was shifted in line with the English November, the traditional Guy figure was not named after the English plotter Guy Fawkes, but was still called by his original name: Aên Boud'lot, boudloe, or Bout de L'An, a name which means 'old year's end'.

The year's end represented the winter consort and his death embodied the death of nature. The folklorist McCulloch has given us quite a detailed description of the customs that surrounded the sacrifice of the Guernsey guy, or Bout de L'An. He tells us that the effigy was dressed up and paraded through the streets in a mock funeral procession, before either being buried or burned on a bonfire. He quotes a certain local writer who took this funeral ritual very seriously. To him it was not a children's game at all, but a religious ceremony carried out with 'classical solemnity' ending in what he called the 'Pagan ceremony of incineration'. This observer spoke of the 'melancholy' duty of attending as a 'chief mourner' the 'funeral of old Bout de L'An', as if he was grieving at the funeral of a much loved friend.

This shows that the old year's end was personified and even highly respected, like the ancient consort. It was not always a lachrymose ceremony in Guernsey, however. On a 'three cornered field' near St Martin's Mill, the Bout de L'An was burned to the blowing of cows' horns and dancing.

The menhir where the Bout de l'An was regularly burnt. Today it is guarded by Guernsey cows

The link between these year-end rituals and the Neolithic rites of sacrifice becomes clearer from another Guernsey ceremony, Le Tronc de Noue, in which the effigy was burnt in St Peter in the Wood – of all places, at the foot of a menhir. Those attending the ceremony danced around the flames. Durand mentions the 'fantastic' dress and blackened faces of the dancers, and suggested that the ceremony was a survival of a 'pagan fertility rite'.

The meaning of Tronc de Noue is, of course, 'Noel' or 'Christmas trunk', a huge wooden log, sometimes known as the yule log. In Jersey, too, a tree trunk would be similarly dressed up as a man, like a guy, and then burned at the end of the year.

According to De Garis, there was another custom in Guernsey that linked the yule log directly to the Neolithic burial sites. On the last day of the year, after the Christmas festivities were over, the half-burnt log would be decorated in greenery before being carried to a Neolithic menhir and solemnly burnt.

The Yule log, in fact, is reminiscent of the ancient Anatolian consort Attis, who was also an Asian tree god. The solemn bringing in of the Yule log to the hearth on Christmas Eve is reminiscent of the bringing in of Attis's pine tree from the woods into the goddess's temple, decked in spring flowers, ready for the sacrifice. As we have seen, the Guernsey Tronc de Noue was also decorated with greenery before being burnt.

A fascinating clue as to the ancient origin of the year's end ceremony might be found in an incident that occurred in Guernsey in 1965, which De Garis describes bluntly as an example of ancient 'sympathetic magic'. A number of disgruntled farmers burned an effigy of the Minister of Agriculture, a man whose policies they regarded as a threat to their livelihoods. As the effigy burned, the farmers fired their shotguns at it. De Garis suggests that 'it was thus that their ancestors dealt with the god who sent them contrary weather and gave them poor crops'.

As we have said, the Bout de L'An or year's end was a winter consort, like Puck. He was associated with the death of fertility, which is why he had to die. As long as this old consort kept living, the fertility would never return to the land. He was therefore to blame for winter's curse.

This infertile, waning consort was known in ancient Greek as the *pharmakos*, a word with the modern meaning of scapegoat – a person blamed for the ills of the community and made to suffer for them. The *pharmakos* would be treated like a king for a short while, maintained at public expense, fed with choice foods and clothed in special garments. At the end of his reign, he was either burned or thrown to his death from a cliff into the sea. Near Athens, during hard times such as pestilence or famine, a *pharmakos* would be chosen for his ugliness. He was driven from the community with curses and blows, and then ritually sacrificed. Only then could the ills be driven from the society, allowing wealth and prosperity to return.

This tradition of sacrifice seems to have been central to the rituals of Samhain until quite recently. Ruling over the enjoyable anarchy of Samhain used to be a mock king called the Lord of Misrule, leader of the games for the duration of the festival. He was free, wild, and anarchic; he would initiate tricks and gleefully upset the status quo, duping and embarrassing high and lowborn alike. Even modern parties still sometimes appoint a so-called master of the revels, whose job is to organize the games and induce people, sometimes by jovial force, to join in the fun.

The Lord of Misrule survived into Roman times, and could be found reigning at the spring festival of Saturnalia. This was a 24-hour period of unbridled fun. The whole day was given up to celebration and feasting, and the normal social order was reversed. Masters waited on their slaves and all form of authority was topsy-turvy.

There seems to be a clear local link with the topsy-turvy world of Saturnalia in this description of 1875 of a celebration in Sark:

> *Masquerades and disguises soon followed. Boys dressed themselves up like girls, and girls put on boys' clothes; aged men even did the same. Some covered themselves with rags of every shape and colour, others blackened their faces, and then tried to embrace the women and girls in order to blacken them as well.* [1]

In a similar way, in the modern Halloween, the normal order of the universe is suspended. The barriers between the natural and the supernatural are temporarily removed, and the spirits of the dead move freely among men and interfere, sometimes violently, in their affairs. This anarchic tradition survives in the ritual of 'trick or treat'.

In the Roman festival, with all normal authority reversed, the Lord of Misrule was truly king for a day. He reigned supreme for as long as the festival lasted, but not an hour longer. His temporary sovereignty ended abruptly as soon as the celebrations ceased.

It all sounds like good fun, but the idea of a king's reign ending suddenly sounds like a throwback to a more violent festival. As it turns out, Saturn (after whom the festival was named) was originally the Roman god of the seed, which makes him counterpart to Adonis, Osiris, and all the other consorts of the grain. Hardly surprisingly, there is every indication that, in earlier versions of this festival, the reign of the king at Saturnalia came to a somewhat crueller end than merely losing his paper crown. According to Fraser, 'A conspicuous feature of the Carnival is a burlesque figure personifying the festive season, which after a short career of glory and dissipation is publicly … destroyed, to the feigned grief or genuine delight of the populace.'[2]

This all sounds very similar to the burning of the figure of the guy. A remnant of this ancient custom clings to the current practice of pulling Christmas crackers: after the muffled explosion of the cracker, the prizes are generally revealed to be a joke, a charm, and the paper crown of the Lord of Misrule. This master of anarchy, trickster and bringer of mischief also strongly resembles the Channel Islands' Puck, another god/consort who delighted in playing tricks on people.

But away from the parties and merry-making of the fire ceremony of Samhain, there is a detailed description of a much older human fire sacrifice in Guernsey. It can be found in a folk story published in 1858 called *The Forest of Vazon*. This fascinating book claims to be an account of a series of events from the eighth century AD, but this sacrifice is clearly from a very much older tradition.

As we have seen, central to the scene is the sorceress Judith, clearly a powerful figure in the Guernsey community of Voisin. We saw her earlier as a member of the triple goddess, performing her healing arts on an injured young girl. Here we see her employ her more sinister arts of death. Judith decides that her daughter's lover, Jean, is a threat to her matrilineal plan for her, and a wider menace to the whole community. She decides that the only cure for her community's ills is to sacrifice him.

> *She held in her hands the strong frame, the stout heart, the ruling mind. All were concentrated in Jean Letocq. He, then, must be offered up as a fitting sacrifice. By such an offering the deities could not fail to be appeased, and by the death of this man in this fashion all the natural exigencies of the situation would be satisfied.*[3]

Preparations for the sacrifice go ahead; it will be a ritual burning on a large pyre. The arrangements sound not dissimilar to some of the Bout de L'An ceremonies described earlier.

A pyre, some twelve feet high, was built at the foot of a huge granite boulder, near the sea-coast: it was constructed of dry wood, and was drenched with combustible materials. Jean was bound firmly to a strong hurdle, made of birch stems and withies securely lashed together.

Before the pyre is lit, a series of eulogies is uttered by the priests. The first of these clearly identifies the sacrificed Jean as an almost classical hero figure: 'He passed a warm eulogy on the qualities of the captive, whom he described in exaggerated phrases as a sage in council, and a hero in battle, endowing him also with every domestic virtue which seemed in his eyes worthy of enumeration.'

Having praised the victim, the tone of the speeches undergoes a change. Jean is now identified as the scapegoat, and every sort of odium is heaped on him, just as was done to the Greek *pharmakos*: 'He was accused, in language which seemed devil-born, of every crime, every infamy, of which the human race is capable; held up to scorn and ignominy, he was cursed and execrated with a shower of blasphemy and obscenity.'

At this point, the writer of the story pauses to consider the apparent savagery of such actions, and comes to a remarkably perceptive conclusion. Jean is being sacrificed to cleanse the community of its evils: *'It may have been that the abhorrence and extinction of evil was roughly typified, or that it was understood that the death of the victim would, as if he were a scapegoat, cleanse the worshippers of the sins with which he was thus loaded.'*

As a final warning against the assumption that, in our modern civilized world we have left such barbarous practices behind, the writer assures us that 'it is not for critics, whose pious forefathers kindled the fires of Smithfield, to assert that their practice was wholly barbarous'.

As we have tried to show, the ritual of sacrifice has survived into the present day – most commonly in the burning of the guy on Bonfire Night and, until recently, the fire of the Yule log in the domestic hearth. However, there is a clear difference between Samhain and Yule.

Samhain is the season of the consort's death. Yule, on the other hand, is the moment of his rebirth. So, whereas the effigy of the guy was always burnt in a public place, to general rejoicing or mourning depending on one's mood, the Yule log belonged exclusively to a private, domestic setting. Its fire was utilized as a source of winter light and heat to the home, expressing hopes in the rebirth of nature and the return of the warmth and light of the distant spring. In a sense, Yule brought a piece of spring's warmth into the home.

Perhaps that is why the log was thought to contain a miraculous renewing power which could bring good fortune to everyone who gathered around its hearth. People would poke at the log, believing that every spark they generated would turn into cattle or a sheaf of wheat. Even the Yule log's ashes were thought to have fertilizing virtues and were sprinkled on the fields to make them fruitful.

Nevertheless, Yule seems to have acquired its own, private rituals of sacrifice. Central to these is the boar. We have already called the goddess a sow, the winter goddess Keridwen. And if she is a sow, it follows that her partner, the consort, must be a boar. This is quite a reassuring thought for those who feel unhappy with the idea of human sacrifice. It is very likely that an animal was sometimes killed in place of a human victim.

This explains why some of the most famous consorts, from the Greek Adonis to Irish Diarmid and the Egyptian Set, have sometimes appeared as pigs or wild boars. The Norse goddess Freyja and the Irish mother goddess Grey Eyebrows had wild boars as consorts.

Apparently pigs and humans are very alike anatomically, so it is hardly surprising that we are mythologically interchangeable. In fact, this close similarity between the bodies of pigs and humans once inspired a secret craft of healing on Guernsey. Pig slaughterers, with their wide experience of carving up carcasses, acquired an intimate knowledge of the bone and organ structure of the human body, superior to that of a doctor or surgeon. As a result, they were adept at osteopathy, a knowledge which they very seldom passed on to the uninitiated outside their craft. To them, pigs, which they slaughtered on a daily basis, had become sacred animals and creatures of healing. They guarded their secret therapeutic wisdom as jealously as the practitioners of the Eleusian mysteries.

The divine influence of the pig on the Channel Islands even extended into the realm of fishing. There used to be a Guernsey superstition that if a fisherman saw a pig on his way to his boat, he would catch no fish that day. The word 'pig' itself was also never used in a boat, for fear of provoking tempestuous weather. The Guernsey folklorist and broadcaster Freda Wolley has an explanation for this. Pigs, she says, were unlucky for seafarers because they were 'sacred to the Ancient Goddess who had charge of the four winds'.⁴ Perhaps that is why Guernsey pigs were also said to be able to see the wind and foretell the weather, displaying the same forecasting ability as the Neolithic sages, who charted the passing seasons through the dolmens.

This explains why the pig has long been associated with divination and good fortune. For example, it used to be possible to buy a silver mascot in Jersey in the form of a 'lucky pig'. L'Amy had no doubt as to the reason: 'The boar, or pig, was the cult, or "totem" animal of Isis, the Mother, or "Moon" Goddess. She was Demeter of the Greeks [and] she was revered as the Queen of Heaven, the mother of all life, and the Goddess of love and war.'⁵

This is the same goddess, L'Amy insists, who was prevalent in Gaul, Britain and the Channel Islands in Roman times, and probably up to the introduction of Christianity. L'Amy calls her Demeter, the Greek grain goddess, but Keridwen is another of her names.

L'Amy also points out that Jersey people never used the word 'pig' itself, almost as if it was taboo. They used a euphemism to name the animal: *avers*, meaning 'possessions', which in Jersey patois was also the word for children. Associating pigs with children and possessions may seem odd, but it could be a reference to the sow's fecundity, suggesting that the title of 'mother of all life' survived in this rather charming island name for the pig.

But there is another reason why the boar, which is basically a most unsightly beast, was the sacred consort of the grain goddess in early societies. The boar is a voracious consumer of corn; his body is largely composed of the stuff. He is a living, breathing, moving embodiment of the corn. His sacrifice and burial at the darkest time of the year was thought to restore fertility to the earth, a sort of symbolic planting of the seed. The ritual of slaughtering and eating the body of the grain consort also celebrated the nourishing powers of the crop, and acted out the hope of plenty of food at harvest time.

The pig may be perfectly palatable as a ritual meal, but it has often been an object of revulsion. The odium surrounding it persists in Semitic tradition; both Muslims and Jews shun it as unclean and forbidden meat. This argues quite strongly that it was once seen as holy. There is a remarkably close affinity between that which is sacred and that which is cursed.

But there might be another reason for this abhorrence. The wild boar is a natural enemy to any society reliant on a successful corn harvest. In gluttonous pursuit of his favourite food, corn, he will, if left unchecked, happily run amok among the fields, devastating the crops. Today, the pig's reputation for ravenous greed is universal; 'greedy as a pig' is a common insult. As a deadly rival for the fruits of the earth, a threat to the land's fertility and the survival of the community, the boar had to be ritually killed in order to ensure a good harvest.

So the grain-gobbling boar is associated exclusively with winter and the dark time of the year. This confirms it as the partner to the winter goddess. When the boar, the king of winter, reigns supreme, the earth and humankind suffer. There is no food and no prosperity. In early British myth, the son (or consort) of the sow Keridwen is even called Affagdu, which means 'darkness'.

The sacrifice of the winter boar consort survived, until recently, in the custom of roasting and eating the Yule boar on Christmas Day. Although we tend to eat turkey these days, there seems to be little doubt about the ritual origin of our much loved Christmas dinner. Sometimes in Jersey the Yule boar was not an animal at all, but a loaf made from the harvested grain. The last sheaf of corn taken from the field would be left standing on the table until Christmas was over, and then mixed with the seed for sowing in the spring.

This is reminiscent of a Samhain practice of regarding anything remaining in the fields after the last harvest as belonging to Puck. Sometimes the last reapers would leave a small portion of the crop in the field, 'Puck's share', to appease the god's winter appetite. The following spring, this now rotting old remnant of the previous harvest would be buried in the ground with the first of the seeds.

There is also a memory of ancient grain customs in this description of a Jersey Christmas sweet cake, made with the flesh of the pig: 'Then finally came the Christmas season and the killing and salting of the pigs, the pork chops or trimmings on Christmas Eve, and the *Fache a Cretons*, which was a cake made with the residue from melted pig's fat, known as cracklings, and apples mixed in dough. [6]

In the Eleusian mystery rituals, it is believed that the product of the corn, in the form of sweet cakes, was eaten, along with the flesh of the boar consort. Portions of the flesh were also sown with the seed to ensure a good crop.

This all relates back to the Halloween custom of eating and distributing sweets – which used to be sweet cakes – made from the harvested corn. Our Christmas sweets, in the form of a heavy pudding and rich cake, are still a vital part of our celebratory meal today, although honey has largely been replaced by sugar and that relatively new winter innovation, dried fruit.

However, there are some older Channel Islands customs in which a sweet cake features as a kind of ritual meal. In Jersey, a girl seeking a husband would bake a cake containing some of her own blood, continuing the fleshy associations of the sacred grain cake. She would offer a slice of this to the man she had chosen to be her husband. Here the ritual combination of sweet cakes and blood forms the basis of a fertility ritual. Presumably this meal formed a kind of marital pact between the woman and her chosen man, who was obliged to marry her in consequence. In true goddess tradition, it is the woman who is in charge.

In a similar fertility cake ritual, a woman would mix flour, soot and salt in a cake mixture and put it in to bake. She would then leave it in the oven and wait, because the man destined to be her future husband would come and turn it over. It is hard to understand the significance of mixing a cake that no one would want to eat, unless the soot once represented the fertilizing ash of the Yule log. Salt, of course, is a primary food and a preservative; like the honey in sweet cakes, it conserves provisions over a long period and helps defeat the winter.

In one version of this story, however, a woman loses her nerve when she hears the footstep of her future husband on the stair. She throws the cake on the fire in panic, an act she lives to regret. She subsequently marries the man, and throughout their life together he endures endless burning pains in his body. Like the Yule cakes, which contained the flesh of the sacrificed consort, this cake represented the body of the chosen husband, which suffered the same burning as that inflicted on the cake.

The Yule log, the Yule boar and the sweet cakes and puddings of Halloween and Christmas all have their origin in the ritual sacrifice of the winter consort. In these winter festivals we are somehow still participating in the ancient mystery celebrations that stretch back as far as the Eleusian mysteries and to the original builders of the Channel

Islands dolmens, and we are incorporating the apparent barbarity of the acts of sacrifice that so puzzled and distressed early visitors to the Channel Islands.

Notes

1   Anon, 1875.
2   Frazer, p. 586.
3   These quotes are all taken from *The Project Gutenberg eBook* of *The Forest of Vazon*.
4   *Guernsey Legends*, p. 9.
5   *Jersey Folk Lore*, p. 174.
6   Blackstone & Le Quesne, p. 296.

Part II:
Myths and Monsters in the Landscape

6 The Isles of Avalon

The writer Marie De Garis has described a fascinating Yule ritual in Guernsey. A local woman once told her that, in her youth, she and her friends used to take the Yule log, the Bout de L'An, to Vazon beach and send it out to sea. This was followed by the lighting of a bonfire and much feasting and revelling on the beach.

The symbolism of this act is unmistakable. If the Yule log represents the dead consort or seasonal king, then the ritual of consigning it to the sea takes us into the realm of Norse and British myth, when the body of the dead king was usually conveyed to the water.

One famous example of this royal ritual comes from the Old English poem *Beowulf*, where the dead Danish King Scyld is placed in a ship loaded with precious things. He and his barge are then placed on the sea, which bears his body away. In Arthurian legend we find the story of Tristan, wounded in battle and laid in a small boat which sails off across the sea. Even more famously, King Arthur himself is mortally hurt in battle, taken to the waterside and put into a barge, which bears his body away. There are many more examples in mythology of a ritual involving a final journey by water, a metaphor for the consort/king's death.

We can presume that the dead king is returning to the realm of the goddess – the underworld that we all go back to. We are told, for example, that *Beowulf*'s King Scyld is embarking on a voyage to 'his distant home'. Home is just another way of describing the place of birth, the primal 'motherland', a symbol for Mother Earth herself. In some variations of this ritual, a small hole is pierced in the boat so that it will sink beneath the waves when it reaches the open sea, a more literal return to the bosom of the goddess.

Arthurian legend is a little more romantic. Tristan ends up in Ireland, where he is healed by Isolde the fair, an encounter that results in one of the greatest love stories in all literature. King Arthur's body is conveyed to Avalon, an island inhabited by a race of women who will eventually heal and restore him. (We know this because the legend says that one day Arthur will awake to rule England again.) These Arthurian stories clearly show the dead hero or king being conveyed to the domain of the goddess, a place of death and rebirth. The king's journey by water is essentially a cyclical journey.

The Norse legends also describe a circular journey, such as the story of Sceaf, who sailed to Denmark with a sheaf of corn in his boat. (In other versions he came with a boat full of weapons.) He was adopted by the local priestess and became king. When he died he was put back into the boat, with the weapons of his birth, and his body sailed back into the ocean from whence he came. (His name means 'sheaf of corn', which confirms that the sacred consort/king was originally the spirit of the grain.)

It is perhaps worth mentioning that King Scyld (whose name sounds rather similar to Sceaf) also came to Denmark, 'as a boy, on a ship laden with treasure from across the sea'. On his final departure by sea, his successor as king is Beowulf, who arrives in Denmark on a ship that brought him from his homeland, Sweden – and so it goes on.

So maybe this ancient seasonal sea ritual survived in the Vazon ceremony of conveying the dead Yule log to the sea. The link with Vazon is important here, because there is another interesting tale associated with the area, to be found in the collection of Guernsey folklore, *The Forest of Vazon*. In it, we again meet the sorceress Judith, the mother in the triple goddess, who presided over the sacrifice of Jean. In this story, she speaks of the day that her beloved husband Haco died because of another man's treachery. Despite her grief and fury at his betrayal, Judith's first priority was to give Haco a fitting funeral.

> *'We must bury him … in a hero's grave, and after the custom of our fathers.'*
> *They brought the choicest of the boats, they put in it the dead man's arms, and food to accompany him to the land of spirits. Then they bound him before the mast, his face turned seaward. At sundown they towed the boat to deep water, so pierced her that she might sink slowly under the waves, and then they left the hero to his rest.*

But this is not the end of Haco's story. Judith is a sorceress and restored her dead husband to life before consigning him to the sea. This means that the boat was carrying a living victim, wounded rather than dead, rather like Tristan or Arthur on their final journeys. Judith also plugged the hole so the boat would not sink, but continue its journey. Where it will end up, however, Judith cannot tell. For the moment, the final destination of her husband is a mystery, even to this goddess.

It is interesting, too, that Judith's victim, Jean, after being placed alive on top of a funeral pyre, is not burned after all. Due to a huge tidal wave that hits Vazon forest at the crucial moment, he is cast out on to the sea, just like Haco, Sceaf, Arthur and many other mythical heroes. 'A second wave crept in, smaller than the former, but overwhelming the pyre. When the pyre was submerged the litter, to which Jean was attached, floated off and formed a tolerably secure raft. In speechless wonderment he was carried seaward by the slowly receding tide.' So he faces two ritual deaths. Fortunately, like the immortal consort he is, he survives both.

A dim memory of these ancient sea rituals might explain the once popular pilgrimage to Cheval Roc, a large sea-girt rock shaped like a horse's head, which is still a prominent feature of the Jersey harbour of Bonne Nuit. On midsummer's day, crowds all over the island used to flock to Bonne Nuit, simply to row a boat once round the rock and back again. It is difficult to explain the popularity of the event, except that the circular trip exposed the participants to the hazards of Jersey's coastal currents and tides. Both Carey and L'Amy believed that it was pre-Christian. John Mallet also had no doubt that the ceremony dates from pagan times.

So perhaps the people of Jersey were inspired by the traditions of an ancient myth as they leaped eagerly into their boats. This symbolic sea journey, with its attendant risk of drowning, was an ancient metaphor for the final journey and a symbolic rebirth from the underworld. Certainly the ritual was believed to have a renewing effect on the fortunes of those who took part. According to a contemporary account the whole purpose of the journey was to ensure good luck for the following year. Spring always follows winter, so from rebirth to renewed fortunes is but a small step.

This ancient sea ritual also appears in some other Channel Islands folk tales, even those that appear to be Christian in content. There is a story from Sark featuring the pupils of a local saint, St Malgoire. His young prodigies were innocently playing on the seashore one day when

The Cheval Roc, Bonne Nuit, Jersey, a large sea-girt rock, shaped like a horse's head, once the centre of a rather dangerous midsummer pilgrimage. Is this another sacred god of the rock?

they came across an old ship that had no rudders, sails, or oars, and which was rotting away. Eagerly they climbed on board, pleased to have something different to play with. At that moment, a great storm arose and the ship was carried out to sea. Terrified, the children called for help and to their relief the saint appeared. However, he did not try to stop the storm or even rescue the children. Instead he guided the ship with his staff to a neighbouring country.

When the children arrived at this foreign land, its people, hearing the tale of their miraculous voyage, loaded the ship with corn, flour, and supplies of all kinds. At this, the ship then miraculously sailed away again, and came to rest back on the coast of Sark, in the same place where it had lain rotting for so many years.

Despite the presence of a Christian saint, this tale has all the elements of a sea-bound trip to the otherworld. First there is the 'miraculous' nature of the children's journey, which takes them into a sort of timeless, eternal zone in which a rotting old boat becomes a seagoing craft. The fact that their ship is filled with ample supplies at this foreign land is also paralleled in the Norse stories, in which precious treasure, or in Sceaf's case sheaves of corn, are placed in the kingly craft. The corn, suggesting a rich harvest and the wealth of the earth, was interpreted in later mythology as treasure and grave goods. Then there is the story's cyclical structure – it ends exactly where it began, on the coast of Sark.

Another, more complicated story from Sark involves three brothers, all of whom were rivals for the love of one woman. Instead of fighting for her, the brothers decided to hold a contest: they would all three walk the whole length of the island at night. This does not sound like a very challenging ordeal, considering Sark's small size, but it carried a serious risk of death. Anyone venturing out at night risked seeing Sark's ghostly walking coffins, a line of sarcophagi that were said to walk across the island between sundown and sunrise. The merest glimpse of these could be instantly fatal. It was agreed between the brothers that whoever walked the length of the island without seeing the coffins and dropping dead from fright, would win the hand of the young lady.

Pierre, the craftiest, decided to avoid the graves by setting out along the island by boat. (Pierre, of course, is Peter, associated with rock, the Blanche Pierre and our trickster Puck.) Pierre docked for a few hours at a place called the Lamentation Caves, where it is said his weeping can still be heard. His weeping was clearly prophetic, the outcome of all his scheming was that he did not arrive at his destination at all. Instead, his drowned body was later washed ashore at a promontory now known as the Three Brothers.

But the story does not end there. A short time afterwards, before either of the other brothers had a chance to marry the lovely lady, a strange craft was seen approaching the island, shaped, of all things, like a coffin. This morbid vessel docked and inside was Pierre, not only alive but completely unharmed. After returning so miraculously from the dead, he naturally won the heart and hand of the local lady. In this story, the mystical craft actually doubles as a coffin, emphasizing the ritual, otherworldly nature of Pierre's journey.

These two stories of sea rituals, both originating in the island of Sark, raise another interesting question. The notion of an island as the abode of the dead, such as Avalon, is common across Norse and Greek mythology. In myth, such islands were known as the Fortunate Isles, or the Isles of the Blessed, a place where favoured mortals were sent to a blissful paradise. In Greek myth they were called the Elysian Fields, home to the dead. These stories suggest that Sark, and perhaps some of the other Channel Islands, were sacred islands of the dead.

Certainly the legend of the walking coffins is significant. The reason for their existence is a strange one. It seems that on Sark, since time immemorial, graves were always dug in the shape of a Christian cross. One day a careless grave digger forgot to make his grave cross-shaped, and this simple oversight was the cause of the walking coffins, this unforgiving procession of the living dead. This story sounds like an attempt to Christianize a tradition that has ancient, much darker associations with an island death cult.

A link with the domain of the death is more starkly clear on the island of Herm. The number of Neolithic burials there has been estimated in

Neolithic burial on Herm. Dwelling place of the 'spirits of the island'

thousands, too numerous, as the guide book points out, for them all to have been of Herm residents. Evidence suggests that the island was a major Neolithic entombment centre or resting place of the dead, and they can only have been brought there by boat.

Perhaps the number of Neolithic burial centres explains why a strange, sinister atmosphere hung over Herm until recent times, a spirit which almost seemed hostile to the presence of the living. Edith Carey eloquently describes feeling a presence that seemed to resent the intrusion of humans. She called it the Spirit of the Island, which must be propitiated at all costs.

The *Guernsey Press* of 18 March 2003 mentions a guided trip to Herm, which offered its visitors tales of legends and ghostly sightings on the island. The guide Annette Henry is quoted as saying:

There are many ghost stories coming out of Herm … myths and folklore. There were tremendous massacres on the island and the remains of Neolithic aristocracy lie under the common. That would make me assume the island has a rich, mysterious past that we are just starting to uncover.

The common on Herm with its dolmens, from which writer Compton Mackenzie fled in terror

The writer Compton Mackenzie, tenant of the island, claims that he felt the elemental spirits come to life one evening as he walked across the common at dusk. As he approached a group of dolmens, he was seized suddenly with a panic. He was unable to describe the terror that he felt, and could only confront it later by performing an act of almost Christian piety. The next morning he returned to the dolmen where he had experienced the panic, and prayed to the spirits of the island.

He had already been warned that there was a 'curse' against him on Herm. A relative of the previous tenant (whose occupancy had ended rather badly) had prayed to the island spirits to bring misfortune to the next tenant. Clearly believing in the curse after his experience at the dolmens, Mackenzie fled from the island and never came back. He turned his extraordinary experiences into a novel called *Fairy Gold*. It contains a strong supernatural element, expressing his own strongly held beliefs in the mystical powers that had frightened him enough to make him leave Herm for ever.

We have already suggested that fairies are a folk memory of the Neolithic people, a belief shared by the residents of the Channel Islands. It is also worth remembering that they are traditionally associated with the world of the dead. In some European folklore, they were seen as the captors and guardians of the dead, and it was not uncommon to describe the deceased as being 'among the fairies'. Fairies have even been called the spirits of the departed themselves. In some stories, fairies actually cause death; the slightest contact can be fatal for ordinary mortals. Clearly, from his terrified reaction, this was a belief that Mackenzie shared.

Nevertheless, he remained loyal to the Channel Islands. He moved to the neighbouring island of Jethou, where he believed that the spirits were far more friendly – indeed, he claimed that the spirits of Jethou looked after him there, which explained perhaps why his years there were among his most happy and productive. Clearly his Herm-based fairy book was inspired by the friendly spirits of Jethou.

Mackenzie's successor on the island was a man called Sir Percival Perry. A more down-to-earth, practical man could hardly have been chosen for the role of tenant. In Mackenzie's own words, Perry was a hard-headed 'profiteer of war', who had made a fortune selling old war vehicles. Later he was to become Chairman of the Ford Motor Company. He was the last man to believe in fairies. In fact, Mackenzie believed that the spirits of Herm had chosen Perry as a direct result of his prayer, in which he asked them to choose a hard-headed man, 'on whom they could vent their ill will'.

The spirits could certainly be said to have vented their will on Perry, but not for ill. During his tenancy, the no-nonsense, matter-of-fact man of business was moved to write his own fairy tale, *The Island of Enchantment*, a whimsical J. M. Barrie-type story about a family of children who meet up with the fairies of the island. It contains this enchanting refrain:

> Yes! Hame [Herm] is the land of the fairies
> You'll find out the farther you go,
> On the beach you'll discover their clothing,
> If you search when the tide is low.

Clearly the feminine fairy spirits of Herm had a softening influence on this hardened old capitalist.

Jethou is also rich in the remains of menhirs and dolmens. One menhir in the middle of Cannon Field was once apparently part of a stone circle. There is also a vertical line of stones to be found on the island, similar to the alignment at Carnac in Brittany. An aerial picture makes it clear again that there is a definite circle marked around this area too, suggesting a complex of stone lines and circles comparable to Avebury. All of this also suggests that the tiny island, little more than a soil-covered rock, was an important ritual centre during the Neolithic period.

The archaeologist Kendrick has conjectured that many of the Stone Age bodies buried in Alderney and Herm had been brought from the mainland of France, and suggests that both islands were therefore sacred. Marie De Gras takes matters further and speculates that the whole of Guernsey may have represented a holy isle, to which the great dead were brought over from the Continent.

Coysh, in his 1974 guide, is sure that Alderney was also once a prehistoric necropolis. It is the closest of the Channel Islands to the French coast, lying just nine miles from Le Cotentin and 'one may well assume that primitive man, regarding offshore islands as places of sanctity, honoured his illustrious dead by ferrying them over the Race for interment'. To support this view, it is worth noting that most of Alderney's Neolithic remains are located at Longy, the area of coast closest to France.

It was long believed in Alderney that the tradition of exempting fishermen on the French coast from tax tribute had been granted on condition of ferrying over the souls of the departed. Still current in Alderney in the 1850s was the conviction that fishing boats from neighbouring Brittany were summoned by mystic voices when they put out to sea, and faced the wild Channel in their open boats, 'mysteriously weighed down by some invisible burden, until they reached Alderney, destined to be the resting place of the departed'.

There is another Alderney legend of the sea-bound dead, this time from the point of view of a resident of Normandy.

> *A fisherman of Auderville was once awakened at night by a tapping at his window and voice that pleaded: 'There are many souls waiting to be ferried over to Aurigny [Alderney], the isle of rest'. He got up and rowed his boat, sunk almost to the gunwale with an invisible freight, where on arrival it recovered its normal free board.* [1]

The Roman writer Procopius has left us similar accounts of the Celtic fishermen who heard low knocking at their doors in the middle of the night.

> *… which ceased not until they arose and went forth; then by the side of their own barks they saw a strange boat borne down to the gunwale by a freight of unseen beings which they were to pilot to the Islands of Rest; and as the boats floated away, wakeful women heard in the midnight hour the chant which proceeded from these spirit-laden boats.* [2]

Durand speculates that the Fortunate Isles – Avalon, St Brendan's Isle, Huy Brasil – lay out in the ocean towards the west, and that not Alderney and Herm alone, but all the Channel Islands 'were regarded as the Islands of the Blest'. The tiny island of Lihou, when cut off by the tide and shrouded in sea mist, looks very like a romanticized picture of Avalon, that hazy, dreamy island evoked by Mallory's description of Arthur's final journey. It has even been called a Holy Island, notably in the title of a guide published in 1972. This status seems to be confirmed by the story of Haco, husband to the sorceress Judith. As we have seen, he was murdered by a rival and sent by his partner the goddess on his final journey to the sea. We are also told that Haco was not dead because Judith had exercised her healing powers on him. Instead of sinking the ship, she ensured that it departed on a journey to a mysterious destination – a destination unknown to her.

We can now reveal where Haco's craft ended up. He arrived on the sacred island of Lihou, where he was healed of his wounds and began a new life as a pious, God-fearing monk. Of course the story has been heavily Christianized, although the journey still sounds remarkably similar to Arthur's last, healing passage to Avalon: 'I am Haco! Drifted hitherward on that lonely voyage, I was released by holy men, now saints above, who healed my wounds and taught me to bury my pride, and to kneel humbly before the Cross.'

As we might expect from this Christianized version of the Avalon myth, this is not an island of women – quite the opposite, it is an exclusively male domain; the presence of the female has been abolished and no woman is even allowed to set foot on it. In fact Lihou, ruled by an ascetic monk, clearly stands for Christian values, and is the male stronghold in a culture clash with the matriarchal Voison people, led by their sorceress Judith, and known for their orgiastic rites and devotion to human sacrifice.

There is an interesting confrontation scene between the two religions in the Forest of Vazon, where the monk has been pinning crosses and crucifixes to the trees in an attempt to convert the pagans. The sorceress orders the removal of these Christian symbols from her forest domain.

'Take with you,' she said, 'yon idol that defaces the sacred oak!'

The good fathers, following their usual practice of associating emblems of heathen with those of Christian worship, in the hope of gradually diverting the reverence to the latter without giving to the former a ruder shock than could be endured, had suspended a small cross on the oak, hoping eventually to carve the tree itself into a sacred emblem; it was to this that the woman was pointing with a sneer.

However, in most other stores of Lihou, it is clearly a feminine island. It even has its own goddess figure: the goddess of the rock, a title virtually identical with the winter presence of Blanches Dames. Fishermen used to pay respect to the goddess, or Our Lady of Lihou as she was also known, as a charm against the dangerous reefs that surround the island. They would regularly lower their mainsails in honour of Notre Dame au Peril de la Mer (another of her titles) as they passed the island. (In this we are reminded of the many Channel Islands folk stories in which fishermen have to show respect to the goddess to ensure a good catch and avoid disaster at sea.)

Ruins of Lihou Priory, Guernsey. It seems that Christianity did not thrive on this sacred goddess island

Perhaps the goddess's strong presence on the island explains why a priory was built here dedicated to the Virgin Mary. It would almost certainly have been established, as were many Christian structures, as a deliberate challenge to the old religion. We are told that it stood on the site of 'an old heathen sanctuary', within a flourishing centre of 'pagan worship'; apparently three or four dolmens and about seven menhirs once stood in its vicinity, an astonishing concentration in so tiny an area. It is said that the priory was even constructed from the dismantled stones of these old sanctuaries. Two other chapels and several crosses were also constructed in the region, in what certainly sounds like a very determined attempt to smother or drive out older religious influences. Despite this, the Virgin Mary of the priory continued to be known, to the local people of Guernsey, as Our Lady of the Rock or Our Lady of Lihou for as long as the priory existed. The original goddess of the stone, the Blianches Dames, was never driven out.

Further evidence of a vigorous pagan presence on Lihou could be found nearby, on a mound of land on Guernsey called Le Catioroc ('castle rock'). This was an area notoriously frequented by witches. A dolmen still stands on this site, La Trepied, a name which refers, it is said, to the three great capstones, but which also reminds us of the triple goddess.

Legend tells us that Guernsey's witches, whom Wooten and Scott call 'survivals of the old priestesses', used to meet regularly at the dolmen, from where they had a good view of the priory, and then they would hurl curses at it. They would chant: '*Tcheit, d'la haout, Marie d'Lihaou*' ('Fall from there, Mary of Lihou'), shouting their anger and defiance at the rival Christian goddess. These priestesses of the old religion clearly found the existence of the priory of Lihou infuriating because they were exiles from the site, ousted by this interloper from their old sacred island.

But perhaps they were not really ousted. For a start, the very name of the island, Lihou, originates from their curses; the name comes from Le Hou or 'the hogue', a sacred pagan site similar in nature to Hogue Bie. Besides, Christianity did not exactly thrive on Lihou. Today there is barely a trace of the priory left. Even in its heyday, the monks suffered from a very dubious reputation. They were reputed to dabble in black magic and to practise what was loosely known as 'satanism'. Under their doubtful care, Lihou truly became an island of death, but not in the hallowed sense associated with Avalon. It was the scene of several violent deaths and

Le Trepied dolmen. The centre of the Guernsey witch cult

murders until 1485, when the prior was removed. Clearly the old ways were still having a strong influence, and not always a positive one.

According to a poem written in the eighteenth century, there were both monks and nuns living on Lihou. They devoted themselves exclusively to the Virgin Mary, whom they called Our Lady of the Rock and, under her guidance, they claimed to work miracles. The first part of this poem, called 'The Trip to Lihou', is a sort of early tourist's guide to the island, recounting the rather bizarre sights that visitors to the island might have seen in the sixteenth century. It describes, for example, a rock placed at the water's edge, presumably the rock after which the *Lady of the Rock* was named. It then adds more graphic detail:

> Two gleaming rocks, with man-made cavities
> Were the places that the nuns and young novices
> In the hot and frenzied days of midsummer
> Did cool their ardent love making.

From this it sounds as if the rituals of the old religion, especially the fertility rites associated with later witchcraft, had not been fully abolished from this sacred isle after all.

The rest of the poem then tells an even more astonishing story, featuring a pastor from Guernsey who goes to the island to fish. He is met by five maidens, who promise to give him an excellent day's fishing. Instead, they merely distract and tease him. Much of the teasing is of a frankly sexual nature, making much of the phallic symbolism of fish, the fishing rod and the very act of fishing itself. One of the maidens leaps into the water and 'gaily retrieves the pastor's hook'. Another sees an eel and 'states that she would like to taste it'. 'Is she not a girl,' the poem then asks, very slyly. A third maiden finds a conger in a hole and 'cries out that she holds the most ferocious piece'. And so the innuendo goes on.

The good pastor, unable to cope with all this raucous feminine humour, decides to flee, but finds that his escape has been cut off by the tide. To his chagrin, he realizes that he is trapped on the island in the company of these five maidens for the whole of the night. He makes up a bed of bracken near the ruins of a church (a very symbolic setting). But then, extraordinarily, he accepts the maidens' invitation to share the bed with them and – even worse – he actually spends the night on top of them, serving as a coverlet to keep them warm. At this delicate point in the poem, the writer speaks directly to us:

> Muse, halt here, and keep the secret,
> And never reveal what was then said and done.
> Know only that when discovering the maidens' mysteries,
> One always deplores a cruelty done.

These deliberately vague lines seem, at first, to be drawing a veil of obscurity over a clergyman's sexual indiscretion. But there might be something deeper going on here. The language – the use of words like 'secret' and the phrase 'maidens' mysteries' (*la mystere des belles* in the original language) suggest a more religious context; perhaps linked to the feminine mysteries of the hidden underworld, the domain of death and rebirth, as revealed in the goddess's Isle of Avalon.

After that, we enter the pastor's dreams, and the erotic element in fishing is given full rein. We are told that he is dreaming of a perfect day's fishing, where conditions have never been so favourable. Amongst his piscine pleasures, he is clasping 'a big fat ormer … all wet from the sea', and holding a 'quivering and shivering' eel. He wakes up to find, to his horror, that the fish he has been so joyfully handling is, in fact, the flesh of the five maidens. He has been bewitched; dreams are one way (the poem then tells us) that 'life plays its tricks'. But he still cannot escape because the tide has risen again, so he remains trapped on the island for a second day with the maidens. He is finally rescued by a passing boat.

Who are these maidens? At one point the poem calls them 'sirens' – those *femmes fatales* of Greek mythology who lead men to their deaths, the Greek counterpart of the Dames Blanches. At the end of the poem, the sirens are identified as 'beauties of eternal fame, "The nuns of Lihou"'. Most surprisingly, the pastor is also now revealed as none other than the Prior of Lihou, suggesting that the island is his true spiritual home.

This poem is obviously not describing an historic event. It is an allegory, and seems to be exploring a fundamental conflict of religious values. The island, with its maidens and plentiful fish, expresses an alternative sacred tradition to the church values represented by the pastor. His agony of choice, between the island and his church, expresses the ongoing clash between Christianity and the old religion, between patriarchy and the goddess.

The pastor sees his very presence on the island as a betrayal of his priestly function. With a sense of guilt, he hears the ringing of the church bells from his feminine island retreat, and fears that his flock will think he loves the island ladies more than his duties. He uneasily imagines another minister preaching a stern sermon and 'lavishing fiery eloquence' on his congregation, as a response to his long absence. At the same time, part of him enjoys being there; he even laments, when first trapped, that his role as priest conflicts with his truly enjoying his sojourn on the island. Ultimately this does not stop him sleeping with the maidens – all five of them.

In contrast to the austere, monastic Christian island described in the story of Vazon Forest, this poem, so rich in allegory, clearly identifies Lihou as the domain of the goddess, comparable to Avalon. Unlike the Arthurian story, where the dying king sails away into the poetical mists and out of our sight for ever, here we are given a tantalizing glimpse into the secret world of the feminine, from the inside. We share the priest's anxious, guilty joys and we see his dreams. We have travelled to the blessed isle and tasted the goddess's secrets for ourselves. We have been to Avalon and back.

The name Avalon comes from the British word *lava*, meaning 'apple', so the name Avalon presumably means 'the island of apples'. Apples, of course, have a long association with the Channel Islands. The farming and marketing of apples used to be one of their principal agricultural industries. Sadly, all trace of the traditional apple crop had vanished by the middle of the twentieth century, and many romantic observers and visitors lamented this loss. In 1956 Leonard Clarke tried to imagine the vanished orchards of Sark, evoking 'dew-soaked grasses' and 'cloudless skies', and describing the apples themselves as 'spheres of Sark sea-light', sounding as if he was describing a lost Eden.

It was very different in the seventeenth century, when the apple actually did dominate the islands' agriculture. The writer Poingdestre had a far less romantic vision of Jersey's apple production; he complained that the whole island was in danger of becoming a continual orchard. In the same vein, another commentator, Falle, bemoaned the fact that, with the endless apple trees, the whole island looked like an endless forest.

It might seem disingenuous to link the Channel Islands tradition of apple trees with the religion of prehistory, although there is every possibility that Neolithic people grew apples and brewed cider. At the same time, the apple seems to have been regarded as a sacred symbol wherever the old religion once reigned.

For example, La Dame Blanche is also known as one of the mythical triad of fairy-women said to live on the Island of Apples north of the Breton coastline. It is therefore appropriate that the festival of her consort, Samhain, is also associated with the winter apple harvest. Samhain, in fact, has even been called the Feast of Apples.

Perhaps that is why apples, along with Samhain, are associated with divination and fortune telling. The arrival of winter and its hardships provoked an urgent need to look ahead to a better future, to more favourable weather or crop expectations. This optimism would have extended into the romantic sphere of life, which is why many a lonely maiden would perform oracular apple rituals at Samhain, to guide her in the quest for a husband.

Such apple rituals included peeling the fruit in a continuous strip and throwing the peeling over the left shoulder, where it would form the initial of the man that the girl would marry. In Guernsey and Jersey, another more elaborate apple love spell was carried out, appropriately, on the eve of the winter solstice, 21 December. Before going to bed for the night, a young girl wishing to marry had to walk backwards towards her bed carrying an apple in her hand. She would then place the apple beneath her pillow and recite the following spell:

> The Day of St Thomas
> The shortest and the darkest,
> In sleeping let me see
> The man who will love me;
> So be it.

In carrying out these practices, Marie De Gras points out that the Guernsey young folk were following a very ancient tradition when they used apples in charms to try to find out their destiny. [3]

Bobbing or ducking for apples is another activity associated with Halloween. To the modern mind, the idea of trying to bite into an apple while it floats in a bath of water might seem like an innocent children's game. But it was originally a divination ritual, used until recently by young women seeking a husband. The symbolic act of snatching a bite from the apple is similar to the act of grasping good fortune. It might also derive from an ancient ceremony called the ordeal by water, which symbolizes the passage of the soul to the hereafter over the waters that separated them; the symbolic journey across water that we have already described, to the mythical 'apple-land', and King Arthur's last journey to the island of Avalon.

The apple, as a sacred fruit, turns up in fairy stories and mythology over and over again. It is popularly believed that eating an apple from the tree of knowledge caused Adam and Eve to be thrown out of the Garden of Eden, having been first threatened with death. In Greek

St Andrew of the Apple Orchard. The sacred nature of apples is suggested by the name of this Guernsey church, which was once surrounded by extensive orchards

myth, the garden of Hesperides contained a sacred tree of golden apples, also fruits of knowledge, guarded by a deadly dragon. Apples also appear in fairy stories, most famously in Snow White, when the biting of an apple leads to the young girl's 'mini-death'. Knowledge and death, these seem to be the two main mythical features of the apple.

We have already come across deadly fruit before in Kore's pomegranate, which resulted in the young maiden's captivity in the underworld. The deadly apple offered to Snow White by the crone is similar to the pomegranate eaten by Kore. It seems that both of these harmless and palatable fruits have associations with death. Perhaps this is because the apple and the pomegranate are autumn fruits. Their harvest time coincides roughly with the festival of Samhain, and marks the beginning of the dark months of winter, the period of death. In addition, the seeds like those of all fruits, are associated with burial. The seeds must be buried for the fruit to renew itself but at the same time, burial means death. These two factors, the buried seeds and winter harvest, explain the association of apples and pomegranates with death and the underworld and, of course, Puck's own winter festival of Samhain.

The apple was also thought to have the power to help other crops grow. At the start of ploughing operations in Guernsey, cider would be poured deep into the earth to make the parsnips to grow. This link is also worth exploring, because it seems that the parsnip once had a status on the Channel Islands similar to the apple. Like the apple, the parsnip is a winter crop. It should only be harvested after a hard frost and before other new growth starts. In fact, the flavour of parsnips is improved by a frost, because it increases the sugar content in the root, which not only makes them tastier but helps to preserve them. This means that parsnips can offer food all year round, like the sacred sweet cakes of Samhain and Yule. Another advantage of parsnips is that they can be fed to cattle. When given to cows, the sweet parsnips would nourish the milk, giving it a particular yellow, almost syrupy richness.

Parsnips flourish deep in the earth, the domain of the goddess's underworld. The seeds germinate so slowly, it is said that the parsnip seed goes three times to the devil before it comes up. Many private rituals and even prayers were once associated with parsnip cultivation. The Reverend George Whitely, for example, recalled a farmer who used to chant: '*Grosse et longue et pas frouchie*' as he scattered his parsnip seeds – an ancient prayer that his parsnips might flourish. [4]

It may not have been used as an oracular fruit, but the parsnip was once valued as a source of healing, and appears as such in an old Guernsey tale. In a story similar to the tale of the sick cows, a farmer once had a sick pig which refused to eat and started to grow dangerously thin. The farmer was convinced that this was the work of a wizard and decided to consult a white witch. However, a neighbour gave the pig a parsnip, despite the farmer's insistence that it would eat nothing at all. Against his expectations, the pig greedily ate the parsnip and was immediately cured. Both its healing properties and the ability to defeat the ravages of winter are celebrated in this archetypal seasonal tale.

Even the Channel Islands consort or Pouque is associated with the parsnip. In Guernsey there is a most odd recurring story of a Pouque who was frequently seen trundling a barrow load of parsnips around. He was so renowned that he became the subject of a formal inquiry by the witch trials of the Greffe. Many accused persons told the court, presumably under oath or more likely after torture, that they had indeed seen this strange figure with his barrow of parsnips and described it as their 'first contact with the powers of darkness'. The inquiry failed to induce the Pouque himself to appear.

In fact the Pouque could not have been a real person, a local eccentric or humorist in disguise because, as De Garis points out, this wandering figure lasted longer than any single lifetime. The very facts that he was called Pouque (associating him with the ancient monuments) and that his other title was the devil, imply that he was an ancient archetype. De Garis suggests that his parsnips represented excessive appetite and a celebration of plenty, linking this devil figure with the fat sow or pig. In fact, the full barrow that he carried around could be symbolic of a full stomach, which means that the sweet parsnips were part of the body of the consort, like the sweet cakes or roast boar eaten at Yule.

From ritual meals to divination rituals, they are all associated with the planting of the seed and the body of the sacrificed consort, the Bout de L'An, which until recently was publicly burnt and then sent out to sea, in a ceremony that stretched back into the mists of pagan prehistory.

Note
1 Durand, p. 124
2 *De Bello Goth* by Procopius, quoted in Lane-Clarke, p. 2–3.
3 De Garis, p. 19.
4 Blackstone & Le Quesne, p. 301.

7 The God of the Rock

There is evidence in mythology that a sacred king was regularly sacrificed by either jumping or being pushed from a cliff, mountain or rock, into the sea. A number of classical writers, for example, have written about an ancient Greek vegetation festival called the Thargelia near Athens, where the scapegoat was killed by being thrown down from a great height. The writer Hipponax also mentions the Attic ceremony of the *pharmakos*, where the victim could either be burnt or thrown from a high cliff.

Similarly, on a Greek island called Leukadia it was an ancient custom, at the regular sacrifice, to cast down a criminal from a white rock into the sea. There is, according to Robert Graves, also some historical evidence that at the matriarchal festival of the Scirophoria, a human victim was hurled into the sea from a great height.

There seems to be a common theme here, and there are plenty of other examples. The Greek hero Theseus began his reign as King of Attica by throwing a villain called Sciron over the Attic cliffs and into the sea. Another mythical character is Hephaestus, a victim this time, hurled from the top of Mount Olympus for being so ugly. He fell into the sea and was rescued by two goddesses, but was thrown down the mountain again, this time with more serious results. Basically, the idea of a victim being hurled from a great height into a watery grave seems widespread in ancient history and myth.

A similar tradition of sacrifice seems to have survived into Jersey folklore. At the southern end of Anne's Port there is a rock from which it is said 'criminals of a certain description were formerly precipitated'. The rock, known as 'Geoffrey's Leap', was once described as 'impending over the sea'. Erosion has reduced its visual impact, but it is still a dramatic sight when seen from below and potentially dangerous if one ventures too close to the edge.

According to Jersey folklore, a certain Geoffrey was convicted of a crime against a woman and condemned to be thrown down from this high rock into the sea. A large crowd, which included many women, gathered eagerly to watch his death. He was thrown down from the rock, but the tide being in, he landed in the sea unhurt, and swam to shore. The people were divided in their opinion as to whether he had been adequately punished. To settle the argument Geoffrey gallantly offered to repeat the event. He leaped from the cliff top, but this time he died when he struck a rock on the way down.

There are some variations on this story. One is that Geoffrey was condemned to death because he had killed another man in a fight over a woman. Another suggests that he repeated his gallant leap into the sea as a tribute to the beautiful eyes of one of the women in the crowd.

Geoffrey's Leap, Jersey. Is this an ancient sacrificial site?

The existence of so many versions of the tale, plus the absence of any record that such executions ever took place on the Channel Islands, suggests that this story must be a folk memory, perhaps based on the sort of ancient ritual we have described. Victim, scapegoat, or criminal – there is little to choose between the names. In ritual terms, the scapegoat, the winter king, was little better than a criminal, after all. Winter was a threat to the community's survival and the old consort personified this threat. His welcome death resulted in the ending of that threat, and assured the survival of the tribe. The notion that Geoffrey's death represented some form of redemption, either for himself or the community, is also implied in another version of the story, in which Geoffrey is said to have leaped from the rock in order to escape death.

The presence of women at Geoffrey's 'execution' and their input into its outcome, again suggest a matriarchal origin. Geoffrey's fate is also strangely reminiscent of the Greek Hephaestus' two ritual plunges, the second fall being more injurious than the first. Even the name Geoffrey is probably generic and could be seen as comprising two words – *geo* meaning 'earth' and Frey, a Norse goddess, also linked to the Germanic Freya or Freyja, signifying that the name means 'earth goddess'.

Significantly, the site of Geoffrey's Leap is at the closest non-tidal sea access to the fine hill-top dolmen of Faldouet. We have already noted that the entrance to this dolmen is aligned to catch the full moon as it rises every September from the sea at the leap. September is the autumn equinox, when the power of the reigning consort starts to wane, and the darkness of winter approaches; it is also the season when the corn god is violently struck down in the harvest. This could have been the season of Geoffrey's sacrifice. Perhaps this is why a straight line can be traced from the entrance to the dolmen along the track of the September moonlight, directly to Geoffrey's Leap. This alignment cannot be coincidence, and seems to confirm a ritual link between the two sites.

From Jersey comes another cliff-top legend concerning the Crooked Man, an unsightly character similar to the ugly scapegoat of ancient times and the equally unsightly Hephaestus. According to the story, this man was 'twisted and mean' and possessed a large treasure of gold. It was the Christian church that conquered him – presumably the priory after which this stretch of land is now named. The Crooked Man was driven to despair by the church's incessant hymns and earnest prayers. He took a final leap from the rocks into the sea, at a place known to locals and tourists – appropriately perhaps – as the Devil's Hole.

It has even been suggested that Jersey's Bonne Nuit Bay got its name from a shepherd saying good night to his beloved, before slipping and plunging headlong on to the rocks below, still murmuring 'Good night' as he departed this life. Again, the association of love, death and the presence of a woman imply an ancient folk memory of a cliff top ritual similar to Geoffrey's. As we have seen the same site is associated with the other sea ritual, in which the consort is conveyed (rather more gently) to water on a boat journey round a sacred rock, a journey that that will lead him to rebirth and greater fortune.

McCulloch mentions a Guernsey Geoffrey, associated with a vanished dolmen called Le Tombeau de Grand Sarrazin. The actual *Sarrazin* or Saracen was also called Le Grand Geoffroi – 'Great Geoffrey'. Apparently this Geoffrey was far more than a mere common criminal; he was a piratical sea-king, a monster, the archetypal enemy of the British Isles. At one time, the word *Sarazin* or Saracen was a standard name for all marauding bands and pirates, regardless of origin, so Geoffrey would have been a perpetual common enemy of the people, a criminal or dark consort. In fact, Castel Church (the location of the Gran'mère menhir), stands on the site of a fortified castle called le Chateau du Grand Geffroy, apparently named after another generic piratical invader.

The archetypical Saracen, the dark consort, was often personified as a dragon, another archetypal enemy, as we shall see later. Interestingly, the word 'saracen', or sarsen, is also the name given to any large rock used by the Neolithics. Specifically, a sarsen stone is used to guard and restrict the entrance to passage graves. So it performs the role of guardian of the underworld – a role performed by the dragon in many ancient myths.

All of this suggests that Geoffrey of the protruding rock at Anne's Port, the hilltop shrine of Faldouet and the sarsen stone, can be identified as Puck, the Neolithic consort of the rock.

We find our local consort again in a strange verse quoted by De Garis, from an old song once very popular in the Channel Islands and neighbouring Normandy. It describes what sounds like a sacrificial rite, centred on the death of a person called 'my goodman' (a 'goodman', of course, is just another title for husband or consort). In the song, the singer's much-loved 'goodman's' dead body is covered in a shroud, and then the shroud is removed. Once that is done, the strange funeral rite ends in the following increasingly familiar manner:

> I then took hold of his big toe,
> And pushed him over the cliff.
> All the gulls and cormorants
> Were mewing all around him.

The consort's leap into water is, of course, an extension of the sea ritual we discussed in the previous chapter, in which the consort is conveyed to water on a boat. Water, as we have already seen, was sacred to the goddess; it was her holy domain. It was the earth-based dominion of the moon goddess, a belief confirmed by the effect of the moon on the tides and the fact that the moon was often seen reflected on the water's surface. Water nourished and fertilized the earth, enabling it to produce food and sustain human life, so it was a key element in the goddess's procreative powers. For an island nation like ours, the sea was also a source of marine life and therefore a vital supply of food.

Therefore the consort's leap into the sea was an act of union and renewal. When he entered the water, he returned to the sacred domain of the goddess. After his plunge into the divine medium he achieved immortality and ultimate divinity.

This was the fate of the Greek Hephaestus. When he was thrown into the sea, two goddesses taught him smithcraft. From then on, Hephaestus was worshipped as the smith god. In a quite separate Greek myth, a woman called Leucothea (whose name means 'bright goddess') flung herself from the Greek Molurian Rock with her son Melicertes in her arms. The boy became immortal as a result of this plunge, and was renamed Palaemon and worshipped by the people of Corinth as a god.

In a very similar Arthurian legend, the famous knight Sir Lancelot, when he was a boy, was abducted by a goddess, the Lady of the Lake, who then threw herself into the lake with the child in her arms. As a result of this water rite, Lancelot became an immortal hero and member of the court of King Arthur. And so it goes on; there are plenty of other examples in myth.

There are also a number of interesting local versions in Channel Islands folklore. Guernsey, for example, has its own counterpart to Leucothea. La Belle Lizabeau was a beautiful girl who had an illegitimate baby. Turned out of her house, forsaken by all, she rushed to the cliffs and leaped into the sea with the child in her arms. She and her baby were turned into the rocks which now stand there.

Bonne Nuit Bay is associated with another divine plunge into water. A man named William found a beautiful white stallion in his stables. Unfortunately, when he mounted the creature, it headed straight for the sea at Bonne Nuit Bay, plunging William to his death. The horse turned into a rock, the Cheval Roc (horse rock), which can be seen there to this very day. It is also known as Le Roche Guillaume ('the William rock') which suggests that it is William, and not the horse, that has achieved immortality. Perhaps the reverence accorded to this sacred rock, or immortal consort, is another explanation of the curious pilgrimage we mentioned in the last chapter.

These stories, and many others like them, all express a particularly Neolithic vision of the sacred. To the Neolithic mind, rock and stone symbolized immortality; they were permanent and incorruptible. They were also seen as nascent life, representing hope of rebirth, like life frozen by winter. By metamorphosing into rocks, our island heroes achieved the sort of immortality enjoyed by their classical equivalents when they plunged into water.

On Alderney's Clonque Beach is a chair-shaped rock where, it is believed, a holy monk once wrestled successfully with the devil. Having defeated him he fell exhausted on to a rock, which at once turned into a chair for his greater comfort. He settled on it and became part of the rock. Another Alderney rock, the Lover's Chair, at Val l'Emauve was once the meeting place of two lovers who, when attempts were made to prevent their union, joined hands and leaped into the sea.

There is also a lover's leap in Guernsey at Pleinmont. This commemorates a young couple, forbidden to marry, who mounted a horse, urged it to a gallop and directed it down the ravine and over the precipice into the raging sea below. A stone barrier now marks the spot where the lovers fell. Once again, as in Neolithic mythology, a stone or rock has bestowed immortality on the mortal victims of the sea.

Guernsey's rock at Moulin Huet is internationally famous as the subject of a painting by Renoir called *The Boat of the Three Maidens*. According to folklore, three young girls bathed here, unaware that the tide was rising. Their cries for help went unheard and they drowned. The rock, symbolizing their death at sea, dominates Renoir's impressionist painting, and the sacred site looks both impressive and strangely spiritual.

Another rock stands off Moulin Huet. It looks like a man enveloped in the gown and hood of a monk. This rock is believed to be a priest of the old religion called Le Petit Bon-Homme Andriou, who plunged to his death into the sea. Fishermen and pilots show their respect to him by taking off their hats when passing the point where he stands. Sometimes they offer a biscuit or libation of wine or cider. There is even a prayer associated with him, which pleads for protection from the wrath of the sea, and contains the pious entreaty: 'Andriou, watch over all', identifying this local sacrificed sea consort as a god. A similar prayer was offered to the rocks off Jersey's La Rozel, giving them the name Paternoster ('Our Father') Rocks.

There are other rocks on the Channel Islands coasts that fishermen salute. McCulloch noticed that the ancient tradition of paying respect to the rocks, the lofty 'stacks' of Guernsey, was still common in his own time. We have already mentioned the honour paid by sailors to the island of Lihou in lowering their top masts while passing the old Notre Dame de la Roche. This lady, by the way, sounds very like the Greek sea nymph Cymodoce, who lived among sea rocks and had power over the wind. Sailors used to pay tribute to Cymodoce in the hope of a safe and favourable voyage. Interestingly, this Greek goddess has a direct connection with the Channel Islands, because the English poet Swinburne, who visited in the nineteenth century, associated the Greek nymph Cymodoce with the island of Sark.

Of course, it is understandable that a maritime people should respect, and fear sea-bound rocks, as they are an obvious threat to both lives and livelihoods. Nevertheless, this fear is always mixed with awe at the calm beauty of eternal rock, 'unscathed by tempests, bidding defiance to the stormy turbulence which thunders round it', immovable and ineffable in this realm of death. The combination of rock and water – expressing immortality and stability amongst fluidity and death – is a vital feature of the Channel Islands' mythological landscape. Daniel Defoe described it most eloquently in a chapter on Jersey in his *Guide to the British Isles*, when he said: 'The rocks are vast and terrible; the tides rapid and strong; here there is no still water at any time, as in other parts of the British Channel.'

Even the allure of the Devil's Hole is a tribute to the deadly power that can result from the partnership of sea and rock. The original 'devil', the wooden statue that once graced the site, was adapted from the figurehead of a boat that came to grief on the rocks below the hole. Most of the crew were saved, but the event was commemorated by using the figurehead to create a devil figure.

Another guide, published in 1840, responded instinctively to the terror of rock and sea on the Channel Islands, and tried in vain to give it a Christian perspective.

> *The overhanging precipices ... the impetuous waves rolling on the beach below and breaking with violence on the rocks detached from the cliff, together with the sudden disappearance of every object indicating the presence of man, will impart to the mind a feeling of solitude and abstraction from worldly scenes, and lead it almost instinctively to commune with itself, with nature and with God.* [1]

The Neolithic reverence for rock has even survived into modern times, and extends well beyond the culture of the Channel Islands.

When the ancient Greek hero Theseus threw Sciron from the Molurian rock to his death, he was not only killing the old king but installing himself in his place. This act defines the rock as a site of coronation as well as a place of sacrifice. It was the sacred spot where the king/consort stood when he began his reign.

A piece of folklore from Brittany seems to combine the double tradition of sacrifice and coronation on a sacred rock. Valay was a monk who lived near the capital of the Diablintes. He annoyed the women of the town by criticizing their gossip, and they decided to stone him. As these all-powerful women gave chase, Valay escaped by running up the high rocks at the top of the valley of the Rance, from where he threw himself off. He landed safely on rock on the other side of the river and eventually settled in Dinan. The right bank of the Rance where he landed was called Lanvallay after his feat. The rock itself is still supposed to show his footprints.

Valay sounds very like another scapegoat or *pharmakos* figure – driven out of the community, finally departing this life with a high leap into water. He did not die, but was reborn, consort-like, to a new life. The significant detail here is the footprints in the rock where his new, immortalized life began.

A sacred stone circle once stood in L'Ancresse Common in Guernsey. One of the stones was said to be marked with the hoof print of an ox, a mark made by the devil when pursued by a saint. After a final tussle on this rock, the saint pushed the devil into the sea, and he left the marks of his hoofs imprinted in the stone. The devil's reign may have ended at this point, but evidence of his kingship remained in his hoof prints.

The Devil's footprint on Balan Rock in L'Ancresse, Guernsey

Another devil story from Guernsey almost reads like a sequel to this legend. In this tale a Normandy duke was once accosted by the devil. They fought and the duke won. The devil then disguised himself as a beautiful maiden and rowed a boat near the water's edge, within sight of the duke, who happened to be walking along the coast at the time. He saw the boat with its beautiful occupant and boarded it, because he had an eye for a pretty maiden. Without a word, the devil pulled out until they were far out to sea, where he revealed his true identity. Eventually they reached Guernsey. The devil put his passenger on a rock at Jerbourg and left him there. Then he anchored further up and climbed the cliff face, landing on a big boulder on the top, where the imprint of his claw can still be seen. Clearly this was a cliff-top battle and sea ritual that the devil won.

Similarly, Jersey's Crooked Man of Devil's Hole was said to have left his cloven mark on the land to claim it as his own, before he plunged to his death. In Jersey, Rocqueberg, the 40-foot high granite Witches' Rock, famously has on one of the ledges what looks like prints of a cloven hoof, those of a goat, the god of the witches. This rock was the place of the king's regular seasonal coronation and sacrifice.

So footprints in stone mark the both the beginning and the end of a divine king's reign. It is known that pagan inauguration stones, especially in Ireland and western Scotland, carried carved footprints where the king or chief placed his feet when he was crowned. One example is the inauguration stone at Dunadd Fort, Argyll, where the Kings of Dalriada were inaugurated. A group of carvings inscribed on the rock below the summit includes a carved footprint and – most significantly – the incised outline of an animal's hoof mark. This is where the most famous inauguration stone of all, The Stone of Destiny is believed to have lain before being taken to Scone in Perthshire, when it became known as The Stone of Scone.

The Stone of Scone is the rock upon which all the kings of Scotland were crowned. It was removed by the English in 1296 and built into the royal coronation chair in Westminster Abbey. Since then, all English monarchs have been crowned on upon this sacred stone. It has since been returned to Edinburgh, but only on the condition that it is returned to London for all future British coronations. The English monarchy, it seems, cherishes a coronation ritual of the divine king that can be traced back to Neolithic times and the rituals of sacrifice. Perhaps the same origins can be found in the old coronation cry: 'The king is dead! Long live the king!'

As we have seen, rocks and stones were sacred to the Neolithics. They were seen as nascent life and represented hope of rebirth and renewal. It is quite proper that it should also be the spot where a new consort begins his reign – the god of the waxing year emerging as new life from the frozen rock.

From La Pouquelaye to Puck or Pierre, the holy stone lays the foundations of kingship, and eventually, the British monarchy. This is one of the greatest legacies of the Neolithic people to our own times. And it is perhaps no coincidence that the whole island of Jersey is still known, locally, by its old sacred title, the Rock.

There was one particular type of rock that was favoured by the Neolithics: granite. Granite was often the preferred material for dolmens and menhirs, even when it was not locally available and had to be moved over huge distances. It was a granite capstone, for example, that the builders of Faldouet Dolmen patiently conveyed to the sacred site up the steep incline from the coast at Geoffrey's Leap.

The appeal of granite to a builder of monuments is obvious: it is hard-wearing, a truly 'immortal' stone. In addition, it contains large amounts of quartz crystal, making it quite distinctive and attractive in appearance.

Faldouet Dolmen, Jersey. Visible on the top is the huge granite capstone. This enormous rock must have been conveyed from the coast up a very steep hill. We do not really know how it was done

But the presence of crystal in granite also gives the rock a more elusive, almost mystical quality to which the Neolithics, with their intense reverence for stone, might well have been sensitive.

It has been suggested that quartz crystals, because of their composition and structure, contain a natural form of electrical energy called piezoelectric energy, from the Greek *piezo*, meaning 'to squeeze'. It apparently takes a very small degree of pressure to release a tiny current from a quartz crystal, which explains why these subtle electrical qualities are now utilized in modern technology. Since the human body is a buzzing electromagnetic energy system, it is possible that our own electrical output is capable of stimulating a comparable release of energy from quartz crystals and, by implication, from granite. To anyone sensitive to the presence of stone, this could produce a sense of a tangible energy, of a presence that seems to resonate with our own body rhythms, and echo our own feelings and desires. Crystal, after all, has long been linked to natural healing, and the oracular art of fortune telling, most famously in the familiar crystal ball.

Perhaps this is what causes some people to feel a divine presence in or near a dolmen even today, a living god, or spirit of the earth and the rock, to which they feel an affinity, and yet which they feel is more powerful than they are. This could account for the sense of healing that some individuals, even in recent times, have claimed to receive while standing in or near dolmens.

One of the most important qualities of granite, especially to the Neolithic mind, is where it comes from. Of course, all rock originates in the earth; rock, as we have said, is the bones of Mother Earth. But granite is special; it belongs to the deepest, nethermost region of the earth, the realm of fire and brimstone; those parts of the underworld that still strike terror in us all. Granite is volcanic rock.

It is different from igneous rock, which is spewed out through volcanoes, runs down the mountainside as lava, and then soon cools down, gradually becoming part of the fertile surface of the earth. Granite never actually leaves the underworld; it stays where it is. It only reaches the surface in a cool, solid state, after the soil above it has eroded away. Therefore in its original location granite is the stuff of the underworld. This makes it truly a sacred rock.

To this day granite is called plutonic rock. 'Plutonic' is a word still associated with the underworld, a region both of death and great riches. The Greek god of the underworld, Pluto, is named after *plutios*, meaning wealth, a word from which we get plutocracy, a label for society's richest and most powerful people.

It is worth knowing that Pluto, the lord of the underworld, was originally known as the god of the fields, because it was believed that 'the ground was the source of all wealth'. Perhaps the granite capstones often found on top of dolmens ensured that the consort's body rested in the plutonic regions – the original underworld and the domain of the sprouting seed. This also explains why in Jersey, the little people, who lived in the ground, were thought to be very rich. That is also why granite has long been associated with fertility. Natural granite outcrops often feature in fertility rites. Rocqueberg in Jersey (the Witches' Rock) is a peaked mass of rose-coloured granite. In Guernsey, Rocque Balan, or Balan's rock, a mass of granite on the plain at L'Ancresse, used to be resorted to at midsummer, when youths and maidens danced together on its summit, where bonfires used to be lit.

A view of the devil's granite Rocque Balan, Guernsey, where youths and maidens used to dance at midsummer

A modern extension of this link between granite rock and fertility could be the marriage stones found in old Jersey houses, in which the initials of husband and wife, sometimes accompanied by a heart or two, are carved on a granite lintel above the front door. Sometimes a marriage stone was a gatepost, such as the surviving Le Brun gatepost at Le Coin, St Lawrence, which stands erect like an ancient menhir, that ancient emblem of fertility. Perhaps it is significant that many ancient menhirs were once broken up to provide gate posts.

In the north-west corner of Jersey is perhaps the most impressive of all the granite rocks in the Channel Islands: La Pinacle. Rising 200 feet sheer from the sea, it has been described as an awe-inspiring natural menhir. Archaeological investigations have placed it as the oldest settled site on the island, although it has not been occupied since around 200 AD. Balleine has expressed puzzlement that such an isolated, inhospitable site should have been lived on for so long. The soil is barren and the whole site susceptible to winds so powerful they almost lift you off your feet. He attributes its popularity to a religious urge, the attraction and mystical appeal of this awe-inspiring place which 'filled men's minds with awe for the unseen'. [2]

It is probable that it was a ritual rather than a residential site. There is no evidence of sacrificial practice there, no signs in archaeology or folklore that victims were thrown from its edge. However, it is significant that the sacrifice at Guernsey's Vazon Forest took place *at the foot of a huge granite boulder, near the sea-coast'*. The funeral pyre was 12 feet high, no mean height – yet it stretched only to the 'foot' of the boulder in question. If such a site ever existed, it has long since vanished beneath the sea. Nevertheless, the setting for the sacrifice sounds remarkably similar to the Jersey site of La Pinacle.

At the foot of La Pinacle, in the same relative location as the Vazon sacrifice, archaeology has uncovered the foundations of a shrine, a pagan *fanum* dedicated to an 'obscure local deity'. It is clearly visible today, a small stone circle, looking rather like a miniature Stonehenge. Balleine suggested that this *fanum*, which probably dates from around 200 AD, was evidence of a late survival of the 'older sort of paganism' where people still offered reverence to holy rock. All over Normandy, it seems, such shrines were being erected in defiance of the new religion. Balleine imagined generations of pagan pilgrims in Jersey wending their way westward along the island to worship the god of the pinnacle. However, there is no firm evidence that a Vazon-style sacrifice ever took place there.

Apart from the site's impressive appearance, the presence of a certain type of granite, dolerite, could be another factor in La Pinacle's holy status. Dolerite, a hardwearing granite, was prized by the Neolithics for the making of axe heads and it is thought that the community of La Pinacle specialized in producing these. All tools and weapons were sacred objects to the Neolithics because they were made out of stone. As well as being the bones of the mother goddess, stone and rock, as we have seen, contained the fertilizing power of her consort, the god of the rock. The god himself was present in stone, so anything made from it would have contained his divine power.

A marriage stone, St Helier, Jersey. A modern Neolithic fertility symbol?

The idea of worshipping tools may seem very strange to us, but in fact it is perfectly natural. A tool is a miraculous object; it gives the user additional, superhuman strength. With an axe in his hand, a man can

La Pinacle, Jersey. An 'awe-inspiring natural menhir' and ancient ritual site

fell trees, fend off an enemy or kill prey with a single blow; he attains god-like strength. The exciting tendency of stone axes to make loud bangs and fiery sparks when struck would have associated them with thunder and lightning, an attribute of divine energy that later developed into the fearsome power of the supreme gods: Zeus's lightning bolts and Thor's hammer. In fact, until recently the nickname for axe heads on the Channel Islands was still 'thunder bolts'.

The stone axe, this repository of the god's divine strength, would have been greatly revered and highly desirable. Everybody would have wanted to own one, so in those far off days of simple barter it could be exchanged for virtually anything. This makes it an early form of currency, suggesting that the Neolithic stone axe represented the first stirrings of commerce.

The axe was so highly prized that its value exceeded its practical use and even its strength. This explains why many axes found in burial sites are such beautiful, ornate objects, far too elaborate to be functional and made of fragile materials such as serpentine, callaïs and jadeite. Some were as tiny as pendants, others were carved patiently out of chalk. Theses must have been articles of prestige, for they would have been totally impractical as tools. They would have been kept for loving display, rather like a valuable old painting or jewel, or maybe they were hoarded away with miserly thrift like money or gold.

It is inevitable that the sacred axe would also have been a tool of sacrifice. Its gory associations with hunting would have made it central to the blood sacrament of the dying consort. Ample evidence can be found in ancient art, myth and folklore that an axe was used in this way. An item called the double axe has turned up in many Neolithic finds, such as the double axes of stone found in Karnac, and the image of the double axe branded into skulls in Neolithic cemeteries in France, not to mention the double-axe image carved on the pillars of Stonehenge.

The double axe was a prominent symbol in Minoan Crete, where it was associated with the sacrifice of the bull god; in Cretan carvings it is shown mounted between cattle horns. There is an engraving on a slab covering the Neolithic chamber tomb of Gavrinis, Brittany, which also shows an axe placed near a figure of a bull. There is even an eerie survival of a similar sacrificial rite in Guernsey, in which a Neolithic axe head was dipped in a cow's drinking water to the chanting of spells, after which the cow's milk turned to blood.

However, one of the most prominent stone axe sacrifice sites in the

Channel Islands has been claimed by the Church. Its victim has not only achieved Christian sainthood, but has given his name to a church, a parish and the capital of Jersey. That man was St Helier.

St Helier is a hero and the saviour of Jersey. When he first arrived on the island, it was suffering terribly from Viking (or Saracen) attacks, which had reduced the population to a mere thirty. When the Saracens returned yet again to continue their depredations, Helier prayed and made the sign of the cross. At that moment a devastating storm appeared, which destroyed the invaders and their ships.

But, like all consorts, Helier had to die, and with his ritual death he became a martyr, which is a Christianized consort figure. Just as the consort was killed to ensure nature's revival and the survival of the people, so a martyr or a tragic hero makes a sacrifice, the supreme sacrifice of laying down his life, to save his friends or the wider community.

St Helier died saving the island from the Vandals, a tribe whose name is still associated with wanton destruction. When they arrived and started to lay waste to the island, one of them found St Helier and cut off his head with an axe. The saint calmly picked up his head and walked towards the shore, presumably choosing the sea as an apt place to die. The Vandals fled in terror at the sight, and the island was saved for ever. Helier died in order that the community could live. His reward, like that of the sacrificed consort, was to be transformed into a state of blessed immortality. He is eternally present in his cliff-top stone 'bed', now marked and covered by an ancient chapel. Behind the main castle's medieval grandeur, St Helier's ancient Hermitage Chapel can still be found, 'perched precariously on the side of a steep rocky outcrop', carefully enclosing his once exposed 'bed', a jagged gash in the bare rock.

St Helier was killed with a stone axe, the sort of sacred axe that was mined and created at La Pinacle. Balleine, as we have said, charmingly imagined lines of pilgrims converging on the site to worship the god of the pinnacle. It seems particularly appropriate that, on 16 July every year, a similar pilgrimage takes place to the Hermitage Chapel. When the tide has receded, a line of people walks across the causeway to the town's sacred rock and the island's own living Christian god of the rock: St Helier.

It also seems appropriate that the emblem of modern Jersey, the celebration of the immortal glory of its hero, and the proud icon of the island's capital, should be two crossed axes; basically a form of the sacred double axe.

St Helier's Bed. View of the oratory in its cliff-top location. Every July, the people of the island undertake a pilgrimage to this Christian god of the rock

But that is not quite the end of St Helier. When the saint was beheaded, he walked towards the sea, voluntarily offering his body it sea, like a sacred king. However, according to another legend, his body was actually placed in a coffin and offered to the sea, which carried it to his home, the Norman village of Breville. The coffin – appropriately for the god of the rock – was made of stone.

Notes

1 *Barbet's Guide for the Island of Guernsey* 1840, quoted in *Renoir, Artists in Guernsey*, p. 6.
2 *The Bailiwick of Jersey*, p. 89.

8 Fiery Dragons and Jersey Toads

The quest for more beautiful and durable tools eventually led to the discovery of a new treasure in the depths of the earth. This discovery was to have a disturbing effect on the Neolithics, who so loved and worshipped their sacred stone. This new substance was metal.

Metal changed everything. The stone axe – even the double axe – would be replaced by another two-edged instrument: the sword. It was the lithe, swift-moving sword rather than the cumbersome swinging axe that was to become the favoured weapon of the knight against the dark consort (such as the dragon). It also became a badge of divine kingship, as with Arthur, who first found his sword lodged in a sacred stone.

The worker in this new magical substance of metal, the smith, was a true magician. Indeed his use of fire, his cauldron-like crucibles and the wand-like waving of his hammer possibly evolved into the wizard of fairy tale – that magic but vaguely menacing operator of smoke, fire and loud bangs.

The smith's flamboyant magic easily surpassed the delicate and pernickety craft of the Neolithic tool makers. He did more than just knock and chip a stone into shape. He could take a rock from the ground and transform it, crushing and destroying the dull stone to create fiery liquid from which emerged radiant new forms and textures which had a brightness, an elegant shapeliness and a robust permanence never seen before. The smith's work involved genuine metamorphosis, comparable to that of seed into flower or pupa into butterfly, which meant that he imitated the creative work of the goddess herself. The beating of his hammer, like the crashing of thunder, brought a new medium of terrifying power and creativity to what had always been a sacred tool. This made the smith a priest, a creator – ultimately a god.

Nowadays we regard the smith as a key figure in the cusp between the Stone Age and the emerging technology of the Bronze Age. But as far as the Neolithic communities were concerned, he was a dangerously radical presence, an object of deep suspicion.

According to Balleine, the use of metals was established very slowly on Jersey. Even long after it had arrived, most islanders preferred to use stone, which means that smith-craft remained a foreign, imported technique. As a result, its practitioners would have been outsiders. Nevertheless, the discovery of a fine copper axe head at La Pinacle has led one commentator to suggest that the site might have been in the vanguard of introducing metal working into Western Europe.

A hoard of axes, swords, knives and lumps of metal were found in an orchard in St Lawrence in Jersey. These artefacts, some of them unfinished, are generally assumed to be the possessions of a travelling smith who had to bury his wares for some reason and never returned to unearth them.

This reminds us that the smith, as well as being an outsider, has always been a wanderer. Because of the difficulty of finding metals, he had to roam from place to place, trading in his wares. As a permanent outsider he would have been both revered and reviled, a source of respect and fear. Basically he is not dissimilar to Puck: an alien figure in possession of supernatural powers of transformation, similar to Puck's gift as a shape-shifter. His unsettled roving also seems uncannily similar to the elusive motions of the moon or the figure of Puck. It is possible that the smith may often have been victimized as a scapegoat or consort figure, and suffered ritual killing. The Greek smith god Hephaestus is famous in myth for his two plunges from Mount Olympus. We have seen parallels with his story in some Channel Islands mythical figures, like Geoffrey or the Crooked Man.

But the key to the smith god in local folklore is his restless wandering, and his employment of fire. Both of these attributes come together in the figure known as the will o' the wisp.

Very few of us can claim ever to have seen a will o' the wisp, the mysterious faint light that could sometimes be seen on marshes and bogs on still nights in winter. It was probably caused by methane seeping from a biologically overactive marsh and catching fire on contact with air. In mythology, it is a wandering spirit, a pathetic figure condemned to roam outdoors on moors and heaths, night after night, and never find rest. In Jersey, he is known as Le Bèlengi; in Guernsey he is Le Faeu Boulangier, 'the fire of Belenger'.

Le Faeu Boulangier was a winter consort; like Puck, he was the partner of the wandering Dame Blanche. His flickering light, the fire of his forge, was a death omen and would always appear, like the banshee, wherever a tragic event was about to occur. It was also said that the path of any night-time funeral was always lit by the small glistening flame of the wandering Bèlengi. But any attempt to approach this flame of death would cause it to recede or vanish, leaving the inquisitive traveller hopelessly bogged down or lost. Bèlengi, with his infernal light, would purposely wander the earth leading foolish travellers astray. Fire, according to Shakespeare, was also one of the manifestations of Puck and it is hardly surprising that the Welsh will o' the wisp is known as a *pwca*.

A similar character to Bèlengi or the will o' the wisp can be found in Samhain or Halloween celebrations, where he is known as Jack O' Lantern. The name Jack, in fact, is a corruption of joker or trickster, a trait associated with Puck. Jack's story is told in an Irish tale, in which he tricked the devil into climbing an apple tree, then cut a cross symbol in the trunk, trapping the devil there. Jack was therefore barred from heaven for his blasphemy and excluded from hell for his trickery. He tried to negotiate with the devil, but merely received as reward a burning coal from hell to guide him on his eternal search for rest. As Kore found out to her cost, making pacts with the underworld can often mislead and even trap you.

The will o' the wisp's name, Belenger, is a variation of the Norse name Volunde or Velint. It is more familiar as Waylund or Wayland, the British Isles' most famous legendary smith, who had a 'smithy' in Oxfordshire. This is a Neolithic burial chamber, a kind of dolmen, situated a short walk along the Ridgeway from Uffington White Horse. According to the local legend, if a horse needed shoeing, it was taken to Wayland's Smithy and left outside, with a payment of sixpence. The smith would do the job when the owner was gone.

In much folklore the smith became a member of the fairy folk, one of the little people, driven out by the patriarchal invaders. Like the fairies, the smith made up for his inferior stature by his art, which was still useful to the conquering nation. Like the fairies, too, the smith lurked on the fringes of society, doing casual service for gifts or small payments.

This reminds us that the little people in Jersey, who lived in the ground, were also believed to be very wealthy. The Jersey Pouques are associated with silver, especially silver horseshoes, with which their own horses were often shod. (Silver, of course, was the colour of the moon.) These Pouques were known to be quite generous with their silver wealth, according to a story about a certain farmer, James Bailhache, who found his own horse's shoes magically turned to silver by the little people. This gave rise to the local saying: 'I will have my shoes shod like James Bailhache's.' It is a story with interesting parallels to the legend of Wayland Smith, and his skill in shoeing horses.

Only the smith, with his magical knowledge, had the secret of extracting the precious metal from the ore hidden deep underground. That is why, in folklore, the smith is believed to guard hidden treasure. In some tales the smith will lead those brave enough to follow him to find this treasure. This brings us to another mythical creature and consort figure reputed to guard treasure – the dragon.

Central to the smith's craft is fire, from the will o' the wisp to the blazing forge. Sometimes the smith is portrayed with flames coming out of his mouth, making him into a dragon figure. Wayland's 'smithy' is situated near an area called Dragon Hill, the place where St George is supposed to have killed the dragon.

The dragon, as winter's dead time, or god of the dying year, is the most terrifying dark consort figure of all. It is comparable to the boar, but has an even greater capacity to ravage the countryside and spread devastation and death than the most destructive boar.

Jersey has a dragon which shares the same swamp-like origin as the Belenger or will o' the wisp. From an ancient marsh in Jersey's St Lawrence, emerged one of the most elaborate and best-recorded fire-breathing creatures in the Channel Islands: Jersey's dragon of La Hougue Bie. We have already seen that La Hougue Bie is the largest dolmen in the Channel Islands, probably in the whole of Europe. The mound is large enough to support a medieval church, and for many years it was also crowned by a tall gothic structure, known as the Prince's Tower.

There is nothing surprising about the presence of a church here; it was not unusual for ancient pagan sites to be Christianized. Yet there is a central nagging mystery about this particular chapel. Apart from the fact that it is a pagan site, there is no other obvious reason why a church was built there at all. The mound is a substantial hill, commanding splendid views (as later guidebooks were keen to point out), but it is not

Plémont bay, Jersey. Another dragon in the landscape

a particularly convenient or safe location for regular public worship. Surely no one wants to climb a hill every time they go to church, however lovely the view. More surprisingly, there are no records, no ecclesiastical documents, architect's plans, or any other written documents telling us why the chapel was built, or how and when it was first used. History is as silent on this subject as it is on the construction and use of the dolmens. La Hougue Bie's first church is as mysterious as these stone monuments.

It is hardly surprising, then, that the same aura of myth surrounds this chapel as the so-called fairy palaces and Pouquelayes of the islands, and it seems inevitable that a fairy story – a dragon tale – is the only account we have of its foundation and early years.

During the Dark Ages a dragon lived in the great marsh of the parish of St Lawrence and caused a great deal of devastation in the island. When news of its rampages reached Normandy, the Seigneur of Hambye took leave of his wife and sailed to rid Jersey of the menace. With him came his squire, Francis. After killing the dragon in a fight Hambye took a well-earned rest. Francis, however, planned to claim the dragon victory himself and win Lady Hambye, so he plunged his dagger into his sleeping lord. He then hid the body and set sail back to Normandy with the dragon's head.

He told Lady Hambye that the dragon had killed her husband, and that he, Francis, had killed the dragon in revenge. He also told her that in his dying moments Lord Hambye had bequeathed her in marriage to his loyal servant. Lady Hambye believed these lies and consented to obey her husband's dying wish and marry Francis. Her new husband, however, betrayed himself by talking in his sleep. Lady Hambye had him executed. Once her concealed husband's body had been found, she had a big mound built over it, topped by a chapel. This is the chapel of La Hougue Bie.

We can see at once that this is another seasonal myth. The dark year (the dragon) is defeated by the god of the bright year (the lord). This victorious knight is killed in turn by a new seasonal challenger (his ambitious servant) who then rises to take his lord's place as the lady's (or goddess's) consort for a while. Eventually this consort is killed by the goddess, and so it goes on. Like the pyramids and dolmens, the chapel at La Hougue Bie is a shrine to the sacred dead, founded by the goddess, and built over the body of her defeated lord and consort. It is a living expression of the ancient Neolithic death cult, identical in purpose to the dolmen over which it was built.

We have said that the dragon represented the dark consort, like the boar. But that does not explain everything. At least a boar is a recognizable animal, whereas a dragon, with its wings, scales and fiery breath, seems completely imaginary; a grotesque invention of nightmare. Where did the idea of the dragon actually come from?

Whole books have been written on this subject. However, an important clue comes in the *Encyclopaedia Britannica*'s definition of a dragon as 'the name given by the ancients to a huge winged lizard or serpent'. The serpent was a sacred animal and is always seen together with the goddess in early art. From Minoan paintings and figurines to the early images of the snake-wearing Athena, the snake-haired Medusa who turned people to stone, and the spiral patterns found at Knossos and dolmens like Gavrinis in Brittany, the closeness of the goddess and the serpent has been well documented.

There are a number of reasons why the serpent was a divine creature. One of the most important was its ability to shed and renew his old skin. To early humanity this must have seemed a miracle of regeneration, almost as if the snake was being reborn out of the womb of his own corpse. It gave the serpent the main attribute of the consort – he regularly died and was reborn, and this made him a fitting partner for the goddess.

The snake also lives near the bowels of the earth, intimately connected with the Great Goddess, through her fissures and crevices. The sexual implications of this closeness, emphasized by the rather phallic shape of the snake, again expresses that of a partner or consort. To live underground like the snake was, as we have seen, to inhabit the chthonic domain of the earth goddess, where only the immortal can live.

Because he lived so close to the goddess and inhabited her underground realms, the serpent was deemed to be privy to her wisdom. He had already learned the secret of eternal life and was able to pass this wisdom on to humanity. That is why the snake was highly respected in the ancient world for its powers of healing. In fact, as a beneficent force, a healing divinity, it survives to this day as the symbol of the medical profession: a staff twined around by snakes.

This reverence for the healing power of the snake is recorded in the Greek/Cretan myth of Polyeidos and Glaukos. During his long vigil by the dead boy's side, Polyeidos saw a snake and, fearing more harm to the boy's corpse, killed it. Another snake promptly appeared, carrying a magic herb which restored the first snake to life. Polyeidos then applied the same herb and, in turn, brought Glaukos back to life. The serpent wisdom acquired by Polyeidos led to the establishment of the world's very first spa town: Epidaurus. The rites of healing at Epidaurus, assisted by the sacred snake, took the form of bathing, fasting and most importantly sleep. The devotees underwent 'A long rest visited by healing dreams', during which they were visited by the serpent.

The association of the snake, herbs and the restoration of life can also be found in the Channel Islands folk tale, *The Forest of Vazon*. We have already seen the Goddess Judith healing a girl with an incurable wound to her head. What is significant about this act of miraculous healing is the role of the serpent. First Judith, in the manner of Polyeidos and his snakes, applies some healing herbs to the girl.

The old woman placed some leaves, which she selected, on the wound: the bleeding at once ceased; squeezing juice from the herbs, she applied an ointment made from it; then, opening a phial attached to her waist-belt, she poured some drops of liquid into the girl's mouth, gently parting her lips.

After uttering some incantations, Judith raises her hands above her head. Then we see the serpent.

On the right arm was a heavy bracelet, composed of a golden serpent winding in weird folds round a human bone; the head was towards the wearer's wrist, and the jewelled eyes which, being of large size, must have been formed of rare stones, glowed and shot fire as the red beams struck on them through the branches. It seemed that a forked tongue darted in and out.

Apart from healing, another of the serpent's most famous roles lay in the strange and secret world of oracles, statements made by a deity in answer to questions from human beings. They are also a way of predicting the future.

Special temples existed for the giving of oracles across the ancient world. Many of them, like those at Argos and Delphi, became world famous. Epidaurus was an important oracular site too; dreams are a very effective way of seeing into the future. At Delphi, the goddess issued her revelations in a chamber deep inside the temple through her consort, the serpent, who also guarded the place. Powerful, noxious vapours were said to issue from the ground, to inspire the prophecies and repulse invaders – one possible origin of the dragons' fiery breath.

This emphasized the secret nature of the goddess's domain, and the mystery and power that resided in those infernal regions. At Delphi, the serpent was called Python, and he guarded the site, in the same way that the dragon was said to guard treasure sites.

The Channel Islands dolmens may not have been oracular or healing centres as sophisticated as those of Delphi and Epidaurus. But if, as we have suggested, a function of a dolmen was to measure time, this alone would have been seen as an oracular craft. Farmers would consult these time-reading sages with questions of life or death: 'How soon will winter come?' or 'When should I sow this particular crop?'

So, in that sense, the dolmens would have been the oracular centres of their day. It might be fanciful to imagine that real snakes dispensed wisdom at these shrines, yet there must be some reason why a full-scale dragon myth is associated with the largest of them, at La Hougue Bie.

Having said that, there is a guarding serpent associated with a menhir at La Rocquaine in Guernsey. According to an old story, a man once dug under the menhir and found hidden treasure. However, he was deterred from taking it away by the sudden appearance of a creature that looked like a big black conger eel, with large, staring eyes. Clearly this serpent was guarding the dolmen's wealth as effectively as any dragon.

However, we are told that the dragon of Hougue Bie originated, not in a dolmen, but in a marsh. Marshland, as we have seen, is the domain of that other winter consort: the will o' the wisp.

Until recently, marshland was a prominent feature of the Channel Islands scenery. Both Jersey and Guernsey had a number of inland marshes, where small hollows would trap rainwater. Some of these natural pools still exist today in some of the more hidden and isolated recesses of the islands. But Jersey's marshland may well have been more extensive than a few isolated lagoons or bogs. Today the island is scored by a number of picturesque valleys that were once deeper and steeper than they are now, and which carried a number of stream systems from the central plateau to the coast. Where these streams met the shoreline the waters spread out, forming large areas of marshy ground. This marshy land would have been concentrated on the south coast, particularly around St Lawrence and St Helier, and must have been a very extensive area.

There is no trace of the St Lawrence marsh today, of course. The lagoon from which the Hougue Bie dragon emerged, Goose Green, is the site of a picturesque old pub, whose appeal is rather spoiled by the intrusion of

Swamp land near Elizabeth Castle, Jersey, one of many tidal marshes. Marsh is an amphibious, dangerous place of half water and half land. Lying between this world and the next, it is the traditional mythical abode of dragons and other 'evil' monsters

a major road intersection right outside it. Today busy traffic roars heedlessly through the marsh, between St Helier town and the airport.

Marshland itself is a strange, amphibious place – a half-and-half world of water and land, neither one thing nor the other. It is a place of death which can extinguish a human life with a more lingering cruelty than the angry violence of the sea. Yet it is worth bearing in mind that the very name 'marsh' – and especially its Jersaiase equivalent *marais* – is very similar to *mère* and *mer*, two French words meaning respectively 'mother' and 'sea'.

Marshland is a place of intense biological activity where death is accelerated, which expresses the activity of the underworld of death in a particularly pure form. Yet a marsh can also preserve human bodies; a bog was often a favoured place to bury sacrificed victims, although there is no evidence of such burials on the Channel Islands.

It is understandable that the methane fires that spurt from marshes were seen as fires from the underworld – for that is precisely what they are. The scorching heat that moulders beneath the surface of this otherwise wet and watery marshland was probably the first model of the burning regions of hell, just as volcanoes in other parts of the world gave the same idea. It is significant that the modern visitor to the Devil's Hole in Jersey is now treated to a model of the fiery devil himself rising out of an area of marshland.

The amphibious land of the marsh was associated with amphibious creatures, those able to inhabit earth and water. This is why the marsh's blazing underbelly gave us the dragon, that fire-breathing amphibian of the swamps. It was frightening because marshland was the great enemy of our prosperity; we were always trying to reclaim good living land from it. Perhaps the defeat of the dragon expressed a battle between the need to settle and farm good land against the devil marsh that made that impossible and could take your life.

But the marshland also gave us a much more innocuous, even beneficial, amphibious creature that has entered the folklore of Jersey. That creature

The Devil's Hole, Jersey. Here the devil himself seems to rise out of the dragon's own marshland

is the Jersey *crapaud* or toad. Ireland's St Patrick can be thanked for Jersey's toad, even though he was the most comprehensive dragon-slayer in European mythology. He was not content with slaying a single dragon. He drove all of the snakes from Ireland, in a total defeat of the goddess and all her symbols and rituals. After this victory over Irish matriarchy, he visited the Channel Islands, intending to do them the same favour.

But the Jersey people were not grateful – in fact they pelted Patrick with stones and drove him away. He fled to Guernsey, which proved to be much more welcoming. In gratitude, in an act similar to the one he performed in Ireland, he decided to rid the island of all its snakes. He gathered them up and dumped them all on Jersey. From that moment onwards snakes and toads could not be found in Guernsey, but Jersey has a double share. However, it is the toad rather than the snake that is the emblem of the island, and explains why Jersey people have been called *crapauds* by Guernsey people for generations.

Toads share many characteristics with snakes and dragons, especially their marshland habitat. There is even a curious myth, from Wherwell in Hampshire, in which a toad incubated a duck's egg and hatched a cockatrice or basilisk – a dragon whose gaze can turn people to stone. The gaze of a toad has also been compared to that of a basilisk.

Another snake-like attribute of the toad is that, when angry, it will puff up and spit poison, as illustrated in this verse from 'Song of the *Crapaud*, which appeared in the monthly *Jersey Journal*, 1835, Vol 1:

> Oh! I'm a Jersey *crapaud*,
> A bandy-legged *crapaud*!
> In my hole I will sit
> And my venom I will spit
> At the bipeds who are freaking around me.
> Cro, cro, cro.

Many frogs and toads shed their skins as they grow, and so, like the serpent, have been revered worldwide as gods/consorts that regularly died and were reborn. Equally dramatic is their transformation from spawn. As we have said, the Neolithics were fascinated by such a metamorphosis, which expressed to them the fundamental miracle of life: the growth of the seed into food and flowering beauty.

Toads, as amphibians, can move comfortably between water and air. They are nocturnal and diurnal – fully adapted to both night and day.

They seem almost to inhabit a secret world, under the rule of the moon, moving in and out of the goddess's domain at will. They are lunar animals because they are associated with water and also are liable to vanish and reappear, like the moon.

The toad is therefore a link to the underworld and a natural partner of the goddess. This explains why, like the serpent, it is associated with magic and healing. As early as the first century Pliny the Elder produced recipes for various frog/toad charms for love, protection and agrarian fertility. He asserted, for example, that a small bone from a toad's right side would keep water from boiling and a bone from the left side would repel the attack of dogs. It was also believed that toad's bone could also be used to control animals such as horses.

With the establishment of Christianity the toad, like the serpent, became demonized. During the Middle Ages, the superstitions surrounding the toad in Europe linked it with the devil, whose own coat-of-arms featured three toads. Like the serpent, the toad became the partner or consort of the goddess in her infernal, negative form. He was the cohort of Hecate the underworld goddess, who in Greek was known as Baubo, meaning 'toad'.

In more modern culture, toads became the imps or familiars of witches, assisting them in their evil designs. One of the witches in Macbeth has a familiar called Paddock, an old English name for a toad. Toads are also among the ingredients for the witches' brew in the same play, a brew which answers Macbeth's frantic demand for an oracle:

> Toad that under cold stone
> Days and nights have forty one
> Sweltered venom, sleeping got,
> Boil thou first in the charmed pot.

Like the snake, the toad has associations with hidden treasure, most notably in the fabulous toad stone, a jewel that was believed to grow inside the toad's head. This stone had many mantic and therapeutic qualities, bringing healing and good fortune to the wearer. To this day there are two 'toad stones' in Scotland, believed to have curative powers. Once again, Shakespeare had a line for this hidden beneficial quality of the toad: *'Sweet are the uses of adversity which, like the toad, ugly and venomous, wears yet a precious jewel in his head.'*

Jersey's *crapauds* are not mythical. They were once widespread, emerging in large numbers during wet or warm weather, according to local historian Philip Falle, who regarded them with horror. J. Stead also referred with disgust to their frequency and enormous size. Sadly, urbanization has almost wiped them out, which is why they have been virtually consigned to myth.

Although Falle did not like Jersey's toads, he had to admit that their reputation for poison was undeserved and even suggested that their presence kept the island population healthy. They sucked out everything bad in the air, and kept the people healthy. Guernsey, which had no toads, did not have such healthy people; such was the medicinal power of the toad.

Stead also lamented the fact that Jersey's toads were persecuted, citing a gentleman of his acquaintance who kept two toads in his garden for months, where they protected his vegetables from caterpillars, slugs and other pests, resulting in the most flourishing garden in the neighbourhood.

An edition of *Mother Earth News* from July 1983 confirms the beneficial effects of toads on gardens. They apparently consume virtually all plant pests; their presence should be welcomed and even cultivated by gardeners, because they ensure a healthy and fertile growing environment. L'Amy says that many country people in Jersey would happily pick up toads in the lanes and bring them home.

Perhaps toads were also regarded by early farmers as beneficial to the successful growth of crops. A superstition that dates back to Greek times might suggest so. Here the ancient writer Apuleius is writing about the secret of the 'speckled toad'. He seems to be quoting plant lore that was old even in his own time.

> As a safeguard unto your seeds, before the digging and casting up of your beds, you draw about the garden the speckled Toad, and, putting him into an earthen pot, you do after bury him in the middle of your garden, which let him there remain unto the sowing time … And the Egyptian and Greek writers of husbandry write, that the young plants shall not be gnawed nor harmed of any creeping thing if the seeds be sown about the first quarter of the moon.[1]

Apuleius makes an interesting connection between toads, fertility and the moon.

Perhaps this explains the toad's association with fertility – its reproductive fecundity. The creature's abundant spawn and profusion of offspring is remarkable – it makes the sow look positively barren. In some parts of Europe small toad statuettes were left at holy sites by women seeking aid in becoming fertile. Within Gypsy mythology, the

Queen of Fairies was said to live in a castle that was shaped like a golden toad and Scottish folklore held that whoever carried a dried toad tongue over their breast would be successful in matters of love.

The toad was a feminine figure, although, like the sow, it was not associated with maidenly beauty. No doubt St Patrick intended the presence of the toad to be a curse on Jersey, rather like Moses inflicting the plague of frogs on Egypt. Of course he was wrong. It was a gift; an appropriate creature for an island which has continued secretly to worship the goddess, albeit in her darker, less glamorous, winter guise.

Recently the toad returned to Jersey, allegedly with a modern curse. In December 2004, a commemorative sculpture of a large toad was unveiled at Charing Cross in St Helier. The artist was Gordon Young, already notorious for having designed, in his home town of Carlisle, a 14 tonne Cursing Stone, a granite block inscribed with a medieval malediction known as 'the mother of all curses'. Shortly after this stone appeared, Carlisle was plagued with disasters of almost Biblical dimensions. At one point, the council considered removing it, or breaking it up in an effort to lift the curse.

On the column plinth of the statue of the toad statue in St Helier is an inscription which, it has been rumoured, contains the words of another ancient curse, leading to fears that a similar run of disasters would hit Jersey. In fact, the words on the plinth do not contain a curse, although no one would pretend that their message is a pleasant one.

In fact, the toad sculpture commemorates two features of the Charing Cross area: it was once a marshland rich in toads. As we have said, this would have been part of the extensive marshland that once covered the south coast of Jersey, which means that it was closely related to the area of marshland from which emerged the dragon of St Lawrence.

The second feature of Charing Cross is that it was the site of a notorious prison. Charing Cross gaol was a huge building, famous for its fearsome underground cells known as Les Basses Fosses ('deep trenches'). It was impossible to leave town at this point without passing through the underground vault. So dreaded was this underground prison that it became the source of an entire culture of fairy tale.

Children were apparently 'stuffed with 100 fables' about the place to scare them into being good. According to another written account, the prison became a virtual underworld, populated by the spirits of the dead and other chthonic creatures, including monstrous serpents that devoured their unfortunate victims.

The column of the toad. The Jersey toad was a prominent figure in Jersey's folk-lore. This modern statue, in the centre of St Helier, was built on ancient marshland

The inscription on the toad's plinth is the Le Geyt code of law of 1698, which lists some of the gruesome crimes common in seventeenth-century society and the equally gruesome punishments administered at the Charing Cross prison. It lists a variety of grisly judicial tortures and deaths, including strangling on the gibbet, leaving the body there 'until it rots', burning the body, and the old medieval terrors of hanging, drawing and quartering. In a final horrific twist, schoolmasters are enjoined to 'bring their pupils to witness … every sentence involving loss of life or limb'.

The words on the plinth are not a curse, but their message is grim. The sculpture commemorates an appropriately dark vision of the island, linked to the underworld and the presence of the goddess of winter as expressed, perhaps, through the figure of the squatting toad, the dark lady and the witch, and the Hougue Bie dragon that emerged from its neighbouring marsh.

Note

1 *Jersey Folk Lore*, p.90

9 Lands Beneath the Sea

Water is the origin of all life; every creature on earth had its origins in the sea. That is why it is the sacred domain of the goddess, and why most creation stories are set in the sea. This is also why the king/consort was conveyed to water after his death – so that he could join the goddess and become immortal himself. From the Lady of the Lake to the treasure trove of the more sinister Grendel, the underwater world is portrayed in many stories as a land of wealth and enchantment, a view confirmed by the fact that the rivers and seas contain an infinite multitude of marine life.

The idea that there is a secret land beneath the water, a miraculous underworld where only the immortal could live, has found its most popular expression in stories of lands that have sunk under the sea, such as the famous legends of lost kingdoms like Atlantis or Lyonesse.

The sunken kingdom of Lyonesse features prominently in Arthurian legend; one of the signs of King Arthur's return is that Lyonesse will rise from the depths again. Atlantis is said to be a place where humanity once dwelt in peace and happiness, and there was no mortality, misery or want. Lands that vanish beneath the sea have the same mythic, miraculous status as Avalon or the Isles of the Blessed – domains of the goddess.

It is hardly surprising that the Channel Islands, which suffered the constant encroachment of the sea over countless centuries, have more than their fair share of drowned lands, and these in turn have given rise to their own myths and legends. One of the best known is Vazon in Guernsey. Today it is a large bay, popular with tourists, surfers and fishermen. However, beneath this bay is a flooded landscape where a large forest once flourished. An aerial view shows the size of the arc of water that now intrudes into the overall shape of the coastline. With its ring of sea foam, the sunken area of Vazon looks almost like an outsize lagoon.

There is plenty of mythology attached to Vazon, as we have seen. It is the place where Keridwen the sow goddess searched for acorns in the vanished forest, as if she had emerged from this watery landscape like the dragon from the marsh of St Lawrence. Vazon beach was also the location of the Yule log ceremony, in which the Bout de L'An was conveyed to the sea on his death. Perhaps he was being returned to the lost lands of Vazon and his partner Keridwen. According to the introduction of the book of folklore tales, *The Forest of Vazon*, this was the most beautiful part of the island. On its low ground flourished oak and sycamore, and on the higher slopes were massed beech, birch, and sweet chestnut. Glades bursting with a wealth of flowers penetrated the wood in every direction; streams bubbling up from springs and forming little cascades lent an additional charm. This is the place where we are told 'merry crowds' regularly thronged for music and dancing.

Although the stories in *The Forest of Vazon* date to around 709 AD, the year that Vazon disappeared under the waves, much of the detail in the story is archetypal. Vazon is associated with an age of innocence similar to that attributed to Atlantis. The book says that it existed before the 'storm clouds' of war and invasion had touched the island and nothing yet had disturbed its tranquillity. Even more significantly, the people taking part in a series of seasonal dances on Vazon seem positively Neolithic in appearance, and radiate an almost puckish charm and mischief: *'They were a small race, lithe and active, with strong black hair and dark eyes now twinkling with merriment.'*

Jersey has its own flooded bay, even larger than Vazon. The 5-mile sweeping coast of St Ouen's borders the drowned, semi-mythical manor of La Brecquette. This lost domain, like Vazon, was surrounded by a forest of oak trees and it is said that the stumps of these vanished trees can still be seen if the tide recedes far enough. A recent website referred to the whole region, rather evocatively, as 'darkest' St Ouen because of the secrets now hidden beneath the waters.

The writer Daniel Defoe referred to this lost land in his *Guide to the British Isles*, claiming that a 'rich vale' could once be seen there, before the sea swallowed it up. Evidence that this lost land was once rich and fertile is provided by the ancient peat beds that are sometimes exposed along the northern end of the bay. These beds are over 5,000 years old, and have yielded pottery, animal bones, an animal's horn and even thunder bolts (axe heads) during a recent archaeological search.

But the legend of St Ouen's flooding does not end at the land now lying under the sea. The higher land that overlooks the bay, a region known as Les Quennevais, also suffered its own deluge. At about the same time that the sea covered the forest of Le Brecquette, a storm of sand swept over Les Quennevais, which explains why the whole area, from the coast road to the facing hills, is a landscape of sand dunes. This mature dune environment is particularly rich in vegetation and wildlife. It is unique in the British Isles in providing a habitat for the bright green lizard – another dragon figure that seems to belong exclusively to these islands. A number of menhirs can still be seen there, known as the Blanche Banques menhirs – probably named after the pale dunes.

The story of Les Quennevais' inundation of sand can be found in an old smuggling legend. Apparently the sand was sent as a punishment for the wreckers at St Ouen's Bay, who once lured a fleet of Spanish

The sand dunes of Les Quennevais, Jersey, with one of the Blanche Banques menhirs

ships on to the rocks to steal their treasure. As the last of the ships smashed to pieces on the rocks, the captain of the stricken vessel, just before he drowned, stood up and cursed the wreckers, prophesying that retribution would overtake them by the end of the year, for what they had done. He did not say what form that retribution would take.

When the year's end came and nothing had happened to them, the wreckers held a feast to celebrate their escape from whatever dire fate had been prophesied. But as they sat around their boiling cauldron of limpets, a terrible storm arose. The sea swept over the land, drowning the wreckers. When it retreated, it left the district covered with the sand that is still there today.

Although this story dates only from Spain's days of empire, several commentators have suggested that its origins are much older. In fact, Bisson cites it as further evidence that many 'folk memories may go back to Prehistoric times'. For a start, the prophecy, uttered by the dying captain from the flotsam of his wrecked ship sounds far too paranormal to be true. The superstitious flavour of his 'dying curse' places it in a more ritual context, particularly the length of the prophecy – one year – which would have been the period covered by all ancient seasonal forecasts. Equally significant is the 'celebratory' (i.e. ritual) meal of limpets eaten by the wreckers at the moment of their death – a meal which takes place over a goddess cauldron of rebirth. Ritual meals usually preceded a sacrifice, or other seasonal rite. The image of these wicked wreckers chortling over the shipwreck they have caused while stirring their boiling pot, is almost reminiscent of Macbeth's witches, who cackle gleefully over their cauldron about the winds they have raised to upset ships at sea.

The ancient origins of this story are also suggested by an astonishing archaeological find in Les Quennevais: a Bronze Age pot, standing upright on a hearth beneath a layer of sand, looking as if it had been buried there by a sudden deluge. Even more interestingly, the remains of the meal also survived the passage of time; the pot was half full of limpet shells, the same meal as that eaten by the wreckers before their death.

The fact that the wreckers were eating limpets is additionally significant. Along with other shellfish, they often formed part of ritual meals in ancient times. Shellfish are sacred because they belong to the sea, yet are able to sustain a terrestrial life on dry rock. They therefore inhabit both domains, and have the same amphibious status as toads and serpents (to say nothing of dragons!). Limpets even live on rocks. Their presence means that the sacred rock, symbol of fertility and the birth-place of the consort, is also a source of food.

The shape of a limpet actually resembles a cauldron; it holds the gift of food in its shell in the same way that the cauldron contains the wealth and immortality of the earth. Certain types of shellfish were even thought to prolong life if eaten. Ground cockle shells were said to produce an elixir called 'mother's milk', which, like the Great Goddess herself, contained the 'milk of wisdom'. Seashells were also worn as amulets to guarantee good fortune. A ritual connection with limpets seems to have survived on Guernsey until recently, when it was customary to go limpet picking on Good Friday, a day that commemorates a divine death in Christian tradition.

We can assume that the Neolithic dolmen builders also identified limpets with the world of the dead. Limpet shells have been found buried as grave goods in a number of dolmens in Brittany and the Channel Islands. In a tomb in Jersey's St Clement, near the famous Blanche Dame menhir, a shallow pit was found, surrounded by a setting of small stones. When investigated, the pit was found to be filled with thousands of limpet shells.

This burial site is a particularly appropriate place for limpets, because it is very near another location where they can be found in abundance and in their natural environment: the huge tidal stretch of St Clement's.

St Clement's Bay fronts another lost area of land, a huge area which once stretched from Le Hocq in St Clement to Mont Orgeuil Castle in Gorey. But unlike Vazon and St Ouen, this landscape was not lost for ever. It reappears every day when the tide retreats. (This reminds us that the Channel Islands have some of the largest tidal movements in Europe.)

Every day, on the bay of St Clement, the sea daily draws back slowly to reveal its lost land of the dead. It is a fascinating sight. Islands gradually materialize from the retreating water, becoming craggy mounds and then fists of rock that shoot and spread out to the distant horizon of a darkly sallow landscape, austerely beautiful and strangely lunar in appearance. Once the sea has abandoned the site, leaving a straggling horizon of stranded ponds and lakes, the exposed land is an inhospitable place to visit; the craggy, slippery hillocks offer no refuge or comfort and will allow no one to climb them safely. It is not a place to linger.

The fascination of seeing whole swathes of submerged land restored to the world of the living perhaps explains why the St Clement area of Jersey was once the favoured place of the witch cult. Above this moon-

St Clement's Bay, Jersey, when the tide is out – an unworldly landscape briefly restored

Rocqueberg, St Clement, Jersey. An isolated mass of rose coloured granite, where witches would conduct their 'Sabbath orgies'

like, rock-strewn sea world rises the 40 foot high Rocqueberg, an isolated peaked mass of rose coloured granite, where the witches would conduct their 'sabbath orgies'.

An important feature of this marine landscape of the dead is the limpet shells speckling the exposed rocks, those same limpet shells placed in a sacred burial near the Blanche Dame. It could be also argued that these amphibious shell fish represent their own version of the dragon cult.

It is worth pursuing this link between shellfish and dragons because of a strange coincidence of names. Dragons in early English are also known as *wyrms*, worms, or (more interestingly) *ormes*. It is so tempting to see in the word *orme* a relationship to the ormer, another shell fish chiefly found in the Channel Islands. This is not as fanciful as it sounds: ormers are not only a rare delicacy, they share the same sacred nature as other amphibious creatures like limpets, toads and (by implication) dragons. Like toads they are aquatic creatures of the moon. They only lie on the open rock at night. Like other shellfish, their home is the rock, the birthplace of the consort.

Ormers even feature in the extraordinary poem of the pastor's trip to Lihou. We have already commented on the primal significance of the maidens toying erotically with eels and congers. In this same scene of primordial sex, one of the maidens baits the pastor's fishing hook with an ormer. 'Throw your bait here – you will catch maidens', the girls call to him. If the fishing rod is phallic (and the poem's rather arch tone suggests it is) then clearly the ormer was a female counterpart to the sea serpents. Later, in the pastor's erotic dreams, he clutches a 'big fat ormer'. When he awakes, it turns into the flesh of the maidens that he has been sleeping with. Both the eel and the conger are, of course, the phallic snake, original partner to the Great Goddess. The erotic inter-play between the nymphs and the eels expresses the primordial rela-tionship between the goddess and the serpent, found in the earliest matriarchal creation stories in which the goddess emerges from the sea and mates with the sea serpent to create the whole world.

On the subject of eels, an old custom involving catching these elusive creatures, vividly described by De Garis, has created a myth and ritual of its own. The eel hunt always took place on moonlit nights; De Garis emphasizes, more than once, the importance of the full shining moon in this ceremony, under which the eels resembled little serpents and would glitter like silver. Once they had been caught the parties would feast and dance all night round a bonfire, like a pagan celebration of Samhain.

The sand-eeling parties, as described by De Garis, were a piece of fun, a modern Guy Fawkes or Halloween party retaining certain ritual elements. But in earlier times, it would have been part of an earnest quest for food. How far would these small moonlit serpent-like eels, with whom the catcher had to do battle in order to survive, have been seen as the spirit of the moon and the sea, and become magnified in imagination into the larger sea serpent, the dragon or leviathan, with whom the hero could do battle?

All mythology, as we have suggested, emerged from the basic need to survive. Here, in our aquatic landscape of the Channel Islands, fishing was given a sacred significance, and it seems that our hunt for sea food nourished our local mythology. As if to confirm this link between eels, dragons and Neolithic ritual, it is worth remembering that one particular dragon/serpent in Channel Islands myth, the guardian of the treasure at Guernsey's La Rocquaine menhir, was said to resemble a big black eel.

Returning to the world of dragons, the moon-like, inhospitable landscape off the St Clement coast is as active biologically as any dragon-infested marsh. It has been estimated that a single square metre of this wetland mud contains as much energy as twenty-five chocolate bars. Tidal marshland is as rich, both in nascent life and mythology, as any other in the Channel Islands. Although no ravaging Hougue Bie dragon has emerged from this swamp, this large tidal area does have its own dragon myth – at least by proxy.

Next to one of the coast's most prominent landmarks, Seymour Tower, is a rock which bears the name St Samson or Sampson. This saint is believed to have lived on this rock, in the manner of that other god of the rock, St Helier. He may not have defeated a dragon on the Channel Islands, but he killed one that lived in a cave in Cornwall. He is said to have led it from its lair and thrown it to its death over the rugged sea cliff on the peninsula. The transfer of this saint and his legend to Jersey must have been inspired by the unearthly landscape of St Clement and La Rocque. Incidentally, he eventually settled in Guernsey and founded his church (which still stands) on what was once beach land – an area as susceptible to the tides as St Clement and Seymour Tower. Clearly it was a landscape that suited him.

Even the legend of St Clement, the parish saint, seems to belong to the marshy, tidal coastline that bears his name. According to some accounts, he was martyred by being '*lashed to an anchor and thrown into the Crimean Sea*'. This is another plunge into water, very similar to the divine leap of Hephaestus and Sciron. After his death, the sea flowed back to reveal his body resting in a beautiful, divinely built marble shrine. This is, again, a more stylish version of the immortality of the rock achieved by Neolithic heroes.

Clement's association with tidal movements and the landscape revealed by the retreating sea is expressed in another version of his myth in which, after his sacrificial death, his bones gradually emerged from the mud and sand of a retreating tide, implying that he emerged from this marshy domain just like the dragon of Hougue Bie.

St Clement is represented in art with an anchor by his side, symbolizing permanence in the unstable element of water; an anchor is also an object which can be plunged into the depths again and again, and therefore

represents immortality. Even into early Christianity, the anchor represented hope in an afterlife. St Paul directly referred to it as the symbol of resurrection: 'Hope we have as an anchor of the soul, both sincere and steadfast.'

Because of his direct association with the anchor, a tool made of metal, St Clement is the Christian 'smith god'. He eventually replaced Wayland in popular hagiography as the patron saint of all smiths.

Vale St Michael's Church, Guernsey, from across the pond – all that remains of the tidal floods that once made the church a semi-island site

There is another site in Guernsey that used to be regularly flooded. Although the land has now been reclaimed, Vale Church used to be cut off from the rest of Guernsey every high tide, turning it into a virtually inaccessible island. Even two bridges could not provide safe access at high tide and many people drowned trying to cross. Because the lowlands around the church were regularly flooded, a mythology emerged from the area, and an aura of death was said to hang over the place. It was reputedly haunted by the Feau Boulangier, the will o' the wisp, who was often seen dancing on the sands or under the bridge.

Le Feau Boulangier was no ordinary will o the wisp; this was not a distant, feeble flicker in a marshland. It was as powerful and terrifying as a dragon. It was a ball of fire that would leave its marshy domain and rampage across country, usually in pursuit of people. As recently as 1920 a man walking down a lane in Guernsey found himself encompassed within a red glow and saw the hedges on either side of him suffused with this red light. *'To his horror he saw bounding across the nearest field a big ball of fire making straight towards him.'* This ball came straight from the area called Rocquaine, a witches' site.

Another sighting of Le Feau Boulangier was at a place called La Rue de la Rocque, the site of a Neolithic monument, where a man saw a large oval-shaped sphere of light floating in front of him about a foot off the ground. Sightings of this unique dragon of the swamps, have been well documented in Guernsey. In view of this, we can almost imagine Vale Church standing as a bulwark against the terrifying tidal forces that lapped all around it. This is not as unlikely as it might sound, as we shall soon see.

The monks of Vale monastery and church originally came from the famous and impressive priory at Mont St Michel in Normandy. Mont St Michel is a huge, towering rock, a sort of island-cum-mountain, towering defiantly 80 metres above the sea and sands around it. Crowned these days by a cathedral and small town, it is a very impressive sight and is deservedly one of Normandy's most popular tourist attractions.

Mont St Michel has one important feature in common with the Channel Islands – the enormous tidal movement of the sea that surrounds it. In fact the tides around it are deadly. They move at about 30 miles per hour, making the land round about a dangerous place. Over aeons of time countless lives have been lost, and whole villages and forests have been regularly inundated, sometimes submerged for ever under the encroaching waters.

Mont St Michel was originally called Mont Tombe ('tomb on the hill'), which actually sounds like a monument to the death cult and the lethal power of the tides. Tradition says that 'a college of druidesses' was driven from there, which could refer to priestesses or even a goddess.

Once the 'druidesses' had gone, the mount was dedicated to the worship of the god Belenus, whose name has the same root as Bèlengi, the will o' the wisp. He, however, was the spring consort, the sun god. (Belenus was a good sun god, unlike the uncontrollable fire ball of the Boulangier – clearly a very bad sun god indeed.) His shrine was built on top of the mount, in order to defeat the tides. He did battle against the great serpent, that familiar creature of the swamps and marshes, the dragon.

At the beginning of the eighth century the mount was Christianized and an oratory built in defiance of the power of the tides; indeed it is said that the dragon of Mont St Michel was driven back into the sea by the building of this oratory. Belenus's name was changed into the Christian St Michael, the dragon-slayer from the Book of Revelation who heads a band of angels which battle against the dragon: 'Michael and his angels fought against the dragon; and the great dragon was cast down, the old serpent, he that is called the devil.'

Guernsey's Vale Church, also called St Michael's, was a miniature version of the Mont St Michel site, a small islet surrounded by hostile tides. In fact, a large number of church sites on the Channel Islands seem to be smaller versions of Mont St Michel: located on high land partially surrounded by water, and becoming an island at high tide. One important site is Jersey's St Brelade's Church, standing remote above its fluctuating tidal marshes. On a larger scale is Elizabeth Castle, built around that island's own god of the rock, St Helier, and still proudly secluded on a peninsular which becomes an island at high water. Like Mont St Michel, a priory once stood on this site too.

There is also Lihou, another tidal island, attached to Guernsey by an ancient causeway at low tide. We have already discussed the priory that once stood on this holy island, particularly its rather unconventional monks. As it happens, the monks of Lihou came originally from Mont St Michel, as did those of Vale.

From the towering Mont St Michel to Geoffrey's Leap and Jersey's Hougue Bie, we find the same mythological battle enacted. It always takes place on a raised area of land, which can be an island, *hougue*, hill, mountain or cliff top, and this high land generally overlooks a sea, river,

The mound of La Hougue Bie, Jersey. The dolmen mound was a place of death and rebirth, 'the womb from which the dead are reborn'. It could also be the site of apocalyptic dragon-slaying battles between the forces of good and evil

marsh or flat land. A battle takes place on this summit between good and evil, light and darkness, winter and spring. Winter or darkness is defeated and this defeat involves a great fall into the sea/water/ swamps beneath.

As we have seen at Mont St Michel, this cosmic battle, this version of the seasonal sacrifice, was eagerly embraced by Christianity. But in Christian dragon-slaying legends, the dragon's death is always final. The beast has been defeated for ever and will never return to ravage the land. Perhaps this particular dragon-slaying myth represents not a temporal seasonal battle, but a permanent conquest – an enforced change to an older culture. This cultural change signified the defeat of the goddess, and her replacement by the sun god.

People preferred the masculine power of the sun over the goddess's feebler, more inconstant moon. The sun god represented the eternal vigour of nature and the healthy outdoors, as opposed to the lachrymose murk of winter, the gloomy underworld of bogs and tides, and the morbid rituals of death. People wanted the sun god to defeat winter for ever. They called him 'king' and 'lord' and prayed that he would reign over the land and all human destinies, bestowing eternal spring and banishing winter's darkness. With its misery and want, winter would never reign again.

Of course, the hatred and dread of winter had always motivated the sacrifice, in which the death of nature would be overcome and winter defeated by the spring. But in the new religion, the victory over winter became the one and only drama. More importantly, the victory had to be permanent.

This change in perspective, resulting in the defeat of the goddess, was probably caused by changing conditions for the farming communities. Agricultural techniques were becoming more efficient with the arrival of metal, and men were gaining greater dominance over nature. We no longer saw Mother Earth as divine. We moved away from propitiating the goddess to controlling the environment and changing it to suit ourselves. We ceased, for example, to see the marsh as a source of rich life; it was an area of useless and even dangerous land which had to be tamed. The seasonal failure of the earth's fertility became a misfortune that had to be fought against and overcome for ever. We lost our harmonious relationship with the earth as nurturing mother goddess. We no longer propitiated her dark side. We fought against it. The ultimate outcome of this change, this ousting of the goddess, was that religion and mythology became increasingly patriarchal.

But Channel Islands folklore seems different. Even Jersey's dragon tale of Hougue Bie does not end with a permanent victory over the forces of darkness. The conquering knight himself is killed and becomes the interned consort, and then his killer is killed – and so it goes on, like the seasons. The only permanent, unchanging presence in this legend is that of Lady Hamby – the goddess herself. This and other evidence suggests that our folklore is still fundamentally matriarchal in nature.

For a further sign that the old pagan beliefs were never fully defeated at Guernsey's Vale or St Michael's Church, we need only look at an extraordinary ritual associated with the priory and the monks of the Church. This was the remarkable island-wide procession called the Chevauchée de St Michel.

This *chevauchée* (a word which means 'cavalcade') was a formal procession of officials and servants, riding on horseback around every field and patch of land on Guernsey. It took place at midsummer every three years and was initiated by the priory of St Michel, who held ownership rights over common land. The official purpose of the caval-cade was to collect tithes and ensure that the roads and boundaries were in good order. However, Durand points out that the custom is older than any of the island's roads and De Garis, who has no doubt as to the pagan origin of the custom, mentions a number of stopping-off points where fertility rites were performed.

There were quite a number of these points. One was the Rocque des Faies in the Forest parish, known also as the fairy ring because it was where the fairies were said to hold their revels at night. The monks' footmen would dance, fairy-like, round the rock. After their dance, they would knock on the door of a nearby house to claim a glass of milk, a drink favoured by the fairies and associated with the nourishment of the moon

The fairy ring which the Chevauchée de St Michel danced around

goddess. Another port of call was a Neolithic menhir on the hill called Les Pointues Rocques. The footmen would dance around this stone too.

The *chevauchée* also stopped at a grass mound at Les Pezeries where, according to folklore, a coven of witches was 'regularly feasted by Satan'. Here the attendants of the monks would sit down and be 'regaled with food and wine' just like the witches. They would then move on to a boulder near Jerbourg, said to have the imprint of the devil's claw imprinted upon it, and perform fertility rites there, again, in much the same manner as the witches of Jersey's goat-imprinted Rocqueberg.

The localities favoured by the monks of St Michel included Le Bourg and Jerbourg. The name bourg (from Scandinavian *beourg*) means a tumulus or standing stone and led the folklorist McCulloch to describe this part of the Guernsey coast, from Jerbourg to Pleinmont, as consisting of bold headlands, *'rising like pyramids and obelisks'*.

This extraordinary cavalcade would eventually come to an end at another menhir near Forest Church, at the King's Mills. This large rock had a partial inscription, *Le Perron de Roy* (the king's mounting block) because it was used as such by the leader of the cavalcade. The ritual tour then reached a truly astonishing climax. Having encircled all the arable land on the island, the cavalcade circled round the miller as he stood on the sacred stone holding in his hands plates of newly ground flour. De Garis is in no doubt that the original purpose of this was to bless the fields and increase their fertility.

What is extraordinary about this ritual is that we are not looking at an obscure medieval practice, conducted in secret away from the disapproving gaze of the Church. This was a public ceremony conducted every three years and only discontinued in the nineteenth century. It was briefly revived in the 1960s, but is now only a memory.

Jersey's Hougue Bie is the centre of a similar pagan cavalcade that was revived twenty-five years ago, and still takes place to this day. At 6 a.m. on 1 May, a group of morris dancers assembles at the *hougue*, and commences a dance that takes them around all the island parishes, finally ending back at Hougue Bie, at six o'clock in the evening. The stated intention of this circular spring dance is to 'ensure that all the fields are fertilized'.

St Michael, the Christian dragon slayer, as we have seen, has his own small mount on Guernsey's St Michael's Church. But perhaps the dragon has not been killed. Today the church has another mythological figurehead, one of the most mysterious rock structures to be found on the Channel Islands. In front of the church entrance, at the brow of the barrow-like incline, stands what looks like a striking natural outcrop of rock, whose top is roughly on a level with the earth at the tip of the hill. A closer examination reveals a dolmen-like structure, a kind of rough capstone straddling two low supporting rocks, creating at least part of the familiar passage grave arrangement. But it is the head, or facing supporting stone that is most striking.

The rock clearly resembles a dragon's face. Large eyes, which appear to be closed, as well as a well-placed nose, are clearly marked. As soon as one has absorbed this astonishing image, it becomes clear that the whole structure resembles a crouching beast. As well as its head, the dragon's rear and front feet can be distinguished from protruding rocks at each side. Its capstone strongly resembles a spinal column.

View of the dragon's head and articulated neck at Vale Church. Great care has clearly been taken with its construction

Even the neck is articulated, with a delicate arrangement of small bones fitting neatly into a carefully shaped aperture at the base of the head. The head is also supported in its position by a pair of strategically placed stones on each side. It is these fine details which suggest that the dragon is not a random pile of rocks, or a wrecked dolmen, or a naturally occurring feature. It was carefully and deliberately constructed in this way.

From many viewpoints, the creature is partly squatting, partly immersed in the land of the island site, as if wallowing in a swamp, halfway between this world and the next. Modern building and tree growth blocks its view of Vale and low-lying L'Ancresse today, but it is clearly guarding its site.

It has been suggested that the dragon's head might be a broken *logan stone*, a natural rock formation that can be rocked if force is applied to it. According to Daniel Defoe, there was once a logan stone in Jersey, at Les Landes in St Saviour, which he compared to the famous one in Scotland.

Logan stones have always been associated with supernatural powers, perhaps because they mean movement and movement implies life, the life nascent in the living rock. The word 'logan' may also have a link with Danish *logre*, meaning to wag the tail. The symbolism of a wagging tale can only refer to animal life. So maybe our sleeping dragon once had the power of movement, as was sometimes attributed to the Gran'mère of St Martin's Church.

So the church's patron saint is the famous Christian dragon killer, but in the grounds of his church, his enemy the dragon, that emblem of the old religion, stands undefeated, clearly feeling that his precious site still needs guarding. The tidal waves, the moon's influence and the spirits of the water have long receded. Yet on this ancient sacred site, the dragon consort of winter stands on guard, immobile, tolerated but unrecognized, leaving us wondering if the time will ever come when this sleeping god of the rock, like the rock-bones of the buried mother goddess, will ever awake.

View of the whole body of the dragon at Vale, which continues to guard St Michael's mound

10 Black Dogs and Guernsey Donkeys

Apart from Vale Church, there is another church on Guernsey that seems to be connected to Belenus: St Martin's de la Bellouse. This church has its own figurehead of the goddess in one of the island's famous crone menhirs, the Gran'mère. But if the name Bellouse is derived from Belenus, the sun god and dragon killer, it seems odd that the crone goddess should be associated with the site.

As it happens, the common root (*'bel'*) is simply a title of the god or consort; it means 'lord' in the same sense of Adonis. A version is found in other god titles like Baal or Beelzebub. In fact, one of the names of the witches' devil from Le Catioroc was apparently Baal Berit. Besides, the winter god of the marshes is Bèlengi or Belenger, so we must be careful about drawing too many firm conclusions about the name. (It is interesting that the swamp in St Lawrence, the birth place of the Hougue Bie dragon, is called *Bel Royal*. However, general opinion has identified it as a Viking name, with the 'Royal' being a reference to the presence of Charles II.)

To extend the feminine connection, Beltaine is also the name of the horse goddess. Her consort is Bel, one of whose manifestations is a white horse, which we have come across several times already in Channel Islands folklore. We have mentioned the white horse that carried William to his death in the bay of Bonne Nuit. Each day at low tide, this horse's head emerges proudly from the middle of the bay, confirming the Cheval Roc as Bel, the god of the rock. A horse is also associated with the lover's leap in Guernsey at Pleinmont, in which it plunged into the sea with its two riders.

In Guernsey there was a horse which used to carry large numbers of young men on his back, and then deliberately deposit them in the muddiest water he could find. In Ireland, there was a fairy horse that did the same, known as the *phouka*.

It is not unusual to identify the horse with the sea. We commonly call the surf riders on rough seas 'white horses'. Perhaps the name for a female horse, 'mare', (very similar to the word for sea) confirms both this link with water and the divine mother.

Perhaps we should call the horse Puck, the title of our Channel Islands consort. According to Shakespeare, one of Puck's favourites was a horse; he boasts about being *'a fat and bean-fed horse beguile, neighing in likeness of a filly foal'*. In Jonson's poem, Puck turns himself into a horse so that he can entice weary travellers on to his back and then gives them a wild and terrifying ride across country before finally dumping them in a ditch.

The notion of a horse consort might explain the extraordinary burial found in La Hougue Boëte, in St John, Jersey, in which a cist was found to contain a man lying on top of a horse. Although the horse's teeth have been identified as modern, this does not invalidate the ritual nature of the find. A similar and probably much older burial was found at Icho Tower at St Clement's, in the vicinity of the witches' neighbouring Seymour Tower, refuge of the dragon-killing St Sampson. The bones of a single human and horse were found on a small ledge behind the tower between 1919 and 1929. In 1912, the teeth of several horses were found in a dolmen in St John, suggesting that horses' heads were regularly buried with the dead in Neolithic times. This again identifies the horse as an ancient consort figure.

We have already mentioned the close association between horses and the Pouques, the fairy folk of the Channel Islands. Horses also formed an important part of Sark's midsummer celebrations. On St John's day, horses would be garlanded with flowers and ridden by young people. On their travels across the island, the youngsters were fêted and welcomed by everyone with offerings of food and drink – almost as if these horse-riders were the spirits of Samhain, who needed to be appeased with gifts.

Another horse myth, the story of the Black Horse of St Ouen, apparently belongs to more recent times. Yet it contains so many mythological elements that it confirms that much oral history, like folklore, contains memories that may go back to prehistoric times. It is dated during the 1460s, at the time of the brief French occupation of Jersey. This was a dark time in its history, comparable to the fate of the island under the Saracens during St Helier's time, and could symbolize a period of extended winter in Jersey's fortunes.

In this story, the Seigneur of St Ouen, fishing in his pond, was surprised by a band of marauding French soldiers. He leaped on his horse to escape, but was cut off by another band ahead of him, so he rode towards a deep ravine known as La Val de la Charrière. Preferring death to capture, he leaped across the ravine. He survived but the horse did not and was given a hero's burial in the Seigneur's garden. As we have said, the story contains a number of familiar mythological elements, including a huge leap. In fact, there is some doubt as to whether the horse burial at St Ouen's Manor really dates from the 1470s, or belongs to a much earlier period. An ancient menhir appears to be built into outbuildings on the manor, suggesting that it might have been an earlier ritual site.

On the subject of black horses, sometimes the Irish *phouka*, the fairy horse, took the form of a jet-black dog with blazing eyes. This sounds very similar to another legendary animal in Channel Islands folklore: Jersey's Black Dog of Bouley, a beast with large, saucer-shaped eyes, which would roam the lanes and cliff paths round Bouley Bay dragging its chain behind it. Less well known but equally menacing was the Jersey black dog that used to run from Ville au Neveu to Cinq Verges, Millais, again with a chain hanging to its neck. It was believed to run the same road, over and over again. This *phouka* dog sounds very similar to the itinerant figure of Puck, especially as described in this old Jersey rhyme:

> Lost on a road …
> Who will release him?
> Black dog;
> Between this world
> And the next,
> Waiting to be redeemed. [1]

Jonson's poem about Puck confirms that another of his favourite animals was the dog.

The island of Sark also had its own black dog, as big as a calf, with flaming red eyes and fiery breath. It too dragged a heavy chain and would pursue a person to death, usually along the narrow strip of land called La Coupée. Guernsey also had a creature known as La Biche, described as a large brown beast the size of a calf, with enormous red, staring eyes.

Guernsey had a number of other black dogs, some of which had a direct association with dolmen sites and the secrets of the sacred dead. There was once a legendary dog that used to prowl round megaliths, known as *la beste* or *la bête*, whose presence gave rise to place names like Rue de la Bête and Courtil de la Bête. Other Guernsey dogs had names directly associated with death, such as Le Tchico, whose name means 'the dog of the dead'. Another black dog, Le Chien Bodu, was said to haunt the area called Clos du Valle and a holy cross was built at Ville Baudu to keep him away. This dog's name, Bodu, is derived from the German *bohdu* and Gaulish *bodu*, meaning 'conductor of souls'. Even if the frightening appearance of these dogs did not kill you, their appearance was usually an omen of death; rather like the banshee or the Dame Blanche.

This widespread association with death is the key to the dog's place in legend and folklore across the world. In ancient Greek mythology, the most famous dog of death is Cerberus, the great sentinel and guardian of the underworld. His bright saucer eyes are associated with his namesake Sirius, the dog star, the brightest star in the sky. In some representations, Cerberus is portrayed as a serpent, sometimes even as a dragon-like figure. Whatever additional guises they may have, dogs as guides or guardians of the underworld are found in mythologies from Greece to northern Europe and even as far away as the Americas.

Dogs are traditionally associated with the world of the dead. They are even supposed to be able to sense death; they are said to start howling when their master is about to die. They are also believed to be able to see ghosts. There is a story in Guernsey of an old man who 'often heard the wheel of his cider-press turn at midnight when not a soul was about and see his cat and dog frightened at something he could not see'.

Basically, though, the dog is a scavenger, which is enough in itself to associate it with the world of the dead. Dogs are infamous for burying and unearthing mortal remains like bones, an action which is, in a very lurid sense, like bringing something back from the dead.

In Neolithic times, excarnation (removing and reburying human bones) was probably a familiar part of religious death rites. It may well have been normal at such times to see dogs gnawing on human corpses, crunching the bones into small fragments. Such a gruesome sight, such intimate contact with the very bodies of the dead, would reinforce the dog as the conductor of souls to the underworld. They are the guardians at the boundaries of the two worlds, providing a link between this world and the next. In mythology, the dog fulfils the mantic role of consort; like the serpent, he is the mediator between humanity and the domain of the goddess.

That is the mythical nature of the Channel Islands' black dogs. They are guides to the underworld because they herald death. They wander between two worlds, like Puck, between this world and the next, their trailing broken chain symbolizing the umbilical link with death and rebirth. Some are even associated with the Channel Islands dolmens, those gateways to the underworld. The dogs' flaming eyes are reminiscent of the bright eyes of Cerberus, and just as Cerberus is a mixture of dog and serpent, so the fiery breath of the Sark black dog resembles that of the dragon.

Perhaps this is why, in Jersey folklore, the master or god of the witches is sometimes said to be a black dog, able to broadcast a call to his witches that is unintelligible to ordinary persons.

Several Channel Islands dogs are also said to guard treasure. There were rumours of buried treasure in the vicinity of Guernsey's La Bête and a black dog was believed to be its custodian. In an old house in Petite Port, Jersey, another black dog was believed to guard treasure. Buried or hidden treasure, as we have seen, symbolizes the hidden wealth of the fertile underworld to which the divine consort, existing between both worlds, had access.

The black dog also appears in a very strange story from Jersey, called 'the Wizard and the Cows'. A farmer once quarrelled with his neighbour. He then noticed that his cows were getting weaker, and that their output of milk was diminishing. He decided that this was the work of a witch or wizard and kept watch the following night, armed with a gun.

At about midnight, a large black dog, belonging to the man with whom the farmer had quarrelled, jumped over the hedge of the adjoining field. It ran towards the cows on its hind legs and began to dance before them. The cows also stood up and danced. The farmer fired his gun at the dog, which ran off with howls of pain. The next day the farmer's neighbour appeared with his arm in a sling. The cows no longer danced at night and soon regained their strength.

The ritual elements in this story are quite clear. The quarrelling neighbour was the farmer's seasonal adversary threatening his livelihood, and he was transformed into a black dog. When the farmer shot at the dog, he wounded his scapegoat, thereby removing the threat to his prosperity. This story clearly identifies the black dog as the dark consort.

Dogs are natural guardians, unlike boars or serpents. They instinctively watch and protect our hearth and home. But they can be aggressive if abandoned or let loose, and the frightening Channel Islands black dog perhaps implies a severing of that co-operative relationship between humans and dogs, symbolized by the broken chain. The black dog no longer graciously escorts and guides people to the underworld; he merely frightens them into an early grave.

The *phouka* also represents a loss of co-operation between humanity and the consort. This wicked fairy horse does not carry his riders safely and comfortably to the next life. Instead he hurls them to a brutal death, usually under water, like a sacrificed consort or the 'criminal' Geoffrey.

In the same way, the trickster Puck, deluder of travellers, does an incomplete job of guiding people to the otherworld. He does not lead them to a celestial destination; he lures them away from their expected life path and takes them on an incomplete journey, abandoning them halfway to the next world. His victims are led astray, left stuck between two worlds, wandering lost and in limbo, sometimes in a state of life-threatening danger.

The Welsh Puck, or Pwca, a 'dusky little figure', is said to have led a peasant to the edge of a great chasm with a roaring torrent of water rushing below him and left him there. The poor man, abandoned in the dark, standing on the edge of a watery precipice, is very close to joining the other world. He is suspended, like a consort about to make the divine leap, but unable to do so. His so-called guide Puck, instead of conducting him there, makes the leap alone and of course survives it: 'The Pwca leapt across the fissure and, let out a malicious laugh, leaving the unfortunate man far from home, standing in pitch darkness at the edge of a precipice.'

According to Bois, there is a theme of metamorphosis in these Channel Islands animal stories. They are not concerned with the real or imagined existence of black dogs or water horses at all. They are about those people who can turn themselves into black dogs, play practical jokes on neighbours or join their friends on the road at night. In other words, these creatures are not real or mythical beasts at all; they are examples of people dressing up as beasts.

In Guernsey, sixteenth- and seventeenth-century records mention plenty of prosecutions of people accused of dressing as animals and running amok around the countryside, or being disguised by night in a most 'hideous and shocking form'.

One of Puck's favourite animals, as we have seen, was the horse. Guernsey records tell us that ceremonies involving dressing up as horses were suppressed in the seventeenth century. A character called Blampied was indicted 'for having by night gadded under the form of an artificially re-skinned mare'. His companions were to be arrested on account of having 'gadded by night' in his company. A later nineteenth-century report states that in Sark's farmhouses 'there was always … a stock of horse-skulls in hand for the occasion', the population being 'wont to disguise themselves in the hides and with the heads of a variety of beasts' in the Christmas season.[2]

Horse ceremonies were not exclusive to Guernsey. Calvinist authorities also condemned similar revels in Jersey. In local records, the word *resneries* repeatedly occurs; it is a local translation of the English 'horse harness', used to mean both 'livery' and 'disguise'. Such dressing-up and trickery were once common in the Channel Islands, and were known as the *vueilles* or *veilles*.

As it happens, the custom of dressing up as animals is as old as humanity itself. Before the development of agriculture, hunter-gatherers would regularly perform rituals in which one of them dressed up as the animal prey and the rest pretended to hunt and kill him. It was believed that acting out a successful hunt would influence subsequent events and guarantee that the next real hunt was equally successful. (It is probable that this mimetic behaviour developed later into the traditions of drama.)

This idea of homeopathic or imitative magic – that you can make things happen simply by acting them out – persisted, as we have seen, into later vegetation fertility rites. There is an obvious similarity between killing prey and sacrificing the consort. It is possible that this form of sacrifice developed out of the hunt, ending with a similar ritual 'tearing apart'. Whether or not a real human killing always took place, the consort would have 'become' the animal for the duration of the rite, which explains why, in much mythology, the human consort 'becomes' an animal, such as a dog or a horse.

Dressing up as the animal would have been as important as the ritual itself. As we have said, the Neolithics revered the phenomenon of transformation in nature. The sight of the planted seed metamorphosing into a flower or crop, or a caterpillar transforming into a butterfly, filled them with wonder at the miracle of life and the divine presence of the goddess. To imitate this metamorphosis, by literally turning into something else, was to celebrate this miracle and become the goddess's partner in the divine process of creation and rebirth.

The Black Dog of Bouley has been dismissed as a fake, a piece of 'horse play' by an eighteenth-century French royalist who dressed up as a dog for a joke. Even if true, this does not deny the animal's mythological authenticity. As we have suggested, it might well have been the same Neolithic tradition of dressing up as the animal which gave rise to myths such as black dogs, dragons and giant worms in the first place.

In Guernsey, at festival times, it was common for a person to disguise himself as a donkey to frighten people. He would carry the head at the end of a stick and place it on his own head, having first covered himself in a sheet. By means of cords, he would make the jaws of this head open and shut with a noise, and then run after people in the house, trying to bite them. Not surprisingly, this resulted in a general turmoil, some people screaming with terror, others laughing at the joke. This is reminiscent of Puck's trick in *A Midsummer Night's Dream*, when he mischievously places the head of an ass on to another character, Nick Bottom. Perhaps Shakespeare was drawing on a similar English tradition when he wrote that scene.

All of this might help to explain the origin of the island's totem animal, the donkey, Guernsey's counterpart to the Jersey toad. Perhaps the Guernsey donkey was the island's Puck.

All this animal dressing might also explain the more sinister tradition of the werewolf. It is easy to see why the wolf might have become a sacrificial animal to the later farming communities. Unlike his domesticated cousin the dog, the wolf was an implacable enemy to humanity, especially farmers dependent on small livestock. To them, a wolf was as destructive as any ravenous boar or fiery dragon; every raiding visit brought them the devastation of a winter. The wolf seems to have left its mark on the north coast of Jersey, with mysterious ancient names for landmarks like the Wolf's Caves and the nearby Wolf's Lair; a name that sounds much older than the Napoleonic guardhouse that currently bears the name.

Sometimes, of course, the enemy was not a wolf. The theft and killing of livestock was often carried out by brigands or poachers, especially in the days when the Channel Islands were assailed by raiding enemies such as Vikings, Saracens and Normans. (Jersey's Geoffrey, the archetypal enemy, has been identified with the Saracens.)

So in the hard-pressed agricultural communities of Europe, the rituals of sacrifice continued to be as popular as before, forging collective solidarity against a common enemy as they had always done. The wolf, and its ritual or human counterpart the werewolf, had become the new dark consort.

That is why the werewolf shows many of the traits of the consort. Like the scapegoat, or *pharmakos*, the werewolf could be as much of a victim as a villain, condemned and driven from society with loathing. He was destined to be an outlaw and outsider, and treated very harshly; often attacked with fists, stones and sticks.

To the eighteenth-century Norman peasantry a werewolf, or *varou*, was an outlaw, existing outside the boundaries of humanity. Wanderer, outlaw, trickster, fairy, or demon, the wandering *varou* is another version of the itinerant Puck. There is even a French medieval legend about a soldier turned outlaw, who changed himself into a werewolf and began a series of attacks on children and adults until defeated by a carpenter. Here, the werewolf has turned into the monstrous boar or dragon.

The Norman–French word for werewolf, *varou*, is also associated with the fairies. Similarly, when one delves into Channel Island folklore, the distinction between *varou* and fairy often becomes blurred, because the *varou* is often associated with the 'underground' fairies living in dolmens and mounds; the original 'spirits of the dead'. There is a cave in Guernsey called the Creux des Varous, which, it is said, leads to a secret tunnel that runs to a dolmen called Le Creux des Fées, from where fairies would dance on a holy hill nearby. These underground fairy folk often manifest themselves as 'big wolf-life hounds, or goats with fiery eyes', guardians of the treasure of the underground caves and menhirs of the island.

McCulloch even suggests that the word *varou* comes from the Breton word *varw* – meaning 'the dead'. In its closeness to death, McCulloch suggests that the werewolf can be traced to ancient rituals of the dead and the beatification of heroes, and even goes on to claim that Guernsey, in the days of Demetrius, was known by the name of the Isle of the Heroes. Of course this reminds us of the ancient status of the Channel Islands as islands of the dead, a sacred function that almost certainly stretched back to Neolithic times.

McCulloch tells us that an alternative name for Guernsey in the time of Demetrius was the Isle of the Demons, which implies that there was an aspect of the Varou or werewolf that was much wilder than the gentle reputation of fairies. As well as being a wanderer and outlaw, the varou has been associated with wandering behaviour of a more predatory, even aggressive kind, of coursing around the countryside by night, chasing women, eating prodigiously, and 'caterwauling' generally. One definition of the word *varouage* is to take 'the course of the werewolf'; in a figurative sense this means to 'rut' or have sex. In fact, the word *varou* in Channel Islands patois can be translated as 'disorder' or 'large appetite'. There was once a local expression, '*il mange comme un varou*', which meant to have excessive appetite.

By displaying such orgiastic, excessive behaviour, the *varou* seems to be closely allied to another mythical name associated with excess: that of Bacchus or Dionysus.

Notes
1 G.J.C. Bois, p.13
2 Olgier

Part III:
Pagan Rites and the Secret Church

11 Bacchanalian Orgies

Bacchus, or Dionysus, is associated in most people's minds with the bacchanalian orgies, popularly believed to have been riots of drunkenness and lust. A number of Roman writers were responsible for this idea. The historian Livy, for example, raged against the orgies, which he said were responsible for every depravity known to man. Those wicked enough to take part in them were guilty of indulging in the very lowest passions, such as wine drinking, debauchery and 'promiscuous intercourse'.

The fact is we do not really know much about the bacchanalian orgies because they were mostly held in secret, much like the Eleusian mysteries. The word 'orgies' originally meant secret rites, not wild sexual excess.

There is some evidence from Roman sources that a version of bacchanalian rites once took place on the Channel Islands. Artemidorus described a little island inhabited by solely by women, who worshipped Bacchus with ceremonies and sacrifices. It seems that no man ever set foot there, so the women had to leave the island if they wanted to join their husbands, although they always returned afterwards to resume their mysterious rituals. Artemidorus was writing about a Greek island called Samothrace, but he compared this to 'a small island near Britain' where he said similar rites were celebrated to the goddesses Ceres and Proserpine.[1]

The Roman writer Strabo also mentioned an island close to Britain, where Demeter and Persephone were worshipped with rites and orgies. The fourth-century Roman Dionysus actually revealed names; he mentioned a group of islands near Jersey and Guernsey, where he said the rites of Bacchus were performed by women crowned with leaves, who danced and made a great shouting.

Bacchus is a sort of half man, half beast, with the body of a man and the head of an animal. We have already come across a figure like this, of course; he is the goddess's consort; dressed as a ritual animal for his seasonal rites. As we have seen, the practice of ritual animal dressing was common in the Channel Island *vueilles*, those often riotous parties in which people disguised themselves as a variety of beasts and got up to all sorts of trickery. Perhaps the *vueilles* were a later version of the bacchanalia. Many writers have thought so. One of the ceremonies in Alderney was called Le Jour des Vitres and in the dialect of Alderney, *vitres*, means 'masks'. Masks, of course, mean disguises, and Durand had no doubt that the wearing of masks and disguises proved that the ceremony had a bacchanalian origin.

This tradition of animal dressing even dates back to Roman commentators on Channel Islands bacchanalia. In Alderney, according to Pomponius Mela, it was a favourite diversion to assume various disguises: 'Men were in the habit of disguising themselves as all sorts of animals – lions, lionesses, crows.' It is very likely that he was referring to the Channel Islands when he wrote about priestesses who were able 'to turn themselves into whatever animal they may choose'.[2]

The Channel Islands *vueilles*, with their parties, dressing up and mischief making, were not too innocent to contain risqué elements. We must not forget the Varou, in which a man dressed as a wolf would venture out on sexual adventures. In Guernsey, the meaning of the word *vueille* sometimes went much further than innocent, orderly festivities, and referred to noisy night-time parties or nocturnal rampages by gangs of young people. It even appears that a verb *vueiller* was used. All of this seems to be getting ever closer to the bacchanalia. In fact, when Guernsey people indulged in debauchery and sexual behaviour it was known as *allair en varouv'rie* – 'going to the devil' or to the Varou.

But it is at the witching sites of La Catioroc and Rocqueberg that we actually meet Bacchus face to face – and find that he has the face of a goat. In Guernsey's La Catioroc, the witches used chant and dance around the Trepied Dolmen, and worshiped a figure sitting on the capstone in the shape of a black goat. At La Rocqueberg in Jersey the witches would meet at midnight at the time of the full moon, for their 'Sabbath orgies'. The man who took part covered his head in an animal mask, dressed up as the sacred goat, 'as the ancient priests had done'. It has been claimed that the dance rituals at both of these islands' sites would end up with the witches copulating with this goat-like figure, in a truly bacchanalian orgy.

The goat has one important feature that distinguishes him from the other Puck-like animals we have looked at. He has horns on his head. As Greek Pan (a small man with the horns and the hindquarters of the goat), Norse Cernunnos and Roman Dionysus, in his appearance as a bull, goat or stag, we are looking here at the most familiar and widespread of the goddess's consorts: the horned god.

To understand the significance of the horned god and what his horns mean, it is important to remember that the Great Goddess was often personified as the moon. The curve of the new moon is horn-shaped, so it follows that the maiden's young partner would have carried the same moon-like emblem on his head. The horned god was consort to the crescent new moon, the young maiden goddess.

The new moon, as we know, represented the spring, and always appeared when the earth was most fertile, a belief which still persisted in Guernsey into the twentieth century. The young horned god, therefore, also represented fertility and potency, and embodied the exuberant energy and bounty of the spring. That explains his association with overtly sexual rituals like the bacchanalian orgies.

The horned god had to be rampant and fertile. His task was to fertilize the goddess and, by implication, the whole earth, an act that required no small degree of virility. That is why male creatures noted for their almost brutal potency, like the bull, goat or stag, represented him. The horned god's sexual member was the most important part of him so it had to be big; in some classical art, his private parts are gleefully exaggerated – like the grotesquely endowed Greek satyr, or Pan.

The power of the horned god was linked to the fertility of the earth and the potency of beasts and humans. That is why his fertility ritual involved a great deal of public sex, at both the planting of the seed and the gathering in of the harvest.

The horned god appears in Guernsey's Pleinmont Bay, another site with powerful memories of ancient ritual and devil worship. The writer Victor Hugo was sufficiently impressed with the spiritual nature of the area to refer to a nearby watchtower as a 'haunted house'. He even featured it in one of his novels, *The Toilers of the Sea*. Several local writers insist that his account of the haunted house has no foundation in fact, while others have identified Pleinmont as another witchcraft site, like Catioroc. Independently of Hugo, the haunted house features in an island poem, where it is visited by the horned god and his lover, the witch crone:

> I've seen the horns, really, and the tail,
> It sends shivers down my spine, of the demon:
> I've seen, stretched out on her broomstick,
> Riding along behind the evil one.[3]

However, in this poem, the horned god and the crone goddess are defeated by the resident of the house – mostly, it seems, by the healing effect of his drinking half a pint of cider.

Since before recorded time, the Channel Islands have revered the cow as a source of food and wealth, which would suggest that a bull cult might once have existed. As it happens, the relationship with the milk-producing cow might have been bloodier in earlier times; it is probable that the blood of the cow was drawn from the living animal, as a source of nourishment. This is reminiscent of the strange rite mentioned earlier, in which a ritual with a stone axe turned cow's milk to blood, a tradition that seems to commemorate this rather more gory relationship. In fact, whole cattle carcases have been found buried at a site in L'Ouzerieré in St Ouen's, which indicates that these animals were ritually sacrificed.

It could be argued that the name Puck is related to the early Irish *poc*, a male goat. A similar link between the goat and the figure of Puck can be found in the Puck Fair held at Killorglin in Ireland's County Kerry every August, where a goat is chosen and decorated as 'King of the Fair', in a tradition very similar to the Lord of Misrule. At the end of the fair the goat would be slaughtered and its meat shared out by everyone, but in these gentler times the animal is generally put out to grass.

The ritual nature of this animal sacrifice, the killing and distribution of the body of the god, shows the 'darker' side of the bacchanalia and might help make some sense of a particularly gruesome Roman description of a Channel Islands Dionysian ritual:

> *Every woman [brings] her load and she who lets fall her load is presently torn in pieces by the rest, who heaping up the mangled limbs with shouts at the temple, do not leave off till their furious transports subside, and it always happens that one of them does let fall her load, and is thus torn to pieces.*[4]

Central to this horrifying account seems to be the action of tearing someone apart, limb from limb. Such actions have long been associated with the bacchanalian rites where, according to contemporary accounts, copious wine was drunk in honour of the deity, followed up by the drunken rending and eating of a chosen victim.

Tearing someone apart seems monstrously cruel, yet it is simply a version of the ancient hunting ritual, in which one of the old hunter-gatherers dressed up as the animal prey, and the rest would pursue and kill him as hunting animals did, by rending their prey apart. We have already suggested that the sacrifice developed out of the hunt kill, and the hunt's dismembering has its counterpart in the ritual dismembering of the scattered broken bodies found buried in the dolmens, and the cult of dismembered Osiris in Egypt. In fact there is evidence that in early farming communities in the Channel Islands, the flesh of cattle was eaten raw, which would have involved the dismemberment and ritual sharing out of the body.

So it is probable that the bacchanalian rites deserved their reputation for wildness and savagery. Indeed, some of the old terror and manic energy of the cult of Pan has survived in modern words that evoke his name: words like 'panic' and 'pandemonium'. Even the word 'savage' comes from Sylvanus, the Roman equivalent of Pan.

One of the goddess names that the Romans brought to Britain was Diana of the Wood, or Diana Nemorensis, better known in the Greek word *nemesis*. She is portrayed as pursuing the sacred king before eventually capturing him at the end of summer and tearing him apart. This notion of the goddess 'chasing' the king and rending him at the moment of capture has obvious associations with hunting, which is perhaps why Diana is associated with the hunt.

A legend of Jersey's La Rocqueberg seems to dramatize this violent ritual of the horned god's sacrifice. In this story a local youth was engaged to a beautiful and very pious local girl. Despite his love for this maiden, the young man was fascinated by the darker things of life, especially the witch cult practised on La Rocqueberg. One fatal evening he yielded to temptation and turned up at the rock site, where he was welcomed by a bevy of beautiful maidens. One of them expressed her love for him and invited him to return the following night.

The next morning, the young man boasted openly about his rendezvous with the beautiful maidens. His young fiancée sought advice from a priest, who gave her a large crucifix, promising that it would protect them both from harm. The good maiden's prudence and foresight paid off. When her man returned to La Rocqueberg the following night, the beautiful maidens had changed into hideous old hags, stoking a large and terrifying fire. They danced round the man, now pinned helplessly to the rock, screeching obscenities and threats to tear him apart. The young girl promptly saved her young man by brandishing the crucifix at the witches, at which they disappeared with screams of panic, and their fires were extinguished. We can assume that the story ends happily, but we are not actually told that. Instead, the story has a different ending, which can be paraphrased as follows: 'It is said to this day that the Rocqueberg promontory bears the imprint of a cloven hoof, and is ever after called the Witches' Rock.'

These hoof prints seem to have little to do with the reckless young man and his miraculous rescue. It is far more likely that a much older story has been clumsily sanitized at the end. Instead of a bloody pagan sacrifice, the tale finishes with a Christian redemption. But in the original story, the young man probably attempted to become an initiate in the mysteries of the goddess. He became her consort as the horned god, and was torn apart at the moment of sacrifice.

On closer inspection, some of the islands' black dogs turn into horned creatures. One or two are described as being as big as calves and one creature in Guernsey, at a house called Le Lorier, is portrayed looking like a calf and as large as an ox. Another Guernsey black dog or calf known as the Coin de la Biche appears in the form of a giant nanny goat.

A ghostly bull was also a common feature in the Channel Islands landscape, and although invisible, it roared. The coast of St Clement's in Jersey, an area associated with La Rocqueberg and the witch cult, used to be infamous for its roaring bull. Every few years at low tide, a low roaring sound used to come from across the sea, resembling, according to L'Amy, 'the barbarous and melancholy bellowing of some gargantuan and presumably amphibious bull'. The eerie sound was eventually discovered to be caused by tidal water running down a pipe or cleft in a rock pool. The cleft was plugged in, and sadly the bull roars no more.

Another ritual site in Jersey, the Devil's Hole, also had a roaring bull, alongside its crooked man. It used to be a sheer-sided fissure connected to the sea through a large cave. At high tide this cave became flooded and the water was forced to and fro in the tunnel, creating a roaring noise. Jersey's crooked man of Devil's Hole was said, after his fall down this hole, to have left his cloven mark on the land to claim it his own; presumably this was the mark of the horned god.

Guernsey's Rocquaine Bay once had a 'beast' that used to roar at the approach of a storm. It was a favoured setting for the ritual burning of the Bout de L'An, as well as being one of the sites used by the witches for their moonlit revels. It is also the location of the menhir whose treasure was guarded by a big black conger eel – the serpent guardian of the tomb.

The Norse name for the island of Jethou is Keitholm, meaning 'place of the roaring', due to the so-called Creux du Diable (or 'devil's hole'), where the tide was pushed up through a small cavern, forcing air up through a small chimney and creating the roaring sound.

Of course, all of these roaring bulls can be explained as natural phenomena, the action of wind and water on rock. But many of these sites have other mythological and ritual associations, and linking them all is the notion of a devil's hole, a cliff-top site, where the god of the rock comes to life as the horned god, and returns to sea in a repeated act of regeneration and sacrifice.

Robert Graves, no stranger to the power of myth, associated this sort of sea noise with the biblical Bull of Bashan.

> And storms, and then with head and ears well under
> Blow bubbles with a monstrous roar like thunder,
> A bull-of-Bashan sound. [5]

There is an odd resemblance between the name of the Bull of Bashan and a curious object called the Bacchan (pronounced 'Bashan'), the very purpose of which is to produce a roaring sound. The word also has a close resemblance to Bacchus – at least, there is no other explanation of its origin. It is a large open metal basin filled with water. Two or more people then rub large damp reeds across the edge, creating ringing vibrations which, as the whole bowl begins to resonate, turn into a loud, sustained roaring. As the bowl rings and roars, the water inside begins to bubble and spit as if it were boiling, resembling the classic image of a bubbling cauldron.

It takes several people, working in close co-operation, to perform this ritual successfully. One needs to hold the edge of a large reed to the rim of the bowl – not as easy as it seems. It is vital not to touch the bowl itself, or the music will be deadened. Sitting opposite him, another person has to pull at the reed to create the sound. The player should never squeeze the reed too hard, because that would stop the vibration.

The ritual is a curiously monotonous, undramatic sight. Yet there is something hypnotic, even cyclic, in the way that the hand gently and repetitively pulls at the reed, dipping in the water for lubrication, then pulling again. It is important to keep the bowl resonating at a constant pitch and volume and ensure that the boiling waves inside maintain a constant rhythm. The intention seems to be to maintain a static motion – a kind of timelessness – in the ringing bowl and the bubbling water. It suggests that the whole ceremony is a celebration of the eternal, unchanging rhythm of life, contained within this symbolic goddess cauldron.

L'Amy calls the bacchan ceremony the *Faire braire les poêles* and explains that it took place on Midsummer's Eve – the day before the summer solstice. Stead also wrote a description of it, pointing out that people of both sexes would share in the activity – presumably stooping over the same bowl, with obvious fertility implications. The bull-like roaring sound produced by the bowl would be augmented and increased by additional groups of people standing around and blowing cows' horns. According to another account, this performance would be followed by parties of young men and boys going round milking all the cows they could get hold of.

In its association with cows, bulls and horns, and its evident ritual and fertility ramifications, the bacchan – the bowl of Bacchus – seems to be a survival of the cult of the horned god on the Channel Islands.

Central to the cult of Bacchus or Dionysus was the grape – the fruit of the vine. Fruit, as we have already seen, was often sacred to the ancients. The pomegranate and the apple were associated with the rituals of death and the underworld. But the joyful bacchanalia did not celebrate winter; it rejoiced in the spring, with its rising sap and rampant animal fertility. Unlike apples, Dionysus's grapes were not sacred for their buried seeds, but for their suggestive, bulbous appearance. In crude terms, the grapes represented the testicles of the tree god who, like his cousin the horned god, was supposed to be manifestly and visibly potent.

Also like the horned god, the tree god was regularly sacrificed. The plucking and crushing of his testicular fruit to make wine was a symbolic sacrifice of his virility. The wine itself was the sperm of the god, and drinking it allowed the worshippers of Bacchus to imbibe the god's supreme fertility and become divine and super-fertile themselves. It is the best possible excuse for getting drunk.

Even late Greek mythology still believed in the fertilizing powers of wine. It is interesting how many Greek heroes or demi-gods were born only after their sterile old fathers drank wine until they were virtually comatose, then made energetic love to a passing nymph or goddess. The drunken delirium obtained from wine was, of course, a further sign of its holiness – it removed the drinkers' inhibitions and gave them divinely inspired energy for participating in Bacchus's religious rites.

We know the Romans cultivated vine as far north as the British Isles, because Europe was passing through one of the interglacial warm periods at the time, making it very likely that an extensive vine-inspired bacchanalia also existed on our chilly islands.

In colder climates like ours, the counterpart of the vine was often the *loranthus* oak mistletoe. Its juice-filled berries, like the grapes of Bacchus, were the genitalia of the oak tree, and were believed to have powers of fertility and regeneration. The bitter juice is not drinkable, but mistletoe is still an emblem of fertility and sexual love today, especially at the midwinter ceremony of Christmas, where the spring rite of 'kissing' is still performed under the plant's testicular berries. The solemn bringing in of the Yule log to the hearth on Christmas Eve is reminiscent of the bringing in of the Asian Attis's pine tree from the woods, decked in spring flowers and covered in the oak mistletoe, ready for the sacrifice.

St Martin's Church is called St Martin's de la Bellouse, which might also mean 'St Martin of the sloe bushes'. The sloe, also called the Blackthorn, is a winter plant which sprouts out in a glory of little white fairy flowers between February and April. These are the months after the solstice, and reputedly the coldest and bleakest months of the year. The appropriately named 'blackthorn' therefore represents life in the depths of winter. Its flowering beauty is both a defiance of winter's death, and a promise of the abundance of the coming spring.

It is sacred to the crone winter goddess. It is known as the Mother of the Woods because it nurtures the ground in the winter, like a loving mother. Its dense and impenetrable thickets, tipped with sharp thorns, keep out all intruders, both animal and human, at a time when the

Blackthorn, a plant sacred to the winter goddess because it flowers in the coldest months of winter

earth is most vulnerable. It therefore protects the ground, allows susceptible seeds to flourish and creates safe nurseries which prosper into new growth.

The blackthorn heals and restores the land in readiness for spring. Perhaps this explains why, in ancient communities, witches, shamans and other healers used a blackthorn wand as their staff of office. In fact, sloe bushes still grow plentifully on the Guernsey coast at La Rocquaine, a local site rich in mythology, where the witches used to meet. Another reason for this magic property of the branch could be the blackthorn's fruit, the sloe berry. These berries, the testicles of the sloe bush, were credited with the same miraculous life-giving powers as the grape or mistletoe.

Sloe berries are a product of winter. They always taste better after the first frost, which softens and tenderizes the hard flesh. Indeed, they seem to ripen better underground, and would have been buried, like the seeds of apples or pomegranates. Today, sloe berries are still used for healing. Herbalists utilize them to help in the treatment of stomach troubles and blood disorders. Like the grape, and unlike the mistletoe, the sloe berry can also be turned into a passable wine. (More famous today, of course, is sloe gin, in which the sloes are pricked by their own thorns, and then steeped in gin to produce a very sweet, blood red liqueur.)

In the Channel Islands we had our own versions of Bacchus's intoxicating wine. We had apples for making cider, and anyone who has drunk cider in its rough form knows that it can be more potent in its effects than wine. In their day, our cider feasts were just as capable of turning into wild rites as any bacchanalia. The sight of an abandoned ruined cider mill and broken press in Sark caused local writer Leonard Clark to rhapsodize about a more Dionysian era: 'Do these simulacra remember the dance beneath the moon, the flapping skirts, the clacking sabots, the half-empty bottles, and all the great, noble days of the dead cider feasts?'[6]

A description from 1860 of the twice-yearly harvest of seaweed *vraic*, contains this vivid description: '*Vraic* gatherers of both sexes have a harvest home, at which much cider drinking, dancing and lovemaking are carried on'.[7] This is probably an exaggerated account (it comes from a 'spoof' travel book), but it must have been written by someone familiar with the local harvest traditions.

Like wine, cider was believed to have powers of fertility. We have already seen how it used to fertilize the earth. At the start of ploughing in Guernsey, it would be poured on to the plough so that the liquid ran into the furrow. As De Garis points out, the farmers did not know that in offering the cider in this way 'they were pouring a libation to the earth goddess to ensure help in securing good crops.'[8]

Another popular fertility drink was the milk-a-punch, a gift from the cow goddess. It has been recorded that 'large quantities of a drink concocted of milk, eggs and rum, the famous "milk-a-punch"' was once consumed in copious quantities in spring. This milk-a-punch sounds like a counterpart to the wine drunk at bacchanalian rites. Again the ritual of the Bacchan is linked to the cow and by implication the fertility of the bull and the horned god.

The associated rituals bring us back to the bacchanalian orgies. In fact, what we are looking at here is a celebration of Beltaine, the festival of spring. Until recently, it was widely celebrated in the Channel Islands. A joyful celebration of the arrival of spring is not the same thing as a triumphal rite over the vanquished winter. This positive welcoming of the warmth of spring, with drinking and fertility ceremonies, is how the Neolithics would have marked the event.

This is what the folklorist McCulloch discovered. After researching Roman accounts of bacchanalian rites, he found plenty of similar public orgies still taking place in Guernsey's spring ceremonies in his own life-time. Like the Roman commentators, he did not always approve of what he saw. He has given us a rather prim description of a spring fire dance performed at May Day, which ended in what he called an 'oscu-latory movement', which often continued into the evening. His rather formal euphemistic term 'osculatory' had two senses: it meant both 'kissing' and 'coming into close sexual contact'. For all his distaste for such rituals, McCulloch had no doubt that they were 'remnants of sacri-fices to gods and goddesses of cereal and furrow, to us unknown or long forgotten.'[9]

The cheerful influence of Beltaine explains why St Martin's Gran'mer stone crone was seen as a fertility goddess. People used to leave offer-ings of flowers or fruit at her feet and brides would put garlands around her neck. She was not ousted or shunned as a winter crone of death; she joined in the spring celebrations. These celebrations would often have been of a sexual nature, celebrating the fertility of the land. So even if the bacchanalian rites were a religious cult, performed in honour of the goddess of the grain, this does not mean that Livy was wrong in accus-ing them of sexual excess.

The feast of Beltaine, the bacchanalian orgies and the horned god may all express the same ancient ritual; a joyful fertility ceremony that once universally celebrated the end of winter and the return of spring. It was not a victory or fight to the death. It was a partnership. It cele-brated the mating of the goddess and her consort and the consequent return of nature's fertility. This exultant ceremony was known as the *Hieros Gamos*, or the sacred marriage.

In ancient times, the sacred marriage was always enacted in the springtime. It was a cheerful counterpart to the grim and sometimes bloody rituals of sacrifice that lamented the death of nature. Winter had now come to an end, the goddess's dead consort/son was resurrected, and the mother goddess, now as bride, was united with him in marriage.

After the requisite dancing and drinking, everyone would have glee-fully joined in the general lovemaking. It did not worry them that this was meant to be a religious ceremony. People had not yet learned to marginalize sex from what nowadays we might call 'spiritual matters', and carnal pleasures would have been seen as a divine homeopathic force for good. Couples would have celebrated their own fertility and made love in the hope that nature would imitate them (at least, that was the excuse).

There was nothing exploitative or abusive about these ceremonies. The sacred marriage celebrated an equal partnership between male and female, a close relationship, without conflict or enmity. It expressed a creative, transfiguring union between the goddess and the consort that transformed winter into spring. There was no question of one partner dominating or defeating the other, they came together as one.

In fact, we believe that the Channel Islands tradition of Dionysus worship was nothing more nor less than a celebration of the sacred marriage. Evidence that all marriage celebrations in the Channel Islands sometimes exhibited certain bacchanalian elements is suggested by a local ordinance of 1611, 'which forbade dances at marriage-feasts and other gatherings, also all immodest or dissolute songs, the villainous and detestable abuses committed at dances and in unlawful games'.

Of course, love has its own familiar goddess figure: Aphrodite or the Roman Venus. She is based on the original sea goddess of creation; she mated with the wind, in the form of the serpent Ophion, and this act of cosmic love heralded the beginning of all life. We have seen this primordial act of procreation enacted in the 'Trip to Lihou', in which the maidens of the island play amorously with the congers and eels in the sea. Later this goddess of all creation evolved into the goddess of love, who rose from the sea and rode in a scallop shell to the Minoan island of Kythera.

The power of Venus/Aphrodite, the goddess of love, was being invoked until recently in a strange ritual on the Channel Islands. Whenever a married couple were known to be arguing or fighting, a crowd would assemble outside their house and 'blow through conch shells upon as many Friday nights as the quarrel lasted'. L'Amy is quite certain as to the origin of this custom: 'These shells were originally considered sacred to Venus, Goddess of Love, and Queen of the Waves … on whose special day … these rites were celebrated'.

A version of this conch shell ritual, called the Chevauchée à l'Âne, was also performed in Guernsey to the benefit of married couples who had forgotten how to love. Interestingly, a donkey was also used in this fertility ceremony; indeed the *chevauchée* was even known as the 'donkey parade'. This means that the island's totem animal the donkey, the *vueilles* and the fertility rites of spring, all came together in a mythological unity.

Notes

1   Artemidorus quoted by Strabo.
2   Quoted by McCulloch p.36.
3   Poem by Georges Métivier.
4   Strabo.
5   Graves, 'I Wonder What it Feels Like to be Drowned.'
6   *Sark Discovered*, p.33
7   Quoted in *Eye on the Past Yearbook*, 1992.
8   *Folklore of Guernsey*, p. 77.
9   *Guernsey Folklore*, pp. 187–8

12 Apollo and the Mystery of Grosnez Castle

Beltaine was celebrated in the Channel Islands as a fire ceremony, just like Samhain. Young men and women would dance around the spring fire and light wisps of straw, which they would throw around like torches. Carey has suggested that this is similar to the rite of dancing round an ancient menhir. Like the maypole, the fire or menhir represents the returning fertility of the land; it is the bright spring god or consort.

If the sloe bush or blackthorn was a winter plant, then the hawthorn was associated with spring. In fact, the hawthorn was called the whitethorn specifically to distinguish it from the dark wood of the winter plant. It features in one fertility ceremony in Guernsey, in which the surrounding grass had to be kept green to ensure the continuation of fine spring weather. It also featured prominently in many Channel Islands Beltaine celebrations. Wreaths and garlands of flowers and hawthorns would be hung all across the highway and people would dance around and under them.

As part of the quest for new green growth, people would raid gardens, plucking flowers, uprooting plants and generally creating havoc where they went. De Garis explains the origins of these ceremonies as 'a near-forgotten folk memory of the old rites of gathering greenery and growth in honour of the pagan god'.

In Alderney the god of spring was a large decorated garland of flowers and hawthorns, known as the May. On the first day of spring, he would be placed in a secret location, and people would set out and search for him. Once found, they would congregate cheerfully around him to dance and sing, much as their English counterparts would dance round the maypole.

The spring god was also known as the Green Man, or Jack in the Green (probably a spring version of the Samhain Jack O' Lantern). He is less familiar in the Channel Islands than in other parts of the British Isles, but Jersey does have its very own Green Man, a mysterious wooden carving in the Les Creux Country Park, on a hill that overlooks the church and fisherman's chapel of St Brelade. This mysterious figure is carved with the shapes of a variety of different types of leaves, including what look like the larger leaves of the vine. In its leafy location, among the many trees on the site, it combines the attributes of Bacchus, Green Man, tree god and – from the forked shape of the head – horned god.

The Green Man once made another regular appearance in Jersey. On 1 May, the island's chimney sweeps would dress up in green foliage and walk the streets. There is a good reason why this performance was restricted to chimney sweeps. The work of the sweep gives him an intimate association with the hearth, another fiery domain. When dressed as the Green Man, he represented the new green life of nature, emerging fresh and new from the spring fires of Beltaine. The hearth is also the place of sacrifice; it is where the Yule log is burned at each winter solstice. The emergence of the living Green Man from the ashes of that hearth represents the restored Yule log decked in greenery, personifying the renewed fertility of spring. Perhaps this link with spring's rebirth explains why sweeps, in British folklore, are associated with good fortune.

Another green plant associated with spring Beltaine celebrations was the bay. This plant features in a song called 'Ah Mon Beau Laurier', which translates as 'Oh, my beautiful Bay Tree.'

A wooden carving in Les Creux, Jersey. A mixture of Green Man, tree god, Bacchus and horned god

> I have a beautiful bay tree of France,
> My pretty bay tree dances,
> My pretty bay tree,
> The lady enters the dance,
> My pretty bay tree dances,

> My pretty bay tree,
> Make us three reverences,
> My pretty bay tree dances,
> My pretty bay tree.

As can be seen from the words, it was more than just a song, it was a round dance and a kissing game, with obvious ritual origins. It was performed by an equal number of men and women – appropriately for a fertility dance. One of the girls would be chosen to enter the circle, while the rest danced round her. The maiden would then choose a man to join her in the middle of the circle, and then the others would start to dance round them both. A kiss and embrace were then exchanged between the couple, and the whole cycle would begin all over again. Standing in the centre of this circular seasonal dance, like a green spring fire, was the bay tree.

The bay tree is among the most sacred of all the green plants because it is an evergreen. Like all evergreens it defeats winter's death and symbolizes forever the warmth and renewing powers of spring. So when the women of Guernsey were singing and dancing round their *beau laurier*, they were expressing their adoration for the immortal god of the spring – the Sun God.

The shape of the bay tree – the way that the leaves and branches span out – resembles the rays of the sun, and this is why its leaves have been used, since ancient times, in another symbolic sun ritual, which is still used today. The leaves and branches were cut from the tree, formed into a round sun shape and placed upon the head of a chosen sun king – basically placing the sun on his head and 'crowning' him as king.

Even the modern crown, with its round shape, gold and bright jewels, imitates the radiance of the sun, reminding us that the earliest kings were sun gods. But crowns continued to be made of bay leaves – or the Greek equivalent, the laurel – well into classical times, when battle heroes, artists and Olympic athletes were crowned with laurels. Even today, the British national poet is called the Poet Laureate – as if he too were crowned with this original symbol of the sun god.

The bay tree or laurel was sacred to Apollo, the god of the oracle in Delphi. Apollo was also a god of light, known as Phoebus ('radiant' or 'beaming') and he is generally identified with the sun god, like the leaves and branches of his sacred tree. Indeed, Belenus, the god of Beltaine, was known as the British Apollo.

But Apollo was a serpent killer. At Delphi he killed the serpent Python, original guardian of the famous oracle. It had been alleged that the snake had destroyed crops, sacked villages and polluted streams and springs all around the area. So Apollo killed it with his bow and arrow and took over the sanctuary. But he was not all bad. The oracle continued to flourish under his guardianship, well beyond classical times. Only with the introduction of Christianity was the sanctuary finally closed and destroyed. So although Apollo defeated the goddess and her partnership with the consort, he does not represent the destruction of the goddess's legacy. The old ways continued under his charge and this, as we have suggested, is what happened to the old Neolithic religion on the Channel Islands.

So it is not too fanciful to look for evidence of Apollo's legacy here too. The wonderful Dehus Dolmen in Guernsey could be named after Teus, a long-horned bull, and the stone carving inside it, called Le Gardien du Tombeau ('guardian of the tomb') might be Mithras. However, the image of a guardian of a tomb wielding a bow and arrows is uncannily reminiscent of the figure of Apollo, guarding Delphi with his bow and arrow after having killed the Python. It is all a matter of names only, because one of the titles of Mithras was sun god – the same as Apollo.

As it happens, there is another site in Guernsey that seems to have a tenuous link with Apollo, at least in name, and that is the little church of St Apolline. It seems strange to link Apollo and St Apolline (also called St Apollonia). She is an obscure woman saint, not a sun or fertility god. Her small, cell-like church on Guernsey, although ancient, has none of the mystery of similar chapels, like Jersey's Hougue Bie. Although early guide books claimed that its date was unknown, we now know more or less when, why and by whom it was built. It was constructed in 1392 by the priest Nicholas Henry in thanks for his escape from death while fighting with the English in naval battles against the French. But these bald facts do not explain its name. St Apolline was a saint strongly associated with Normandy, which at the time was very much part of the enemy, France.

The church features in a folk tale called 'Lisbeau and the Emerald', which links it directly with Lihou Priory, a site with its own impeccable pagan credentials, going back to the Neolithic culture of the Trepied Dolmen and the witch cult. In this story, Lisbeau and her mother return from benediction at St Apolline, after which Lisbeau makes friends with a nun from Lihou Priory who is of fairy ancestry, and becomes bewitched. One night her mother returns from confession to find her daughter gone and subsequently discovers she has eloped to marry a fairy prince.

A recent description of the chapel claims that no earlier church building stood on the site.[1] However, it says nothing about the possible existence of a pagan shrine and is prepared to admit that the association between it and the pagan Lihou is 'interesting'. It is worth noting that the church stands very close to an area of coast called Perelle Bay, which lies neatly sandwiched between Vazon and Lihou's witching coast of La Catioroc. It is hard not to imagine an unbroken continuity of ancient tradition stretching across this coast.

The life of St Apolline is also of interest. She was martyred, and her martyrdom contained some illuminating pagan elements. Rather mundanely, she is called the patron saint of dentists, because during her martyrdom she had all her teeth knocked out. This bizarre incident is paralleled by the dragon myth of the Greek Cadmos, who killed a dragon whose eyes 'shone like fire' and who vibrated a 'triple tongue', and showed a 'triple row of teeth'. Having killed it he knocked its teeth out and planted them in the earth, upon which they immediately grew into a large population of men. Clearly this is an example of a dragon story that does not end in the final, sterile triumph of the victorious sun god, but in the renewal of the earth and its life-giving fertility.

Having knocked Apolline's teeth out, the authorities threatened to burn her alive if she refused to recant her Christian beliefs. She refused, so they piled up a bonfire outside the city and dragged her towards it. But the saint told the mob that no one would have the satisfaction of throwing her old body on the fire. Of her own accord, she leaped on the pyre before it was lit, upon which it instantly burst into flames.

This is a bizarre martyrdom. In fact, it is not a true Christian martyrdom at all because St Apolline threw herself voluntarily on to the pyre. This makes it more like an act of suicide, breaking all the rules of martyrdom. It is virtually identical to the burning of the effigy of the guy and the human sacrifice at Vazon. The fact that Apolline kindled the fire herself, and that it did not consume her, also identifies her with Apollo the sun god, creator of the light, worshipped here until recently by spring fires.

Although we no longer celebrate the power of the sun with spring bonfires, our bonfire party on 5 November, the old Samhain, is a celebration of the death of the sun. Part of the bonfire's traditional function is to provide a pyre for the sacrificed guy. However, it also serves another purpose: to mimic the sun's dying light, and to rekindle it for the coming spring. In this dual purpose, it is very similar to the 'martyrdom' of St Apolline.

And it is this ritual element, rather than the burning of the guy, which explains why a public winter bonfire still holds an extraordinary fascination for us, even today. Although fireworks might thrill us more, and tempt us from our homes at night, it is the bonfire that binds us together while we are there, standing firm like a homely, comforting hearth in the centre of our communal gathering. We may no longer dance around it in bacchanalian frenzy. Instead we stand enthralled, basking in the blaze, admiring it with a truly apollonian calm.

Everyone knows that a well-constructed bonfire, once it has matured, ceases to look like a fire at all. The spiky, waving flames, the leaping of sparks, soon die down. The fire calms and moulds into a glowing ball, deep red in the centre and flickering palely at its rim, looking uncannily like the sun. Its constant, glowing heat, which can warm the body through the bitter chill of a winter night, also feels comfortingly like the sun. Even today we feel a curious satisfaction to stand around a huge fire. It is easy to understand why the ancient fire celebrants believed that they had captured the power of the sun god, or – even more evocatively – that the dying sun had fallen to earth, and was expiring in front of them, in his winter death throes. And when the dances were over, they may well have stood, with hands linked, in a giant imitative circle around the sun as we do today, and prayed for the return of spring.

La Pinacle was a pagan ritual site until around 200 AD. There is evidence that the last temple structure to be built and used there was a *fana* – a secret temple used for the rebellious continuation of banned pagan rituals. We may assume that the site was eventually closed and the cult abolished. But it is possible that its adherents moved somewhere else, not very far away.

Near to La Pinacle, on the north-west tip of the island, is another small coastal settlement, less ancient, but abandoned for centuries and even more steeped in mystery. It is Grosnez, today the site of a ruined castle about which we know virtually nothing. (Surely no other comparable area of land has so many structures and locations so steeped in mystery as the Channel Islands). The earliest record of a castle at Grosnez can be found in a map from 1540, where it is already referred

Grosnez Castle, Jersey, perched on its own sacred coastal mound. Was this once a temple to the sun god?

to as being in ruins. No picture of an intact working castle exists; no written description of its appearance or function has survived. We do not know when or why it was built, or when it was destroyed. All that we can tell, from the scattered location of some of its stones, is that the destruction was deliberate, and not due to age or neglect.

Its very existence is a mystery. Why was it built? It could not have been as defence against invasion. Its coast faces in the opposite direction to the enemy, France, but gives a clear view of all the other Channel Islands. Yet if Jersey once lived in fear of an invasion from Sark or Guernsey, history has been silent on the subject.

Not only is the castle's location pointless, but so is the building itself. It is clear from the ruins that it had no secondary walls. As a defensive structure it was very poorly fortified and once its outer walls had been breached, it could have been taken easily.

An additional puzzle is the lack of any convenient water supply. The nearest spring is 200 yards away. This would have made it impossible to sustain a siege for more than a few days. All of this discounts the idea that it could ever have been seriously built as a strategic defensive structure.

Stead has a possible explanation: that it 'was formerly the abode of some religious order'. Local opinion also identifies the site as possibly monastic. Monasteries, especially on the Channel Islands, were often founded on older pagan sites, so maybe an ancient pagan ritual is associated with the site, as we first suggested.

The site today reveals none of its secrets. A possible clue comes in the name, Grosnez which probably means 'rocky point' (originally Grotness, from the Norse *grjot*, a rock), a name with similar associations to nearby La Pinacle. There is also an undated 'Geoffrey's Leap' type story associated with the place. There is a block of stone near one of the ravines, possibly a fallen menhir, called the Stone Plank, from which a young man once fell into the sea to his death. So again we have a mysterious site, with vague rumours of a vanished Christian institution, but populated more vividly by the ghosts of an older sacrificial ritual.

There is also, as it happens, an old Neolithic site near the castle: La Hougue des Grosnez, a 3-foot high mound with a diameter of 50 feet. Excavation in 1923 revealed a paved floor of red soil, round-bottomed pots and fragments of pottery. It is still unknown exactly what the structure was, and today its few remaining granite blocks are almost entirely covered in gorse. There are very few clues here.

Oddly enough, there is another fortified site a little further along the northern coast. A bank and ditch cut at the opening to nearby Plémont Point are generally regarded as being part of an Iron Age fort, but the puzzle of why a fort was built at such a point is still unsolved. However, Plémont Bay has another feature. A jutting rock next to the popular beach has the unmistakable shape of a sleeping dragon. There appears to be no surviving folk tale featuring this phenomenon so it just remains as another fascinating aspect of Jersey's mystical landscape.

We cannot prove any link between the abandonment of La Pinacle and the settlement of Grosnez. But it is not too fanciful to suggest that this fortified place, in all appearance a defensive structure, was intended to discourage casual visitors to a cult which had once been conducted secretly at La Pinacle's *fana* temple. If so, Grosnez's ruined battlements could represent the site of an elaborate mystery cult, guarded as jealously as the old Eleusian mysteries. This would also explain why all history associated with the site seems to have been erased.

We are helped in this idea by one other clue to the sanctity of the site; one piece of living evidence has survived the ravages of time, and which is obvious to any visitor lucky enough to turn up at the right time of day and year. The sunsets at Grosnez are spectacular. A website dedicated to the castle and its views calls them 'among the best in Europe', and claims that to stand at this location and watch the sun go down is an experience not to be missed; the afterglow creates an almost lunar landscape.[2] Perhaps this is the key to the site. On Midsummer's Day, as any meteorologist will confirm, the sun rises in the north-east and sets in the north-west. Grosnez, on the extreme edge of the north-west tip of Jersey, is the perfect location to bid farewell to the setting sun at the summer solstice.

Midsummer is central to many Channel Islands pagan rituals. The ferrying round the Cheval Roc in Bonne Nuit took place on Midsummer's Day, and so did the Chevauchée de St Michel. Midsummer's Day was the time when the nuns and novices of Lihou 'indulged their pleasant lovemaking', when youths and maidens danced and lit bonfires on the granite summit of Rocque Balan at L'Ancresse, and when the bacchanalian bowl ritual of the bacchan, the *Faire braire les poêles* sent its horned music echoing around the groves.

All over the Channel Islands, the summer solstice, the very point when the sun began its decline, was marked by a lively and almost bewildering variety of pagan rites and rituals, some private, others overt and noisy. And the heart of them all, very possibly, was this perfectly situated rock site of Grosnez, which confronted the sun at its height, and whose fallen menhir may have expressed its fast-waning power.

The idea of a castle being built over a pagan site is not as unlikely as it sounds. Many Channel Islands castles seem to have been built over once sacred ground. Elizabeth Castle, as we know, evolved around the god of the rock, St Helier, and a later priory also once stood on the site. Other castles, like Jersey's Mont Orgueil, are steeped in prehistoric mystery. Local historians tend to agree that something existed on that coastal hill before the castle, but no one is sure exactly what. Nor has anyone yet explained the regular pilgrimage that takes place to the castle, similar to that which is still undertaken to St Helier's bed at Elizabeth Castle.

Guernsey's counterpart to Elizabeth Castle, Castle Cornet, has a name which strongly evokes the rituals of the grain – corn, horn and cornucopia. Elsewhere on Guernsey, the area most famous for the presence of the witches is called Catioroc, which means 'castle rock', extending the sacred associations of castle sites. One of Guernsey's churches is called Castel, or St Marie du Castro – 'St Mary of the castle'. One modern guide book points out the extensive view the church commands from its high position and suggests that the site had another use before it was built there. This is confirmed by the fact that one of Guernsey's Gran'mère menhirs was discovered buried under the floor of the chancel. It is called La Gran'mère du Castel or Câtel Gran'mère, the grandmother of the castle. The castle was actually called Le Chateau du Grand Geffroy, named after Geoffrey, the dark consort and god of the rock.

St. Clement's Icho Tower, that castellated islet where a horse and rider burial was found, was regarded as a sacred spot long before the appearance of the fortification that stands there now. From the evidence of a large cross that once stood on the rock, it appears to have been Christianized. It can be seen on old map references, where the so called Croix de Fer ('iron cross') was represented standing above an inverted cone (the existence of a cone seems especially significant, too). Apart from these old map markings, there is no other record of a cross or any other structure before the building of the tower, which means that this islet is yet another mysterious Channel Islands location, with vaguely Christian associations but much more powerful pagan ones.

A more recent structure, the Gothic Nicolle Tower, was also built over a recumbent standing stone, another place with vaguely sacred or profane associations. Until recently an air of menace hung over the tower. Mothers never allowed their children to go near the place because of rumours of rampant witchcraft. It is remarkably similar to another Gothic structure, the Prince's Tower, which once crowned the sacred mound at La Hougue Bie, absorbing the ancient chapels into its structure. The tendency to build towers over feminine structures seems to have persisted into fairly recent times. Jersey's Archirondel Tower, also stands on the site of a long vanished Neolithic monument.

The story of Guernsey's *Forest of Vazon* extends this apparent link between castle structures and the Neolithic world of the feminine. It contains a description of a castle or tower as the dwelling pace of Judith, the sorceress or Goddess of the island. This is how the story describes the tower.

A wooden partition divided the room on the lower storey into two chambers of unequal size: the larger, in which he stood, was the common dwelling apartment, the other was given over to Hilda. The upper storey, approached by a ladder and also by an external staircase, was sacred to Judith. The seats were rude and massive: one of them, placed by a window fronting the setting sun, was evidently the favourite resting-place of Judith. Above this seat was a shelf on which lay some of the mysterious scrolls of which Jean had seen specimens in the possession of the fathers. Instruments of witchcraft, if such existed, must have been in the upper storey: none were visible.

A castle evokes an idea of a hidden landscape – enclosed and forbidding, a domain as secret as the underworld. In Ireland the counterparts of dolmens, the cairns, were fortified by stone and could stand to a height of up to 20 feet, becoming castle-like in dimensions. From fairy mound to fairy castle, therefore, is not a huge step. With the damsel living on the top storey, the dragon lurking in the subterranean vaults and a wizard on the scene performing explosive magic, they all seem to evoke memories of secret cults in covert places. Perhaps that is why, in so many old tales, the castle is seen as the entrance to the otherworld. The mythical castle of darkness, or castle of no return, inhabited by a black knight (or dark consort) symbolizes the underworld, like Guernsey's Geoffrey in Le Chateau du Grand Geffroy.

The knight, we have already suggested, is an extension of the goddess's consort, of which Lord Hambye and the buried knight at Notre Dame are examples. The idea that knighthood and chivalry, born from the

Arthurian legends, were a development of old fertility cults has been suggested by many writers in the past. Knights lived in castles, which makes the idea that castles were centres of a secret cult seem less unlikely.

Particularly suggestive of mystery cults and the secretiveness around them is a castle in Guernsey, known evocatively as the Castle in the Marshes, or Le Chateau des Marais. It stands on a raised mound in what was once marsh land, and was once believed to be haunted by a white knight on horseback. Although no one ever claimed to have seen him, his ghostly sounds were frequently heard and reported. This begs the question, as De Garis suggested, that if he has never been seen, how is it possible to describe him as a specifically white knight? One possible answer is that it is a half-suppressed memory of forbidden secret rites.

From knighthood grew the notions of chivalry, which can be defined as dedication to the service of one particular woman. In the chivalric tradition, the bold knight – the hero – performed deeds to win his lady's love. He would defer to his lady and obey her in all things, because she was both his mistress and his queen. The knight was filled with a holy passion for his lady. He would never touch her. Instead he put her on a pedestal to worship her and perform mighty deeds in her honour. He was even prepared to die for her. Romantic poetry is full of the miseries and agonies of the knight who has lost his lady's favour, or who meets his death at the ruthless hand of 'La Belle Dame Sans Merci'.

Romantic love was a religious rather than carnal emotion, and has even been traced back to an older religious tradition, the so-called Manichean movement which spread through the Holy Roman Empire in the eleventh century. It was also known as Catharism. One of the Cathars' beliefs was that true love between a man and a woman was the eternal expression of the worship of a feminine saviour, a mediator between God and man. Earthly love, they believed, was an allegory for the spiritual love of the Queen of Heaven.

In the early thirteenth century the Pope declared Catharism a heresy and launched a crusade to repress it. It was consequently driven underground and, it is believed, re-emerged in a 'secular' form, in the cultural flowering of the songs and poems of the troubadours, who sang the praises of their mistresses and the mystic emotions of love. It is possible that their romantic traditions were a deliberately secret and thus overtly 'secular' continuation of Cathar religious practice. Despite this need for secrecy, their elegant and attractive songs became universally popular, sweeping into the courts of medieval Europe, where the worship of the

The Castle in the Marshes in Guernsey, believed to have been haunted by a white knight on horseback. Could it be the site of another ancient pagan cult?

feminine matured into something called 'courtly love', which developed later into romantic poetry.

Jersey had its own troubadour poet. Robert Wace, born in Jersey in 1115, wrote two epic sagas, comparable in scale to Homer or Virgil, which linked the regions of Britain, Normandy and Brittany into a cultural whole. The more famous of his two great poems, *Le Roman de Brut*, narrates the history of Britain from King Lear to King Arthur. In his accounts of Arthur, Wace introduced, for the first time, the legend of the Round Table and was also the earliest writer to give Arthur's sword its now famous name: Excalibur. He helped popularize the Arthurian legends by writing them down in a popular language. In so doing, he also established the Arthurian myths as very much part of the pagan legacy of the Channel Islands.

The legacy of Robert Wace was an inspiration to the later island poets of the nineteenth century. Fascinated by him and the whole heritage of the troubadours, they wrote in the same feminine tradition, and even called themselves troubadour poets. They took their inspiration directly from the pagan folklore of the islands and wrote a kind of 'folk' poetry.

One particular poet, Métivier, who became an expert in folklore, asserted that his poems were all composed from *'orally constructed fragments'*, and annotated his lyrics with comments on local folklore and custom. Fascinatingly, he compared his orally inspired poetry to the evolution of the gospels, saying that they too were sacred poetry created from *'individual oral units'*, later turned into written verse. This was a very revealing statement indeed, comparing his own poetry to the books of the Bible.

Clearly these poets regarded their work as a viable alternative to Christian holy texts. Certainly much of their poetry overtly mocks the established Church, and seems to champion a more feminine tradition. The poem *A Voyage to Lihou*, as we have seen, portrays a near fatal culture clash between the matriarchal and patriarchal religions, and there is little doubt which is on the winning side. Another example of a clash in which matriarchy is victorious is a song called 'The Curate's Black Cassock':

> Coming back from church one evening
> Everyone was laughing, parlafrandine,
> Asking the neighbour and his wife:
> 'Why is there a rip through
> The hem of the curate's robe?

It transpires that the curate tore his robe while secretly 'kissing our Susan'. It must have been a violent and prolonged kiss, because in the process he tore Susan's fine lace. So, in fair retaliation, the girl ripped the hem of his robe to shreds.

This clearly shows the vengeance of the feminine against the patriarchal authority of the church. The violence implied in the fertility act of kissing is directed against the curate's robe. A robe, cloak, or mantle, is as strong a symbol of male authority as the crown. It is associated with the magical power of wizards, and even modern superheroes like Batman or Superman are helpless and naked without their cloaks or capes. In the Bible, Luke's gospel mentions a sick woman who heals herself by touching the hem of Jesus's cloak. We are told that Jesus notices at once that 'some power has gone out of him'. Elsewhere in the Bible, in the Book of Samuel, David symbolically kills his rival King Saul by cutting off a piece of his cloak. The tearing or cutting of a cloak is also associated with another Channel Islands saint: St Martin, who shares his cloak with a beggar. Perhaps one reason why he was not martyred in the usual sense is that the rending of his cloak and the humbling of his status to that of beggar was seen as a good substitute for a ritual killing. So the attack on the hem of the curate's cloak in the Guernsey poem similarly symbolizes a defeat of the priest's sacred authority by the feminine – even a sacrifice.

It is hard to believe that the poet was unaware of the powerful symbolism of what seems, on the surface, a harmless and mischievous tale. It clearly places the Channel Islands troubadour poets in the same tradition as their forebears: the guardians of a covert belief system that is alternative – and hostile – to the ruling church.

These poets, heirs to the troubadour tradition, nourished the pagan heritage of these islands. They made it clear that, for a nation to define its identity, it needs to value and understand its folklore, which is part of the very fabric of the land and the speech of its people. Due to their influence, much ancient folklore has survived, and because of this a true sense of Channel Islands culture and modern nationhood was made possible.

We seem to have come a long way from Apollo. But whether or not Grosnez was really a temple to Apollo, it is not hard to imagine this place, with its spectacular coastal setting, concealing a cult whose richness we can perhaps begin to appreciate. Just as the red sun blazes into the Hougue Bie chamber at the equinox, and the people dance round their fires of the dying sun at Samhain, so perhaps they also once bade

Dehus dolmen – close-up of the guardian of the tomb. Another god of the rock. Or is it Hermes?

farewell to the sun at this coastal temple, perhaps with dancing, perhaps with prayers or sacrifices. On this jutting point, unencumbered by surrounding land, they would have stood as close to the sun and the sea as the mountainless landscape of Jersey allowed. Their temple cult, however secret it was, would have stood proudly in the coastal landscape, in the manner of the famous Greek temple to the sun and the sea, which still stands today at the tip of the corner of the Athenian coast at Sounion.

Notes

1   www.guernseyheritage.com
2   www.freespace.virgin.net/edward.clarke1/page2

13 The Sun God Rules

Perhaps the stone guardian in Guernsey's Dehus Dolmen is not Apollo at all. Expert opinion, including that of V.C. Collum, one of the excavators of the dolmen, insists that, with his bow and arrow, he is the legendary Hermes. As it happens, Hermes and Apollo were brothers in Greek myth and are virtually interchangeable anyway. Hermes is more familiar to us under his Roman name of Mercury, the winged messenger, constantly flitting to and fro between gods and men with messages. This makes him a mediator between the divine and the human, basically the archetypal consort. The word mercurial also refers to something erratic, volatile or unstable, derived from Mercury's flitting around from place to place – all of which is very similar, of course, to the figure of Puck.

In his fascinating guide to the Dehus Dolmen, Collum linked Hermes, his guardian messenger, to other mythological god/consort figures, such as Ishtar and Tammuz, and called him a 'dying god of vegetation' and 'son and lover' of the goddess, as well as a serpent figure: '*This image of the true or faithful messenger is related to the role of the serpent, as messenger between the Goddess in her underworld domains, and humankind. Both Consort names, Ishtar and Tammuz, were called "the great serpent dragon".*'

Among his other mythical qualities, Hermes was famous for bringing healing dreams to mortals, like the serpent at Epidaurus. (His symbol of office was a rod entwined with two serpents.) Hermes was also a psychopomp, the conveyer of souls to the underworld. He was the prince of tricksters, devious, able to change his shape and notorious for misleading travellers. One of his titles was even Lord of Misrule. All of this sounds remarkably similar to the Channel Islands' own god of the rock: Puck.

In fact, one of Hermes' titles in Greek myth was also 'god of the stones'. The stones that bore his name, the *hermas*, were used to mark

roads and boundaries in ancient Athens. To the Athenians, these boundary stones were more than mere signposts or directions in the landscape.
They were sacred embodiments of the fertility god and were
worshipped with offerings of fruit, wine and cakes. This reminds us of
the offerings of flowers or fruit left at the feet of the grandmother menhir
in St Martin's. Clearly, to the ancient Greeks, the boundary stone, the
hermas, had the same sacred status as a menhir to the Neolithics.

There is evidence that boundary stones were equally sacred in the
Channel Islands. One of Guernsey's black dogs was known to haunt the
sites of boundary stones, which reminds us that Hermes, the guardian
of the Dehus Dolmen, was also a psychopomp like the dog Cerberus. In
more recent times, whenever a new boundary stone had to be laid in
Jersey a handful of small rocks, called *témoins*, would be thrown into a
hole, and then would be covered by the boundary stone. This might be
a practical drainage technique, but bearing in mind the symbolic relationship between bones and stones, this action of scattering the *témoins*
and then burying them under a large standing stone is an uncanny
reminder of the scattered bones found in Neolithic burial sites. It is
worth adding that the word *témoin* is believed to come from the Roman
Terminus, a god synonymous with *Mercury* and *Hermes*.

The Chevauchée de St Michel is another ritual that connected
ancient fertility rites to boundary stones, because the official purpose
of the ceremony was to survey all of the boundaries and roads on the
island. At the conclusion of the procession, the menhir upon which the
miller stood was also a boundary stone, and the reverence in which it
was held could be surmised from the fact that carts were forbidden to
cross over it.

From all this it could be argued that dolmens and menhirs, in addition to telling time and measuring the seasons, also existed as markers
in the landscape, creating a sense of place as well as time. By defining
boundaries and declaring territorial rights, they gave each individual a
clear sense of community and family identity; people 'knew where they
were' with these landmarks. As we have said, the tradition of settlement
and land ownership, as opposed to the nomadic wandering life of the
earlier hunter-gatherers, was one of the most important legacies of the
Neolithic farming communities. This new permanence would have
been expressed by the fixed durability of their standing stones.

Clearly then, these ancient monuments 'tracked' the landscape in the
same way that they tracked the sky. Just as the menhirs plotted the

moon's path in straight lines, or later navigation technique drew straight lines (called constellations) across the stars, so it is very likely that these monuments were also linked up on the landscape in a similar series of straight lines. If this is true, it could partly explain the phenomenon known as ley lines.

According to the original book on the subject, *The Old Straight Track* by Alfred Watkins, ley lines are a series of alignments in the landscape, linking ancient sites such as dolmens, menhirs and other sites of ancient sacred importance in a straight line. Watkins claims that it is quite easy to trace these straight alignments by finding all the sites on a map, getting out a ruler and linking them up.

The local writer Bisson, inspired by Watkins, made a serious attempt to track ley lines on Jersey. He identified thirty-three historical monuments and twelve parish churches on the island, and assumed that these had all been built on pagan sites. He tracked these sites with a ruler and a map, in the manner suggested by Watkins, and found that all of them fell into at least one alignment, and most came into more than one. He also discovered that wells, crossroads and stream crossings fell into line, as did most of the recorded watermills. (It is obvious why watermills were once sacred places: they were natural water sites, where the work of the goddess of the grain was carried out.) Some of Bisson's alignments met at places which seemed to have no ancient significance, such as Archirondel Tower at St Martin, but which later research revealed as the site of a lost menhir.

It is not only Jersey that seems to have ley lines linking its ancient monuments. Near Herm there is a strange rock called the Pierre Percee, meaning 'pierced rock', now standing on an islet. A chapel is thought to have existed on this site, but no physical trace or historical record remains. Like so many other Channel Islands sites, its vaguely 'sacred' nature probably has more to do with ancient pagan traditions than Christianity. However, the pierced rock is still there and plain for all to see. On Jethou there is another rock with a hole in it, at the edge of a place called the Fairy Wood.

One explanation of this alignment is that it was the gateway to an ancient road – one that predates the flooding that now separates the islands of Herm and Jethou. Perhaps ley lines were literally paths or roads, providing easy access between the sites at certain ritual times of the year. This idea that they are old routes used by the Neolithic dolmen builders is partly confirmed by their name: fairy paths. The literal driving underground of the old religion also could explain why some fairy paths were thought to lie underground. In Guernsey, it is said that a number of subterranean fairy communities were linked to each other by a series of underground passages, in the same way that roads connect human settlements.

This memory of a sacred ritual journey may explain why it is thought to be unlucky to build on a fairy path, and that any home located on a ley line can expect to be disturbed by strange noises and even stranger happenings. We have already mentioned that a straight line can be traced between the entrance to Faldouet and the sacrificial site of Geoffrey's Leap, a line that seems to follow the path of the rising equinoctial moon. In fact, to this day, part of an ancient track still exists. A clear path, worn down perhaps by thousands of prehistoric feet, still scores a line from the entrance to the dolmen to the edge of the field, where it is cut off by a modern hedge and a large cultivated field. But this tiny stump of a path, which now leads nowhere, might be the fragment of an original ley line which once stretched in a straight line down the steep hill to meet the modern coast road. At the point where the line meets the road, the road proceeds in a surprisingly straight line directly to Geoffrey's Leap.

A certain mystical power attaches to the dolmen to this day and the writer Chris Lake has no doubt that this is due to the presence of the ley line. He describes how, in 1982, people living in houses nearby told a local clergyman that their homes had been invaded by something terribly 'cold and evil'. The clergyman, who blamed it on the activities of local witches trying to tap into its power, was called out on two separate occasions in the 1980s to conduct full-scale exorcisms at the dolmen.

It has also been noted that the pierced rock of Herm and its counterpart on Jethou apparently line up with the sunrise at the summer solstice. The movement of the sun and moon must be the key to the nature of ley lines.

One purpose of the dolmens and menhirs was to track time, originally by observing the moon. But the sun became increasingly important in people's vision of the divine – and the sun was a very effective aid in measuring time and the passing seasons. That explains why most megaliths are carefully aligned to point towards the rising sun on certain days of the year. The entrance to La Hougue Bie, for example, catches the sunrise at the summer and winter equinoxes.

The equinox is a vital seasonal marker; a signal that things are about to change, before the change becomes obvious and it is too late to plan for it. The spring equinox tells us that winter has ended; conversely the autumn equinox warns us that it has begun. So, on the morning of each equinox, the dark tunnel of La Hougue Bie magnificently erupts with brilliant red light, as if a huge fire had been ignited in the chamber. This 'fiery' event, often imitated by the fires built at the solstice sites, would have marked an important day for the farmers; it was time to start planning their planting or reaping.

Ley lines are also evident on Guernsey, where many of the church sites around the island seem to be linked together by a series of radiating straight lines, passing through St Michael's Church to Fort Le Marchant, the most northerly point of the island. This geographical counterpart to Jersey's Grosnez might also have been the home of the sun god, which is why his rays radiate out and bathe the whole island through its sacred sites.

The idea of holy sites co-existing in straight lines might have expressed a common link between them; a mystical unity embraced by the straight rays of the sun. There is evidence that a ley line, corresponding with the line of the sun at the equinox, stretches from La Hougue Bie to Nicolle Tower – which was built, as we have said, over a recumbent standing stone. There was once another stone or tomb about 500 yards away, which pointed directly towards the recumbent stone upon which the tower was built, in an east–west alignment. This same straight line stretches to the Blanche Dame of St Clements and ends at Rocqueberg, which is a very surprising destination for La Hougue Bie's ley line. It seems that the witches of St Clement's are directly linked with the feminine traditions of one of Jersey's most ancient churches, Lady Hambye's burial shrine to her hero husband.

Interestingly, our Faldouet line, linking the entrance of the dolmen to Geoffrey's Leap also leads in a straight line to La Hougue Bie, suggesting that this major dolmen is situated on an intersection of ley lines across the island. Perhaps this meeting of two lines – one tracking the sun and the other the moon – expressed a true marriage between the sun king and the moon goddess in the landscape. The sun king, like the consort, was the bringer of the spring and renewed fertility of the land. The dolmens and menhirs, aligned in honour of the sun, therefore enhanced the fertility of the land.

The straight lines on the earth enabled the king's spirit to radiate through the kingdom. Straightness, after all, is the symbolism of power and kingship. Even our modern language equates power with straight-ness. Word roots such as 'reg' and 'rect' mean 'movement in a straight line' and can be found in modern words such as regular, rectangle and region, and words associated with kingship and order such as rectitude, righteous, regal, reign – and the word 'ruler'.

Ville es Nouaux. Two ancient monuments in the grounds of St Andrew's Church, near St Helier. A straight line seems to pass through the long chamber and circle to the entrance to the church ground. A tree in the back-ground adds to the sense of alignment

But the goddess was not deposed. These stone monuments were still rooted in the earth and dictated by its shape – the hills and valleys that decided where they would be built. Many menhirs and dolmens continued to track the wandering moon. The principle of ley lines expressed a marriage between the fertilizing power of the sun and the moon goddess on earth – a sacred marriage that was eternal and would always guarantee the return of spring.

With ley lines we had no need of sacrifice or the orgiastic rites typified by Dionysus. We were sure in our faith. We moved to a calmer, gentler, more balanced Apollonian view, comforted by the ever-present sun. Even in the depths of winter we knew that there was no cause for despair. The sun might have vanished from our temporary gaze, but it was always present, mated for ever with our feminine landscape. Safe within our network of holy sites, a network which in itself expressed the totality of the enclosing womb, we had faith that spring would always return.

The continued presence of the goddess in sun ceremonies is confirmed in the Story of Vazon Forest, which contains a vivid depiction of a sunset rite, carried out on the evening of the summer solstice, under the auspices of the sorceress and goddess Judith. The description is so beautifully written it is worth quoting in full.

The sun was nearing the horizon. The scene was one of unsurpassed loveliness. Behind lay the central and southern portions of the island, hushed as if their primaeval rocks were still tenantless.

Straight from the sun shot out across Cobo Bay a joyous river of gold, so bright that eye could ill bear to face its glow; here and there in its course stood out quaintly-shaped rocks, some drenched with the fulness of the glorious bath, others catching now and again a sprinkling shower. On each side of the river the sea, clear to its depths where alternate sand and rock made a tangle of capriciously mingled light and shade; its surface, here blue as the still waters of the Grotta Azzurra, there green as the olive, here again red-brown as Carthaginian marble, lay waveless, as with a sense that the beauty was too perfect to be disturbed. Suddenly the scene was changed; the lustrous outflow was swiftly drawn in and absorbed; a grey hue swept over the darkening surface; in the distance the round, blood-coloured, orb hung above the expectant ocean.

Then all assembled fell on their knees. The music gave out sharp plaintive notes which were answered by the voices of men and women in short, wailing, as it were inquiring, rhythm; this continued till the sun was on the point of disap-

pearance, when music and voices together burst into a sad chant, seemingly of farewell; the kneeling people extending their hands seaward with an appealing gesture.

We are left in no doubt that the goddess Judith is in control of this ceremony because she actually makes it happen. At the beginning, she harries her hesitant audience into beginning their obeisance to the dying sun: ' "Why linger you here? Are you unmindful of your duties? See you not how the shadows lengthen?" These words produced a magical effect.'

At the end of the ceremony, the presence of the goddess is clearly described in this closing description: 'On the projecting boulder ... stood the sorceress, her arms also outstretched, her figure, firm, erect, sharply outlined.'

Religious awareness was to change in the thousands of years that followed the Neolithic age, when men started worshipping a father god. Nevertheless, the ancient religion, the Great Goddess, was never really erased from human minds. Her overarching presence and that of her mortal consort remained central to the religious consciousness of what we may call the 'pagan' consciousness. This consciousness is rooted in the landscape, and acknowledges the maternal, all-nurturing nature of that landscape. Even the ceremonies that appear to worship the sun still perceive it terms of the rocks, green plants and trees, and the sea; still rooted in earth. This, for want of a better term, is what we mean by the term 'pagan'.

14 Crypts and Undercrofts

In a book-length version of La Hougue Bie's legend, published in 1837, it is not a dragon that Robert Hambye fights, but a rival prince called Ducaen.[1] Ducaen started life as a good and bold knight, Robert Hambye's equal in graciousness and military merit. But his great love for the beautiful Lady Hambye drove him to revolt against Lord Robert's rule and become an outlaw. He took refuge on the island of Jersey with his bandits, bringing 'violation, fire and rapine' to its land and coasts, behaving, to all intents and purposes, like a dragon.

As it happens, his ensign was a black flag which showed a fiery dragon. Actually, it looked so realistic that, to the terrified Jersey residents, it seemed alive. *'It was even said that he wrapped himself up in its horrid form, when he went to consult the nameless one … from whom he received his power'*. From being the dark consort and the enemy of the ruling lord, is a short step to becoming the enemy of mankind. Ducaen is now associated with the devil.

After the 'dragon' Ducaen had finally been conquered and killed, it was another knight called Malfort, who killed Hambye and became the lady's new consort. Like Ducaen, Malfort's love for Lady Hambye had become a ruling passion and it now led him to challenge Lord Hambye, just as Ducaen had tried to do. We can see that this is a cyclical, seasonal tale, dominated throughout by Lady Hambye. Every male role is defined and identified by an intense relationship to this overarching goddess figure.

Lady Hambye is given a name in this version of the story. She is the fair Gisla, described as the beauteous wife whose elegance and softness was *'of another age'* (the Neolithic perhaps). It was her task to reward valour and acts of chivalry. As we shall see, the ability to judge, reward (and bestow) the gifts of chivalry are qualities associated with the Lady/Goddess.

After Lord Hambye's death, Gisla founded a marble temple dedicated to the Virgin over his remains, with his tomb as the altarpiece. She made frequent visits to it. For the admiring Jersey people, these visits from the goddess had a sacred, almost supernatural aspect. Her sudden visits and disappearances gave La Hougue Bie a peculiar blessedness because it was now believed that the Holy Virgin herself would appear there.

La Hougue Bie – entrance to the dolmen. Above is the church crypt – in exactly the same alignment as the entrance

So now, Lady Hambye and the Virgin Mary were identical. They were both Notre Dame de la Clarté, Our Lady of Light (sometimes called 'the dawn'), to whom the chapel is dedicated. This is a direct reference to the alignment of the ancient dolmen, which receives the glory of the dawning sun at the equinox, the turning point of the season when it can be said that the sun god enters the goddess's sacred domain.

L'Amy also suggests that Notre Dame de la Clarté is the title of the moon goddess, who is worshipped 'even today' in the village of that name in Brittany, and whose veneration was prevalent in the Channel Islands until the introduction of Christianity. He also describes the dedication of La Hougue Bie chapel as *another instance of the assimilation by the Church of ancient pagan rituals*. In fact, la Clartè really translates, not specifically as 'dawn', but as 'luminous' or 'shining', a title of the moon goddess.

There are now two chapels on top of La Hougue Bie. The second, Jerusalem Chapel, was added in the sixteenth century by its priest, Dean Mabon, after a pilgrimage to the Holy Land. Despite this later addition, the whole structure is still uncannily similar in shape to the dolmen underneath it. The width of the main tomb is the same as the internal width of the chapel. It has even been suggested by Rodwell that the rectangular recesses in the Jerusalem Chapel were inspired by the side chambers in the Neolithic tomb.

Most fascinating of all is the crypt. A crypt is the part of a church dedicated to storing the dead, so it has a function similar to a dolmen. Philip Heselton has even suggested that all church crypts have their origins in Neolithic burial chambers.[2] How apt, then, that the crypt of the Jerusalem Chapel should have a window situated in direct alignment above the entrance to the dolmen below it, looking like a small doorway to the Christian tomb.

Such a clear relationship between this window and the dolmen entrance cannot be a coincidence. It can only mean one thing: that the pilgrims to La Hougue Bie were encouraged to see their own crypt as a modern counterpart of the Neolithic structure underneath it. What other purpose could this window serve, but to imitate the entrance to the tomb?

For years it was assumed that the dolmen of La Hougue Bie had been blocked up since Neolithic times and its existence unknown until excavations revealed the ancient site in the twentieth century. But this crypt window suggests otherwise: that the Neolithic tomb was open and accessible at the time that the chapel was built. Certainly the entrance at least might have been visible, perhaps recessed into the hill, even if the dolmen itself was hidden from sight.

Whether or not the medieval builders of the chapel were fully aware of the existence of the ancient dolmen, its matriarchal cult of the dead continued to inspire worshippers on this holy site right up to the Reformation, after which all cult activity ceased and the chapel fell into ruin. In its glory days the crypt, originally built in imitation of the tomb of Christ in Palestine, was a shrine where pilgrims worshipped at the sepulchre of Christianity's very own dying god. This means that La Hougue Bie continued to function as a centre of the death cult, long after the entombment of Lord Hambye had been consigned to fairy tale.

The designer of the Jerusalem Chapel, Dean Mabon, was a man with a strong belief in the miraculous power of the Virgin Mary. History has been unkind to him, accusing him of being a fraud who fooled credulous pilgrims out of their money by devising weird optical illusions in the crypt. He encouraged people to believe that the Virgin Mary appeared there. He also claimed that the Virgin performed miracles, and it is believed that he concocted these miracles by means of concealed wires and artificial lights.

The only evidence that Mabon was a rogue, however, can be found in the many hostile accounts of his actions, written in the aftermath of the Reformation. A different interpretation of his behaviour could be that he succeeded, for a while, in restoring an oracular dimension to the maternal site of La Hougue Bie. Maybe his practices were not so very different from the chthonic rituals of the Neolithic site and the cryptic oracles that might have been dispensed from there. Surely it was an extension of the miraculous tradition of Lady Hambye's and the Virgin's visits to the tomb, echoed by the visits of the Virgin and the Magdalene to the tomb of Christ.

The history of La Hougue Bie does not end there. In later years the site became secularized by the building of a large Gothic tower, when it eventually became the island's earliest tourist attraction. F. Stead approved of the transformation: 'The cell of superstition has become the Temple of Taste; a gloomy cemetery the favourite abode of the sylvan deities.'

It then became a pleasure ground, with a well-planted wood, a hotel, a bowling alley, and a general reputation for revelry. The view from the top of Prince's Tower was recommended by contemporary guide books as the most spectacular on the island – worthy of a mountain top. When the Neolithic tomb was rediscovered and excavated in the early twentieth century, the Prince's Tower, perched on top of the mound, was demolished 'for safety'. It is perhaps to be regretted that the site of La Hougue Bie is no longer a secular palace bringing pleasure to islanders and visitors. The sacred function of this Neolithic site was, surely, never intended to be narrowly Christian. The hotel, pleasure gardens and Prince's Tower are long gone and La Hougue Bie now stands again, stripped of its glamour, as a rather sober monument to past times, good and bad.

There is no trace of a buried hero or consort on the site today. However, a chapel of similar date at Jersey's Notre Dame des Pas, once revealed a very interesting secret. This ancient chapel has given its name to the attractive resort that has grown up around it: Le Havre des Pas.

The chapel was very similar to La Hougue Bie, not only in its age, but in that it occupied the summit of an ancient mound, and was of roughly the same size and proportions. Near to this church lay a pile of large stone, believed to be the debris of a destroyed chamber. The idea that a dolmen once existed here is confirmed by the local name, Le Pouquelaye des Pas. It is believed that the name *Notre Dame* refers, not to the Virgin Mary but to the *fée*, the fairy, whose habitation was once here. Her name, Our Lady of the Stones, is of course a title similar to White Lady or Dame Blianche, the ancient title of the goddess.

According to Sidney Bisson, the Virgin Mary frequently appeared at Le Havre des Pas, as she did at La Hougue Bie. He presumes that the lost chapel was built to commemorate her miraculous appearances. Her footprint, apparently, can still be found in a rock nearby. Sadly the remains of the dolmen have long vanished and even the chapel was destroyed in 1814.

Nevertheless, its disappearance revealed something of interest in its foundations. When it was demolished, a burial was discovered underneath in what may have been an ancient passage grave. The body was said to be clothed in chain mail. It would appear that this chapel, like that at La Hougue Bie, was founded upon the tomb of a man, the buried consort of the goddess. His chivalric chain mail identifies him as the knight, the dragon slayer of legend, and counterpart to the buried hero Lord Hambye.

But that is not the only discovery made underneath the ancient churches and chapels of the Channel Islands. Guernsey's La Gran'mère du Castel or Câtel Gran'mère menhir, stands in the cemetery of the church of St Marie du Castro. But it was not originally found in the graveyard. It had, in fact, been buried a foot beneath the chancel step of the church, presumably at the time the very first Christian chapel was built.

Of course this implies that the church was built, as so many were, on an ancient goddess location, and that this carved menhir must have been an important centre of cult worship. It is surprising, therefore, that the church founders did not smash it up, or at least remove and dispose of it somewhere a long way away. Surely such an overtly feminine, utterly non-virginal icon could not be incorporated into patriarchal Christianity. Nevertheless, the early Christians chose to incorporate this image within the structure of their church. This was not an act of destruction; in a strange way it was the opposite. It was a discreet incorporation and preservation of the goddess, to lay her down carefully as part of the foundations of a new faith.

The church's original name, the Church of Our Lady of Deliverance, also suggests strongly that the influence of the goddess remained here long after it was built. As it happens, the name has another, more unexpected association. There is a fairy tale connected with the building of this church. Apparently the original intention had been to build it somewhere quite different, near the centre of the modern parish. However, the fairies kept removing the stones and transferring them to the present site. Eventually it was decided to give up and construct the church on the site chosen by the fairies. This story is not unique in Guernsey. De Garis tells us that the churches of Castel, St Saviour's, the Vale and Torteval were all built on sites chosen by the fairies as alternatives to the ones originally decided upon.

Carey believes that these church legends might be a folk memory of a controversy between the new religion and the old about where churches could be built. However, their sheer number might imply a long-term compromise between the two religions, perhaps culminating in an agreement that a site could be utilized by the early church so long as its original sanctity was not defiled.

L'Amy tells us that the tradition of fairies moving building materials in this way is known as *la delivrande*, and adds that there is a village in Normandy of that name. There is an important and impressive Marian shrine in Normandy called the Notre Dame de la Delivrande. This ancient site, a favourite place of pilgrimage, is still venerated today. Similarly, Our Lady of Deliverance, or Castel Church, is still guarded over by the figure of the goddess: *La Gran'mère du Castel*.

In Jersey, there is a church with the same fairy tradition of moving stones. St Brelade's is also famous for the ancient Fishermen's Chapel that has stood on its current site since time immemorial. Its origins are as obscure as La Hougue Bie's; almost nothing has been recorded about its early history. Wild guesses have been made about its age, but estimated construction dates vary from the thirteenth to the sixth centuries.

It stands alongside St Brelade's on a rocky ledge in what was once a remote corner of the island. Because of the marshy nature of the land around the site, it was probably cut off at high tide, and at such times would have stood in proud isolation like a holy island. Even today, with fortifications keeping the waters at bay, the chapel and

The Fisherman's Chapel, St Brelade, Jersey. Mystery surrounds the name and origin of this chapel which could have been founded anytime between the sixth and the thirteenth centuries

church still seem to peer down at the beach and sea below from a kind of raised circular enclosure, like a Neolithic *hougue*. We do not even know for sure why it is called the Fishermen's Chapel, although the feminine associations of fishing might give us a clue. Fishing is as rich in ritual and ancient symbolism as farming. On our small islands it is inevitable that fishing would be as important a source of livelihood as tilling the land. Both involve a close negotiating relationship with the goddess's domain.

We have already mentioned the close relationship between Channel Islands fishermen and the goddess, their acts of deference to her, and frequent offerings of a portion of their catch. The Lihou Goddess of the Rock also demanded obeisance from sailors and fishermen. The site of the Fishermen's Chapel in St Brelade, Jersey, is another exposed *hougue* site which once, like Lihou, became a full island with every high tide.

The ancient association of the fish with femininity is widespread, of course. Long before Christianity, the fish symbol was known as the great mother. A cult of the fish existed in ancient Europe and ancient Greek had the same word for 'fish' and 'womb', *delphos* or 'dolphin'. (Interestingly, Delphi was also the site of the Greeks' most famous oracle.) In Syrian and Greek myth, ichthys (another Greek word for 'fish') was the partner of the sea goddess (Aphrodite or Delphine) and he is associated with the consort Adonis.

Archaeological evidence supports the idea that, like La Hougue Bie, the semi-island of the Fishermen's Chapel was sacred to the Neolithics, and that a megalithic structure stood somewhere on the site. Recent excavations suggest a fate similar to that of the Gran'mère du Castel. A fallen menhir, found on the church land, is thought to have served as the threshold to a Dark Age building. In addition, a number of large stones of Neolithic origin were found underneath the main church and the chapel. Although not as striking as the buried Gran'mère du Castel, this looks like another example of the deliberate and careful use of menhirs in the foundations of Christian structures.

A similar find was made on a group of tiny islands situated between Jersey and France, called Les Écréhous. There used to be an important priory on one of them, on the site of an early chapel similar in size and date to the Fishermen's Chapel. Both chapel and priory have long since fallen into ruin, but excavations have revealed that a large Neolithic menhir, probably the only one that had ever existed on this tiny island, was deliberately toppled and buried on the site before the chapel was built.

So it appears that many old Channel Islands churches are founded upon the ancient stones of the goddess. The builders of the churches must have realized the full implications of this. They must have known that they were, in effect, building an edifice over the goddess's buried bones, which represented a 'kore' rebirth to the Neolithics, and implies that the goddess was expected to rise again upon these church sites. Perhaps this was the true nature of *la delivrande*, that strange deal struck by the early church with the followers of the old religion.

Something else was found on Les Écréhous, which confirms that the early Channel Islands church was built on sacred Neolithic foundations. Excavators discovered a bone burial under the chapel and priory: a cache of disarticulated, cleaned bones, similar to the sort of broken incarceration found at many Neolithic burial chambers. Yet this was not a Neolithic burial; carbon dating placed it in the seventh century AD, well after the arrival of Christianity. Warwick Rodwell did not overlook the significance of this, suggesting that this early Christian shrine was built on a prehistoric religious site. [3]

The ancient chapels at La Hougue Bie and Notre Dame may have been built as shrines to a buried hero. But the site at Les Écréhous is different. Here the body has been identified as female, described by the excavators as a *locus sanctus* or saintly woman. It implies that the bones of a goddess figure had been buried, in both a symbolic and literal sense, as the root of a Christian church, and an extraordinary act of devotion by its builders. It symbolizes the burying of a menhir on the foundations.

As if acknowledging the peculiar sanctity of the site, its owner, when granting the land for the priory, asked that it be built 'in honour of God and the Blessed Mary, and the Divine Mysteries celebrated therein daily', a benediction which almost sounds like a cryptic reference to the goddess and her consort. Even the name of the island is significant: La Maître Île. *Maître* translates in Jersey French as 'master', but this 'maître' has a feminine article (*la*). Female 'master' does not translate into the rather degrading term 'mistress'. Instead, it is a title that associates femininity with power and influence; female sovereign perhaps, or even ruling goddess. One of the small islands is called 'Nipple Rock', which reminds us that the Neolithics often saw the goddess's body in the shape of the landscape – and they were not usually prudish on the subject either.

So the symbols and monuments to the goddess remain at the foundation of many early Channel Islands churches, apparently at the instigation of those who built them. Maybe, as the fairy stories suggest, this was only a compromise, to divert loyalty to the new faith. But it ensured that the goddess was allowed to remain in her true domain, in her underworld chthonic realm, now represented by the church crypt and the undercroft. She was not overthrown; she remained as a secret, a mystery accessible perhaps only to the initiated or her remaining clandestine worshippers, a subversive presence.

Some Channel Islands church sites have virtually disappeared from sight. All trace, historical or physical, seems to have been erased, and they only exist in folklore, which record more of the pagan origins than the Christian function of the site.

Overlooking Bonne Nuit Bay, the location of the Horse or William Rock, stood a chapel and a nunnery, which may once have formed a very important ecclesiastical centre. The chapel disappeared in the eighteenth century and the site is shrouded in the same mystery as the Church of Notre Dame at Hougue Bie, or the Fishermen's Chapel at St Brelade. But several stories are attached to the area, including at least two accounts of ritual sacrifice: the plunging of William to his death in the waters by a Puck-like horse, and the plunging of a shepherd from the high cliffs, with the name of his beloved on his lips. Stronger than the memory of any Christian liturgy is the archetypal pagan myth attached to these earlier rituals.

The Bonne Nuit area of Jersey retained its associations with the old religion until quite recent times. It was said that warlocks, witches, ghosts and fairies haunted its high cliffs, and people would keep away from an area known as the Becquet es Chats because they believed that the witches celebrated their Sabbath there.

Even stranger is the priory at the Devil's Hole, which also seems to have vanished without a trace. Despite the impact it was said to have on the devil, driving him to leap into the sea, there is no historical evidence that a priory ever existed here. What we have instead is this sacrificial ritual, similar to the other rituals we have discussed.

In the foundations of the very centre of the Church of England, the cathedral at Canterbury, we find the most evocative of goddess shrines. Deep underground, in the hidden vaults of this ancient seat of clerical power, sits Our Lady Undercroft, resplendent in candlelit glory, in her large pillared crypt that looks so like the goddess throne room at Knossos. Here the Great Goddess reigns in secret, in her underworld or undercroft, unobserved by the Reformation and largely forgotten by the grand cathedral that still harbours her.

Notes

1 Bulkeley.
2 *Earth Mysteries*, p.71
3 *Les Ecréhous*, p.95

15 Subversive Images

The Reformation did its best to erase all memory of the goddess from Christianity. The reformers declared war on religious art and destroyed nearly everything beautiful in our churches. In the Channel Islands, this led to an even more thorough destruction of our ecclesiastical heritage than in England.

A lot of the devastation was caused by simple greed. The ancient churches were full of chalices, candlesticks, crosses, chasubles, copes, altar frontals, palls and reliquaries, the irreplaceable work of generations of craftsmen. Whole cartloads of these cultural treasures were quickly melted down and converted into ready cash, to be spent on fighting wars and building stately houses.

But the reformers were fanatical and took the devastation further. What they could not melt down they burned, and what they could not remove they defaced or smashed to pieces. They shattered the medieval stained glass in the churches and plastered whitewash over the wall paintings and frescoes, obscuring them for ever.

Such vandalism seems hard to credit nowadays. Why were the reformers so determined to obliterate an entire heritage? One possible motive is that they were partly driven by a need to eradicate something subversive in the Church, an influence buried in its liturgical foundations, like the fallen menhirs. This influence seems to have manifested itself in much church art, especially the wall frescoes.

Of course, many of these old wall paintings were straightforward representations of themes and events from the Bible, displayed for the benefit of a church congregation unable to read or understand the Latin liturgy. Other frescoes, however, are harder to explain. They do not portray biblical scenes, or any other events or characters familiar from the bible or Christian liturgy. They seem ambiguous in their message and this alone would have been repugnant to the literal-minded reformers, to whom the truth was pure and simple. Even worse, these paintings, with their mysterious and often sophisticated imagery, are clearly doing more than educating an illiterate congregation. They seem to convey a sort of secret code, the hint of an alternative and a much older religious sense that would have been a direct challenge to the Reformation. We can examine this code, if indeed there was a code, in the few fragments of wall paintings that have survived in Channel Islands churches.

The paintings in the Fishermen's Chapel are a good example of a hidden message. The east wall is decorated with a picture of the Annunciation of the Virgin Mary. Mary is at the centre of this picture and the Archangel Gabriel seems to be kneeling to her, along with family members of the donor of the painting. Even these powerful and influential island people are seen kneeling, and with their hands raised in prayer to Mary.

This scene, which shows nothing less than the full worship of the Christian goddess, is situated right above the altar, the spiritual centre and physical apex of the church. This is where the eyes of the worshippers automatically settle and to which all prayers are addressed. Although

Fresco of the Virgin Mary inside the Fishermen's Chapel, St Brelade, Jersey. Everyone in the fresco shows deference to the Queen of Heaven in this ancient temple

God is present in the picture, hovering delicately above the Madonna like a shy summer sun, it is Mary who dominates this scene, the whole east wall, and therefore the entire chapel. The queen of this ancient shrine is receiving the prayers of her humble petitioners.

Sadly, Mabon's famous Marian shrine, the Jerusalem Chapel at La Hougue Bie, has no surviving art. There are the remains of two frescoes, which apparently represent female figures, but there is no clue as to their identity. Luckily, a series of frescoes in Jersey's St Clement's Church survived centuries of destruction and neglect very well. These extraordinary works of art feature not only Mary, but also a pantheon of other goddesses too. On the east wall are the remnants of two wall-paintings, each showing a woman saint. One portrays St Margaret, with a wing of a dragon, and the other has been identified as St Barbara, standing beside her tower.

St Margaret is also known as Marina; a name very close to Mary, to *mère*, ('mother') and *mare*, ('the sea'). Because of her association with the sea, Margaret/Marina is often depicted with pearls in her crown. She is sometimes shown standing near a cauldron, that symbol of fecundity associated with the ancient dolmen. In this fresco however, she is accompanied by her consort, the dragon.

Sadly, in some legends, Margaret's relationship with the serpent/dragon is not a harmonious one. She is often shown trampling all over him, a most unfriendly act similar to the goddess kicking out Ophion's teeth, or Eve's crushing of the serpent beneath her heel. But there is no violence in the St Clement's fresco. Here St Margaret appears to be emerging from the dragon's body, a much more harmonious relationship that recalls the great serpent Ophion embracing and seducing the Great Goddess while she danced on the sea, creating the world. So in this single fresco, three pre-Christian symbols of creation, the goddess, the serpent and the sea, appear to be unified in a single image.

The other figure, St Barbara, is much less well known. Legend tells us that she was a maiden of such beauty that her father locked her in a tower to hide her away. One day in her father's absence, Barbara visited a new bath house that was being built for her, and decided that a large pool in it was a perfect place for Christian baptism. Barbara told the builders to make a few changes in the design; instead of two windows there would be three – in honour of the Holy Trinity. When her father returned and discovered what she had done, he cut her head off. He was immediately struck by lightning and died.

St Barbara and her castle and sheaf of corn – a figure that resembles the Roman Goddess Nemesis

Like many saints' legends, this is almost certainly an older tale, describing a culture clash between the masculine and the feminine, a conflict which took place when the domains of the goddess were invaded by the new masculine sky gods. There are many examples in myth and legend of a maiden being imprisoned in a tower. Rapunzel of the long golden hair and the Arthurian Lady of Shallot spring to mind. Perhaps here the tower represented male power, an emblem of the sky god, phallic and unyielding, imprisoning the feminine principle like the soaring church spires that replaced the goddess's shrines.

But we have already discussed the possibility that the tower was also a feminine symbol of the underworld. The imprisonment of the maiden could be a version of Kore's abduction to the underworld. This would turn Barbara into the goddess of the grain, imprisoned in the earth like the buried seed, and then cut down when she emerges, like the harvested crop, which makes sense of her violent death in the story.

This second interpretation is confirmed by her fresco, in which she is holding a sheaf of corn in one hand and a sickle in the other. Here she is the grain goddess at the very point of the harvest and the slaying of the crop. The tower that accompanies her could also be a phallic representation of the fertilizing consort, about to be brutally chopped down at the turn of the season.

Like her companion St Margaret, Barbara is a rather unorthodox figure to be so prominently displayed on a church wall. Certainly the hidden meanings and dangerous feminine codes implied in the painting of these myths had no place in the 'pure' Protestant church.

On the west wall are the remains of what looks like a hunting scene. There is a verse underneath it in French which reads: 'Alas, St Mary! Who are these three corpses who look so grim?' This painting represents a story called 'The Three Living and The Three Dead'. Three kings are hunting in the forest when they meet three corpses or skeletons. These turn out to be counterparts of themselves, who give them a warning that they must all die.

So it is it is the hunters themselves, not their prey, that are the victims. This is a reminder that the hunt evolved into the fertility sacrifice in which the male king/consort met with his death in the service of the goddess. This death was celebrated in the bacchanalian ritual, associated more with the witch cult at La Rocque Berg than a church wall. Although the lament 'Alas St Mary' is directed to the Christian queen of heaven, this is an image that recalls a much earlier, grimmer goddess of sacrifice, Nemesis, who pursued the sacred king before eventually capturing him and tearing him apart.

The hunting fresco at St Clement's, Jersey. Are we looking at an ancient sacrifice scene?

This fresco is an appropriate counterpart to the picture of St Barbara as goddess of the grain, holding her sickle, a figure that would eventually develop into that other judgemental creature of fate, the grim reaper. It all comes back to the Neolithic tradition of the Blanche Dame, or *fata*; the death goddess in charge of the turning seasons, the bringer of winter in the height of summer.

Maybe this was behind the fatalism that was so much part of the world view of the medieval peasant – the belief that things were 'meant to be'. A belief in fate (*fata*) is basically a version of goddess worship; it was in a similar 'fatalistic' spirit that the matriarchal Neolithics accepted the oncoming winter. The reformers wanted to replace this belief in 'fate' with a more controlling vision of the divine: a belief in the exclusive rule of the father God.

Another fresco on the north side of the nave shows St Michael attacking the dragon, oddly without his helmet and holding a broken sword. The tip of his sword is at the dragon's feet and the dragon appears to be stamping on it. Usually it is the dragon that is trampled underfoot – originally by the goddess, as we have seen. Now St Michael's sword – his symbol of sacred victory – is receiving the same treatment from a very defiant-looking dragon. This offers us a very strange sub-text indeed.

The east corner of the nave of St Clement's shows us the image of another woman in a headdress, holding a container in her right hand and lifting the lid with her left. On the side of the painting is a banderole, bearing in Gothic letters the name 'Maria' followed by a longer word beginning with 'M'. The container suggests that the 'Mary' was Mary Magdalene (more properly Mary of Bethany), promoted, in this sympathetic fresco, from the 'fallen woman' image usually associated with her. The container of oil that she holds, like St Margaret's cauldron, is one of the traditional symbols of the goddess's plenty. Even the Bible describes the perfume, which was *worth a year's wages*, in vivid detail: 'Then Mary took about a pint of pure nard, an expensive perfume; she poured it on Jesus's feet and wiped his feet with her hair. And the house was filled with the fragrance of the perfume.'

This reminds us that the cup, the cauldron and the cornucopia all represent the bounty of the earth goddess and the source of all wealth. When Mary anoints Jesus's feet, she is bestowing her divine favour on him; like the gifts received by Hephaestus, the 'sacred fluid' symbolizes the power which the goddess of the land transfers to the rightful king. In Jesus's case, it is preparation for his divine death and burial – again, the same baptism as Hephaestus and Lancelot. As Jesus himself said about Mary and her ointment: 'Against the day of my burying hath she kept this.'

This image of the girl holding a vase is an archetype of the goddess familiar from pre-classical times. Would its pagan context and meaning have been familiar to the congregation? It is probable that the destructive reformers thought so. Anyway, the dominance of strong female images in this church, whether in or out of scripture, would have been offensive to them.

On the west side of the Magdalene picture is another representation of a woman, wearing a headdress and surrounded by an aureole. She is seated on a Roman chair and the word '*Sancta*' can be deciphered. It has been suggested that this figure represented the Virgin and Child. If so, with its trappings of temporal power, it gives a central reigning position to the Christian queen of heaven similar to the fresco in the Fishermen's Chapel.

Another Channel Islands church with some surviving frescoes is Guernsey's Castel Church, the location of the Gran'mère. These three frescoes, placed in a series on a high wall of the church, are not as well preserved as those in St Clement's, but are equally intriguing.

The fresco on the left shows another version of the hunting scene, in which three riders clearly meet their own death. On the far right, a more biblical scene is portrayed, probably the Last Supper. Yet a female is present here; a person with long hair can be seen at the front of the picture, apparently in some serving role. Luke's gospel refers obliquely to servants being present at the meal, but no mention of a woman. Again the message of the frescoes is different from that of the biblical text.

The hunting theme in this fresco in Castel Church was very popular in old church artwork

A mysterious feminine presence at the last supper. Are we looking at the Holy Grail?

The female presence is thought to be the same Mary we saw holding the sacred jar in St Clement's Church. Perhaps here the 'serving' act of the woman is not that of a simple servant, but closer to the 'anointing' role we discussed earlier.

The presence of a woman at a sacred feast is usually highly significant in Norse and British myth. In the feasts in the poem *Beowulf*, Queen Wealhtheow appears mysteriously from nowhere to offer a 'flowing cup' to the warrior who has reached a crucial point in his destiny. On one occasion, Wealhtheow offers the cup to Beowulf, who then utters a formal oath to accomplish his deed or die – an expression of his final destiny. Clearly what appears on the surface to be a simple act of hospitality is really a kind of anointment, or even coronation.

The brimming cup of the Beowulf story becomes, in Arthurian legend, something even more mystical and awesome.

> *Therewith there was such a savour as all the spicery of the world had been there. And forthwith there was upon the table all manner of meats and drinks that they could think upon. So came in a damosel passing fair and young, and she bare a vessel of gold betwixt her hands…. This is, said the king, the richest thing that any man hath living … this is the holy Sangreal that ye have here seen.*

How similar this sounds to the expensive nard referred to in Luke's gospel, 'worth a year's wages', which fills the house with its fragrance.

The grail, along with the cup, the cauldron and the cornucopia, represents the bounty of the earth goddess. This is why it is the young woman – symbolizing the maiden of the spring of the new year – who always handles the cup of sacred fluid. The Holy Grail, that feminine symbol, was the centre of Arthurian legend and perhaps also the cult of those mysterious castles. It is that same cult, the secret reign of the feminine, that is manifested here in many of the surviving frescoes of the church.

A darker message is conveyed in the third fresco, reminding us perhaps of the closeness of death to many of these rituals. Prominently displayed on a high vaulting arch between the other two paintings, this single-figure fresco shows what looks like a woman wearing a white scarf, holding a jug and a cup or glass. On first sight she is another 'serving' woman, holding the sacred grail symbols of cup and chalice.

However, apart from the white scarf, this figure is dressed in black and this association with death is even more strongly shown in the shape of an axe drawn across her figure. The axe is a tool familiar from Neolithic times, and was often used for sacrifice. In the fresco, the axe handle is painted

The axe suggests an explicit sacrificial scene, also linked with a Grail symbol

across the woman's neck and the sharp blade points directly over the large container, as if that cauldron of plenty was also the source of death. Perhaps this is meant to remind us that the difference between anointing a king and sacrificing him is small.

From this, and ample other evidence, it seems that the feminine often reigned supreme in these colourful and eye-catching works of church art. We do not know if there was a deliberate 'code' working here; probably the artists were motivated by what today we would call unconscious forces. But these images of the eternal feminine would upset the early reformers. These men knew that the average unlettered churchgoer would have received a subliminal message from these frescoes, a message emphasizing the secret supremacy of the goddess in a divine kingdom that was supposed to be ruled by the authority of the father God.

The reformers knew that the eyes of the churchgoers were being entranced by the colourful images, their ears lulled by the unfathomable but harmonious Latin liturgy with its often beautiful music, and their minds filled with a sense of the wonder of creation and its mysterious female creatrix. No wonder the reformist zealots were so cross. No wonder they whitewashed the walls and translated the bible into English so that the literal 'word of God' could cut through all this feminine imagery.

They did their best to destroy much of the outside of churches too. Most of the old figurines, gargoyles, and other stone carvings that once decorated medieval churches were ruthlessly smashed off. They were considered too unchristian to be allowed on a religious building. Very few medieval decorations have survived on Channel Islands churches because, apart from the Reformation, these ancient structures were continually altered and developed with changing times and needs.

One of the exceptions seems to be St Martin's in Jersey, one the oldest churches on the island. It is located on a hilltop, leading down to the coastal resort of Rozel, which probably makes it the site of a pagan shrine. Among its rather intriguing architectural features are two gargoyles, one on the east and one on the west of the church, both of which double as water spouts. There are also two mysterious, anonymous human faces built into the structure, one over the vestry window and one on the south wall. The latter face looks remarkably like the face of the Gran'mère in the churchyard of Guernsey's St Martin's church. If so, it is intriguing to see this female head, the face of the white lady of the stones, embedded in the structure of the church.

It is not the only female head found on the site. During recent restoration, the smiling head of a girl (assumed to be a saint) was found under the floor of the church. This fragment of its feminine past seems to have formed the foundation of the modern building, much as the Gran'mère did in the similarly named church in Guernsey.

Among the most fascinating decorative features can be found perched on the edge of the east window. Here are two dragons, whose wings are complemented by curling, snake-like tails. One is more weathered than the other, but they seem to be more or less identical in shape. Both appear to have boar-shaped faces and they are sitting in a squatting posture, very reminiscent of a dog. So perhaps the animal consort figures of boar, dog and serpent are unified in these strange carvings, both of which stand guard at the window over the high altar, the church's spiritual centre.

A carved face. Several Channel Island churches have carved faces in them. What is the identity of this feminine face, now displayed at Hamptone House museum?

The dragon over the east window at St Martin's Church, Jersey. A mythical combination of dragon, boar and dog

Slightly above one of these east windows is another stone figure, a very weathered (or possibly damaged) human form that appears to be squatting and facing the visitor, with the arms draped around a part of the body suspiciously close to the genitals. This might be a knightly figure or even a heraldic device; the prominent bulge in the suspicious area could represent the head of a horse. But if the bulge is phallic it could be a satyr, not an uncommon sight on medieval churches and among the first (hardly surprisingly!) to be destroyed by reformers. On the other hand, we could be looking at something even more shocking: the female counterpart of a satyr – the truly astonishing *sheela-na-gig*.

A *sheela-na-gig* is a stone carving that shows an old woman shamelessly exhibiting her sexual organs by squatting with legs apart and pulling open the lips of her vulva. It is not difficult to understand why such images were destroyed wholesale by the Reformation. One can imagine many a Puritan congregation swooning with horror at the sight. The name *sheela-na-gig* possibly means 'old woman with vulva'. It was often placed over the buttresses and doorways of medieval churches, so that entering the church was like entering her womb. It was also like entering the dolmen, whose dark restricted entrance, like the parted vulva, offered another rite of passage into the goddess's underground realm. The *sheela-na-gig* is the earth mother in her winter aspect as the crone.

According to Marija Gimbutas she also resembles the early frog goddess, who often combines a woman's head with the body of a frog, with outstretched bent limbs and a human vulva. This gives it a strong link with the Jersey toad, another creature of great fecundity, similarly associated with the underworld, and sitting in an exhibitionist squatting posture similar to the *sheela-na-gig*.

We may never know if the St Martin's figure was a *sheela-na-gig*. But the building has something else to claim our attention. On one of the buttresses, looking out on the main road through the village, is a carving so bizarre that it defies all analysis. It is such a random confusion of images that

Was this once a *sheela-na-gig* – an explicit sexual carving?

it is tempting to dismiss it as a joke, a stone-mason's piece of idle doodling. Its top looks like the head of an animal wearing a kind of triangular hat, perched on a square block shape, inside which can be seen what looks like a boat, with two people either in it or next to it. The head, from the large eyes and pointed shape of the ears, looks like some sort of cat. The nose and mouth curve in an unmistakably feline shape and even the tiny nostrils are clearly marked. The creature appears to be staring straight out at the world, with the kind of passionless indifference of a cat at a window.

Then, with closer study, confusion sets in. What at first appeared to be the cat's fat or puffed-out cheeks turn out to be two tiny human heads, located on the creature's sloping 'shoulders', which on further examination, turn out to be two small animals. The creature on the right could be a dog or a sheep; the one on the left looks like a pig, from his more obvious snout. Dogs and pigs are familiar creatures from Channel Islands folklore, and we have already seen them in the dragon figures adorning the east window of this church. So far then, this stone collage displays a wealth of familiar pagan imagery, although what such imagery is doing on a church buttress is another question. But first we need to look at the head again and the significance of the cat.

An elaborate and mysterious carving at St Martin's Church in Jersey

The cat, like the toad, is known for its associations with witches. But perhaps this is not a cat at all. Looking more closely, it appears that the ears are in the wrong place. No creature on earth has ears in the middle of its head; this is the place where horns usually grow. Perhaps this is not a cat at all but the head of the horned god.

This seems more likely. With an animal perched on each shoulder, this figure is not dissimilar to other Celtic representations of the horned god Cerunnos. In many statues and figurines, he is shown flanked on both sides by different animals, to symbolize his fertility. Some pictures and carvings in Celtic art similarly show the Great Goddess accompanied on each side by totem animals.

Instead of a recognizable body, this horned god has, as we have said, a square arched block, with corbels in lieu of feet. As it happens, this is also compatible with ancient Celtic carvings. The Celts gave enormous importance to the human head; to them it was sacred, capable of independent life and movement, and endowed with the gift of prophecy and wisdom. So when the early Christian Celts came to carve figures on churches, they carved

This strange carving of a dog inside Guernsey's Vale Church is similar to the image on Jersey's St Martin's Church

them in the traditional pagan style, giving prime importance to the head, and portraying the body as a secondary distinct unit, often just a single block as here.

We can see further examples of this early Celtic Christian art on White Island, County Fermanagh, in Ireland. Attached to the north wall of a twelfth-century church is a set of stone figures from the ninth or tenth century, all looking very similar to our carving. The bodies are similarly oblong, with corbel-shaped small 'feet' at each corner. Like the St Martin's figure they have carvings inside these square bodies. If the head was the seat of reason to the Celts, the body was the centre of the passions, creativity and

© JACQUIE RUTTER

Fig. 1 Ninth- or tenth-century Celtic stone carvings

rebirth. Many of the symbols in these bodies symbolize the womb, or transition to the afterlife.

A closer examination of the body on St Martin's Church reveals rather different images. There is a triangular object which looks like an anchor, wielded by two human figures. Alternatively it could be a boat, viewed from the prow, the two figures being passengers and the high pole being some sort of sail. We can see similar images in a piece of Celtic art. Fig. 2 shows a model of the sort of ship commemorated in burials, used to ferry souls across the sea to the otherworld. There is an uncanny resemblance between the crooked top of the pole in the model and in the carving on the church. Another piece of art, fig. 3, is a bowl handle resembling a miniature version of our statue. This was a votive offering found in a ship burial.

This same shape was common in small votive figures. Again the head dominates, as the source of real symbolic power, while the stylized square body displays a number of quite confusing symbols, which seem to form a sort of labyrinth. This gives us an important clue. The labyrinth was the route to the underworld. It represents a passage to the womb, the centre of all life; the mystery of rebirth, similar to the long entrance to the chamber of a large dolmen.

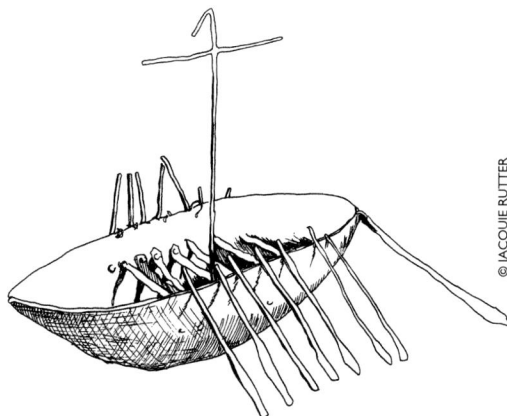

Fig. 2 A model of the type of ship depicted in Celtic art, which transported souls across the sea to the otherworld

Fig. 3 A bowl handle which was a votive offering found in a ship burial

So everything seems to fit together. We appear to be looking at a horned fertility god, with a prominent head and a womb of plenty which symbolizes the journey to the otherworld, in the form of a boat ferrying souls across water. This is an image of death and rebirth we have examined before. The whole carving is not incompatible with the *sheela-na-gig*, flaunting her own passage to the womb of death and rebirth.

A sea-bound dolmen on Jersey. Ships and sea journeys symbolize the passage of the dead to the otherworld. Perhaps that explains why so many dolmens are located on the coast and resemble large ships

However, there is another possible explanation. Most modern books on Jersey, even the voluminous guide to St Martin's parish, ignore this carving completely. But some older books do give it a brief mention. A 1920s Black's guide book describes the figure as a set of 'sculptured arms', a family's heraldic crest. It even identifies the family to whom the crest belongs: Ingelramus de Furneto, Seigneur of the Jersey district of Rozel in the time of King John. According to this book, the mystical boat is, in fact, a heraldic shield supported by two angels, on which is a lion rampant. Above that shield is the family's crest, which is a flag on a pole.

It is hard not to feel some disappointment at the thought that the mystical figure is nothing more than a mundane coat of arms. However, this description is worth taking seriously, largely because the sculpture was in a much better state in the 1920s, even though the book still describes it as 'much defaced'. Certainly, a lion-like shape can still be distinguished on the boat/shield. Although very badly worn, a head can be traced at the same line as the base of the 'flag'. The body continues down to the bottom V-shaped corner of the shield and two pairs of legs are outstretched on the left side of the creature's body. The creature closely resembles the image of the lion rampant from the Scottish flag, which perhaps explains the link with heraldry.

Nevertheless, there are two problems with the guide book's explanation. First there is no trace of the Ingelramus de Furneto family in Jersey family records, so it is hard to know how that particular name can be linked to any heraldic device. Secondly, the plaque looks nothing like a family crest. An example of a real crest on a plaque at St Clement's Church makes this clear. This shows a design with four clearly identifiable armorial bearings and – more importantly – an accompanying, explanatory text, all of which leaves us in no doubt as to the purpose of this plaque. This slab dates from as long ago as 1597 but is far less eroded, which suggests that the St Martin's figure either is much older, or at some time was deliberately damaged.

A publication by the Sociétié Jersiaise, *Parish Churches of Jersey*, also suggests that the device is the crest of a vanished family of Rozel. But it has an alternative theory – that it was a memorial to a donor, a patron stone that once stood over a porch. There is no mention of a cat's head, and no reference to a horned god figure in these descriptions. It is as if these earlier writers are looking at a different image from the one that perplexes the visitor today. It all adds to the deep sense of frustration, and makes one desperate to travel back in time. If only one could see the figure as it once was. In this faded, weathered state, it will never reveal all its secrets.

Amazingly, it might be possible to do that – to travel back in time and get a real-life glimpse of how this figure might once have looked to earlier generations. For such time travel, a sense of timing is very important. One must visit the church at a certain witching hour of the day, close to the onset of twilight and preferably in the middle of winter.

Most visitors only see the carving in summer. Under a high sun, the top of the sculpture is bleached into the appearance of a cat's head, wearing some sort of curious triangular hat. But on a late winter afternoon, when the setting sun illuminates the figure from a lower angle, emphasizing its fading contours, it metamorphoses into what might have been its original form. It is a truly startling experience – a taste of time-travel.

The cat's eyes fade into the background, the nose becomes the base of a standing figure, the crown is transformed into outstretched hands and the eye in the triangle is now a head. Suddenly Lemprière's description of the top of the sculpture makes sense. He describes it as 'a chalice supported by a winged angel'.

Another description in *Parish Churches of Jersey* describes the upper portions of the figure as 'surmounted by the bust of a woman' and the triangle shape at the top of the woman represents the 'sign of the trinity'. So it might be an angel or a woman. But if it is a woman, who is she? The mystery deepens, but a sense of something feminine pervades this whole stone figure.

The universal image of an outstretched woman, her arms raised and holding aloft an important symbol, can be traced across Europe to the Ukraine, where the goddess of life and fertility Beregynia (their version of Britannia) is depicted as a woman with upraised arms. Modern pagans have also claimed this feminine image; it can be bought in New Age shops as a kind of good-luck charm, holding a birthstone in her outstretched arms. So perhaps we are really looking at an image of the goddess.

We may never know and perhaps we are not supposed to. No inscription or acknowledgment is included with this figure, and this cannot be an accident. It can be no accident either that, wherever it originally stood, it has been placed on a buttress, which may be our most important piece of evidence. All the buttresses were built after the Reformation. We know that many broken relics of the old church were used to build them. Are we looking at a collection of broken images, a collage of fragments rescued and transferred from other parts of the church?

If so, this may have been more than just a random hotchpotch of assorted rubble. It conveyed, to those who understood it, a deliberate but subversive message of defiance against the destruction of images.

We began our description by suggesting that this composite image was a sort of joke. Perhaps it was – but a joke with a serious message. It was also a joke so subtle and secret that the reformers would never decipher it, even though it flaunted its defiance from the very public fabric of the church. Its defiance consisted of an exaggerated, satirical surfeit of pagan symbols, stretching from Neolithic to Celtic times. Its defiance has defied time itself, because as the image has aged and faded, its mystery and allure has increased. It is now so ambiguous that it can change its shape and meaning with the movement of the sun, and respond flexibly to the liberal imagination of the visitor. It is a fitting revenge for the rigidity and literalism that temporarily took over the church. Its creators certainly had the last laugh over the Reformation. Most importantly, perhaps this stone image expresses the elusive and mischievous spirit of the god of the stone himself, as if the trickster Puck has also been laughing at us.

Part IV:
Back to the Fairies

16 Happily Ever After?

As we have seen the word 'fairy' in the sense of 'fairy tale' comes from the Latin *fata*, a feminine word meaning 'fate'; *fata* takes us back to the standing stones of the Channel Islands, those ghostly figures which trace the path of the moon and human destiny. Related to them are the goddesses Nemesis and Fortuna, traditionally shown turning a large wheel, symbolizing the moon and the cycle of the seasons.

The idea of the goddess being in charge of this seasonal wheel is linked to the image of story telling – of spinning a yarn or a tale. Spinning and weaving have traditionally been female pursuits. Spinning a tale, weaving a plot; the metaphors illuminate the relationship. From Mother Goose to Scheherazade, from the Wife of Bath to *The Decameron*, tales have usually been told by women.

An important accompaniment to the spinning of the wheel and the telling of the tale is the warm, glowing hearth. The hearth is the centre of domestic comfort, the meeting point of the whole family and the centre of female domination. The hearth, with its ashes and fire, is also the entrance to the underworld, from which the Green Man chimney sweep emerges in the spring, like the sprouting seed.

The hearth is the modern counterpart of the oracular shrines; those infernal, fiery altars, presided over by the serpent, in which the goddess bestowed her oracles. Later, it was the place where the Yule log would dispense his lucky sparks, with the same fertilizing power represented by the Green Man. Stories have been traditionally told round the fireside. The whole family would gather around the hearth, entranced and spellbound, watching the fire as if its luminous, hypnotic dance were the source of the tale itself. Many of Guernsey's folk tales are introduced by the spinning of a wheel by a warm hearth.

Louisa Lane-Clarke also talks about the fairy stories of her childhood in Guernsey told over a faggot fire, which gave 'a glow and a truth to the tale'.[1]

The Guernsey story of the fairy bakers begins with a woman called Colette settling herself on a green bed and starting to spin. The soothing sound of the wheel sends her into a trance from which she suddenly awakes to the realization that she is no longer alone in the room. And so, with the spinning of the wheel, Colette is transported to the half-real netherworld of the fairies.

In addition to the hearth and the spinning wheel there was, as Colette has said, a piece of furniture in the room called *lit de fouaille, vueille*, or 'green bed'. This was a wide bed-frame raised about 18 inches from the ground and covered with dry fern or pea-straw, on which the women knitted or sewed during the winter evenings. These gatherings in Guernsey were named after the green bed, and traditionally known as *vueilles*. In Jersey, the meetings were known as *veilles* (spelt without the 'u') and the equivalent of the green bed was the *jonquiere* or the *filyie*. Sharing the seat and the light from an oil lamp above, 'busy knitters worked and chatted through the long winter evenings.'[2]

The spinning wheel has been replaced by the more modern knitting, an activity which was the 'chief employment of the women'. Because of the sheer quantity of wool produced by the Channel Islands, woollen Jersey and Guernsey pullovers were to become world famous. This weaving industry, ruled by women, replaced the spinning wheel, but its oracular nature still remained. While the women knitted, a 'great deal of gossip', and 'traditional stories' of fairies, bogeymen, werewolves, will o' the wisps, the ghostly dog of death, ghosts and phantoms, were exchanged. Sitting round a cottage hearth with only an oil lamp hanging from a beam, and the firelight sending flickering shadows on the granite walls, must have been an eerie setting for tales of black magic.

However, the rooms where the *vueilles* were held could also be colourfully, even elaborately decorated. The green bed was often decked with fresh flowers and greenery. L'Amy gives a vivid picture of Jersey *veilles* near Bouley, where the company would assemble around the kitchen hearth: a place of ghostly shadows where furze, golden rods and palm leaves covered the walls and surrounded the *jonquiere*, where the women sat knitting and weaving.

In addition to all this, coloured wickerwork crowns were suspended from the ceiling, decorated with coloured paper and artificial roses, an almost overwhelming profusion of natural and artificial adornment. Similarly in Guernsey, according to Lemprière, the walls against which the green bed was placed and the roof above were covered with flowers and greenery: laurel, myrtle, rose and sunflowers.

So this centre of story telling was often decorated, perhaps almost to excess, to resemble an alfresco, natural setting, a sacred grove perhaps, to celebrate the coming of spring. In the summer, the Channel Islands knitters sometimes moved outside to a real woodland location or sacred grove (here called an avenue), and formed sororities and covens.

To understand the almost religious nature of these knitting gatherings, we need to look again at one of Jersey's mysterious sacred sites: Bonne Nuit. This is the location of the Cheval Roc and various other myths of cliff-top sacrifice. But that is not all. It is believed that there was once an important ecclesiastical centre in the region, now occupied by a farmhouse called St Blaize. This mysterious saint has an important and surprising link to the Channel Island *vueilles*.

He suffered more than one sacrifice, which suggests that, like many other saints and martyrs, he represents an idealized consort figure rather than a particular individual. First he and his 'infidels' were burned, but fire would not consume them. Then he was ordered to be drowned, but he walked on water. Finally he was beheaded, which seemed to do the trick.

There is nothing unusual in any of these gruesome forms of sacrifice. But one part of the story is unique – and particularly horrific. Legend tells us that his flesh was torn from his limbs with iron combs. There would seem to be no historic precedent for such a ghastly punishment. It must be a symbolic death, something confirmed by the fact that St Blaize is the patron saint of weavers and wool workers, one of whose tools is the iron comb, used for creating threads out of raw wool. His fame extends over all areas that have benefited from the woollen industry, especially the north of England. At Bradford and Leeds his festival is celebrated with great pomp and ceremony.

L'Amy found some fascinating evidence that the secret of wool combing and efficient knitting first began in Jersey, from where it travelled to Yorkshire. He quotes a fragment from a verse from Leeds that seems to affirm this quite unmistakably.

> Then let us not forget the good,
> The worthy Bishop Blaize,
> Who came from Jersey here to us
> As ancient history says.
>
> He taught us how to comb our wool
> The source of all our wealth.
> Then let us still remember him
> While we have life and health.

The verse refers confidently to 'ancient history', which apparently confirms the view that the traditions of combing and knitting originated in Jersey. This association between the overtly pagan Channel Islands *vueilles* and a consort/saint, suggests a ritual, religious origin to the act of knitting and weaving.

In fact, the *vueilles* often sound remarkably similar to the ancient traditions of the sacred marriage. They frequently celebrated betrothals and engagements – and not necessarily those sanctioned by the Church. When Charles Trumbull visited Guernsey in 1677, he made a note in his travel journal about the behaviour of the women, who used the meetings to attract young men, 'who are never wanting to make up the consort', and contract marriages with them. Stead also mentioned the young men who attended these meetings, who, 'seated in the middle of the ring, pay their offerings at the shrine of beauty, and yield their souls to the impulse of love'.

But perhaps the most charming ceremony of all was performed at midsummer inside the makeshift groves: 'It was customary to elect a girl from among the inhabitants of the district, and seat her in state beneath the floral canopy, where under the name of La Mome she received in silence the homage of the assembled guests.'

This is the crowning of the goddess herself, La Mome or the great mother of the fertile earth. This dignified and beautiful coronation represents the bestowing of the goddess's robes of glory at the height of the spring. Most importantly, it is the glorification of the fairy-tale, with its magnificent royal marriage and 'happily ever after' ending. After the winter period of darkness, when Cinderella languishes among the cinders of her hearth (in her underworld, like Kore), she metamorphoses into a radiant bride. She discards her rags and goes to the ball in glorious array. The same splendid ending is enjoyed by other fairy-tale heroines, such as Snow White and the Sleeping Beauty. This glorifica-tion of the main character at the end of fairy tales is a celebration of the beauty of spring and the miracle of nature's reincarnation after death.

So the *vueilles* made the fairy stories real, through rituals and dramas that had their origins in the dawn of time and the birth of mythology. Carey, among many other writers, has mourned their disappearance, and lamented that so little record has survived of their often secret and arcane customs. We would go further and say that their loss is symbolic of the defeat of the goddess.

Notes
1   *Folklore of Guernsey and Sark*, p. 3.
2   Société Jersiaise Newsletter no. 10.

17 The Golden Age

What exactly was the Golden Age? The myth of Osiris, the consort figure from ancient Egypt, describes it as follows:

> *Osiris and Isis descended on the earth to bestow gifts and blessings on its inhabitants. Isis showed them first the use of wheat and barley and Osiris made the instruments of agriculture and taught men the use of them. After he had made the valley of the Nile a happy country, he assembled a host with which he went to bestow his blessings upon the rest of the world.*

Basically, then, the Golden Age is that 'happy ever after' time that follows the sacred marriage. It is an ideal world, in which the goddess and her consort rule together and bring happiness to all humanity. It is a world full of blessings, in which the art of agriculture brings prosperity to all, the soil needs no labour and men live in peace. It would seem that the European tradition of the Golden Age is really a nostalgic ancient memory of a long-vanished matriarchal society.

There is plenty of evidence that the Channel Islands once symbolized this lost feminine paradise. We have already compared them to Avalon. At one time, because of their plentiful springs, it was also possible to describe them as another Eden.

According to the Bible, Eden was a place where the earth was watered, not by rain but by natural springs, 'streams that came up from the earth'. Spring water, which emerges from the depths of the goddess's earth, is the antithesis of rain, which falls from father sky. No rain ever fell in Eden and this was part of its attraction. Everyone knows that spring water is much purer, colder and sweeter than water from any other source; it is the best water on the earth. In local mythology, this gift from the goddess, this pure, unsullied water from her secret domain, was also a source of healing and had the power of giving oracles.

This was certainly true of St George's spring in Câtel parish in Guernsey. Girls visiting it could expect to see the reflection of the man they were going to marry if they stared into its pool long enough. Water from this spring was also believed to heal eczema, and if consumed on nine successive mornings, was also a cure for barrenness. An old post-card shows a well with a cross placed on top; a clear indication that its sacred character was recognized – and perhaps briefly annexed – by Christianity.

Natural springs were also a feature of the Jersey landscape at one time. Many of them were built up into attractive stone structures located by the wayside for the use of passers-by. A visitor in the 1920s commented on the large number of springs on the island, describing them as 'wonderful'. One in particular, called La Fontaine des Mittes, was said to have the power of healing the blind and curing the deaf. It could also give speech to the dumb, so long as the water was taken before sunrise (i.e. in the moonlight). In an old Jersey fairy story, this miraculous spring is credited with restoring the sight of a blind girl known as Anna Le Brun. In modern times, its miraculous claims have been modified; it is now believed to be good for treating eye complaints, rather than curing blindness.

There is also a fairy story associated with it. Two nymphs once lived in its grotto, enjoying a life that sounds very like biblical and mytho-logical descriptions of a Golden Age. During the fairies' sojourn in the grotto we are told that nothing spoiled the peace and joy of their lives. They lived in flower-filled meadows, in perfect happiness.

Fairies living in the Garden of Eden might sound rather like a mixed metaphor. Yet according to a large number of writers, the Channel Islands were once so idyllic that the Garden of Eden, the Land of the Fairy and the Golden Age could all be said to have existed together on their happy shores. Sidney Bisson, writing in the 1950s, compared pre-war Jersey to fairyland. He described such magical (and long-vanished) sights as cabbages on 10-foot stalks, cows with leather collars and pretty milkmaids with crinkled sun bonnets. Any visitor catching a sight of these, he said, 'would have assumed that their ship had gone astray and brought them instead to fairyland'.

The painter Renoir found inspiration in the Guernsey coastline and compared the island's beaches to a mythological scene by the artist Watteau, whose pictures conjure up a vision of an earthly paradise of grace, leisure and sensuality amid idyllic natural surroundings: 'We are on these enchanted islands … whose inhabitants stroll aimlessly and languorously about, matching their leisure with that of the clouds and the tide.'[1]

Renoir's vision of Eden on Guernsey was inspired by the 'casual undress' of the bathers at Moulin Huet. The easy-going inhabitants of Guernsey bathed in mixed company with an innocent freedom that he found enchanting, and seemed very similar to the lack of shame felt by the original inhabitants of Eden before the 'fall'.

Another nineteenth-century visitor to the Channel Islands, Octavius Rooke, believed he had entered the Land of the Fairy. He described Jersey as a place of Eden-like innocence: 'There was then no sin to mar, no crime that could pollute … and bright glad spirits wandered, where now man slaves to gain his daily bread by the hard labour of his toil-worn hands.[2] He was so entranced by the landscape that he appears to have been converted to what he calls the 'true religion' of the fairies: 'Were the fairies not bright embodiments of true religion, which whispers peace and consolation to the whole race of man?'[3]

Rooke bemoaned the ruination of his homeland of England and the new 'material age' he lived in: the smoky towns, and the mechanic's drudgery. He referred to the hateful new industrial race that 'fills the valleys with tall chimneys and dulls the bright water with unnatural hues, while the very air itself is poisoned by the noxious vapour'. He spoke with great respect of the 'old religions' of the fairies, which made the defiling of the landscape, even the sullying of a pool, a crime. In the Channel Islands, which had not completely lost the old fairy ways, Rooke found a paradise, an Eden that England had lost again, because of industrialization. To him, the rapid mechanization of the whole European landscape was nothing less than a second 'fall' of man, which the Channel Islands had been fortunate enough to escape.

Rooke also looked back with longing to his own time of innocence, and the 'sweet tales that beguiled our youth'. He is not the only one to associate the fairies, those spirits of the old religion, with another universal 'golden age': the blessed state of childhood innocence. The realm of the universal earth mother is also the caring, nurturing domain of the nursery; a golden age of innocence that most of us once shared, and which we still call 'fairyland'. When we encourage children to leave an offering for the tooth fairy, or find chocolate eggs in a church grave-yard on Easter Sunday (a tradition clearly linking the symbols of birth and death, and which is still observed in Channel Islands churches), we see in these ancient rituals an expression of a universal innocence we have all lost.

Another more famous visitor to the Channel Islands in the 1870s was the poet Algernon Swinburne. He wrote a poem called 'Guernsey', which also contrasted the beauty of the island's scenery with the waste-land created by nineteenth-century technological progress. Like Renoir, Swinburne's source of inspiration was a Guernsey beach, and there he called for a rebirth of innocence and freshness, which he compared, like Rooke, to our pre-fall state.[4] He advocated a return to the 'soothing love' and 'breast' of 'Mother Sea', and expressed a desire to return to the primordial older religion, and the innocence and security of infancy. According to him, the combination of worship and 'Mother Sea' restored lost innocence. Like Rooke and many other visitors to the Channel Islands, Swinburne became a true pagan.

It should be remembered that the nineteenth century's rapid industri-alisation, our second expulsion from Eden, took place against the back-ground of the growth of science and Darwinism and the consequent crisis of faith that affected the Christian religion. The theory of evolution had questioned belief in the Bible's story of creation and undermined the supremacy of a God of nearly 2,000 years. It may not be surprising that some men turned to an earlier alternative religion, that of the matriarchal fairies, and it is significant that some of the greatest minds of the nine-teenth and early twentieth centuries seemed to find it still flourishing in the Channel Islands.

But, as Bisson pointed out in the 1950s, this fairyland is now only a memory. The Channel Islands paradise was cruelly shattered in 1940 by the German occupation, when the islands were forced to experience at close quarters one of the most evil political regimes of the twentieth century. Traumatized by this clash with hideous reality, the Channel Islands lost their fairy innocence for ever. Even now, they seem unable to recover from this dark legacy. Virtually all the old German bunkers and tunnels have been preserved, with almost superstitious care, as monu-ments to a modern underworld of evil. Jersey and Guernsey both have their sprawling tunnels and underground bunkers – vast snaking, infer-nal domains of steel and concrete, echoing with the ghosts of a lost time, preserved in a timeless limbo for all eternity.

These tunnels have even earned the Channel Islands a prominent entry in a guide book called *The Visitor's Guide to Underground Britain*, sharing company with fairy grottos and palaeolithic caves. The German bunkers have become the new land of the fairy, and it is a truly murky one. Many are only opened on certain days of the year, as if in an attempt to create a seasonal 'mystery' around these new dolmens.

We need to move away from the rather negative identity the Channel Islands have acquired in recent years, as the only part of Britain that was ever occupied by the Nazis, before they lose their identity altogether. Modern society is becoming increasingly global and anonymous. In one sense this is a good thing. A global society can create global understanding and universal tolerance. It can help abolish wars, poverty and tyranny. However, globalization can also mean global hegemony, a world-wide cultural invasion from the superpowers. Today American culture and influence is swamping everything we eat, read and watch, but there are other new superpowers waiting to swamp us too.

That is why a sense of smaller scale, of nationhood, is so important. This applies especially to a tiny landmass like the Channel Islands. We do not need nationhood in the narrow nationalistic sense of building barriers, hating all foreigners or wanting to exploit them. Creative nationhood is not imposed from above; it is not the domain of government, the property of a small elite, nor does it belong to the Church. It can only be achieved by cultivating a country's folklore and pagan past. National identity grows naturally out of the landscape, history, heritage and speech of the people themselves; it is the only way to maintain diversity and prevent a creeping uniformity in this global world. With a firm sense of personal and national culture we can learn to accept and value other cultures.

So if the Channel Islands are to maintain a clear and positive sense of identity for the next century, and remain a welcoming destination for visitors and new arrivals, we must follow the example of our troubadour poets and turn to our ancient past, a heritage which grew out of the very land and the people who first lived here and shaped the landscape, thousands of years before the marauding German armies built their sea walls, fortresses and underground labyrinths.

Perhaps a good example is the figure of Puck, the spirit of the Blanche Pierre, the rock and stone, the Pouques. Puck has entered our customs and everyday lives in many ways. He is the god of hearth and home. On his special midwinter day of Christmas he appears, via the topsy-turvy underworld of the chimney, bearing gifts that celebrate the riches of the earth. He is Lord of Misrule at our parties. His joyful festival of Christmas has restored winter into our affections and preserved what is best in our Christian heritage: universal peace and goodwill.

Puck rebels against the settled, the expected, the orthodox. His is the spirit of humour; his laughter undermines the powerful and pompous. He drags us out of our set paths into new ways of thought. He represents creativity because he is always reinventing himself. He is the beautiful sculpture that is waiting to be released from every shapeless lump of rock. He is free and individual, yet he exists only through his sacred marriage to the goddess of all creation. We need to embrace the mystery and inscrutability of our earth, the domain to which we all belong, but which we can never fully understand or control. We need to share Puck's closeness with our common mother so that she may continue to nurture us.

Many readers may still be unconvinced that there is any connection between our folklore, the Pouques and the religion of the ancient dolmen builders. But what cannot be denied is that we need them equally today. Our physical and cultural survival depends on our perceiving the earth as nurturing mother, and on learning to value the folklore that grew naturally out of this nurturing landscape.

The Neolithics or Pouques left us a very important legacy. Their deep closeness to the earth is something we are becoming increasingly hungry for, in our post-industrial age, on our now dangerously spoiled planet. Green politics and the Gaia movement represent a desire to return to the matriarchal Eden which we lost when we began to exploit the earth and fight each other for ever-scarcer resources. Maybe, when we rediscover our pagan roots, people will again see the Channel Islands as Eden, fairyland and Golden Age all in one, embodying those ancient feminine values that the world is increasingly turning to.

When we walk the Channel Islands, we are treading a beautiful landscape that has given birth to a mythology as rich and varied as any in Greece, Rome or Egypt. It is a hidden heritage that has remained hidden for too long and one which we should rediscover, and learn to enjoy with pride.

Notes
1 House, pp. 10–13.
2 *The Channel Islands, Pictorial, Legendary and Descriptive*, p.55.
3 Ibid. p.54.
4 Shayer, p.8.

Bibliography

Ahier, Philip, *Jersey Sea Stories* (La Haule Books, 1984)

—— & Ashworth W.S., *The Historical Hotels & Inns of Jersey* (Ashton & Denton, 1978)

Anstead, D.T., *The Channel Islands* (W.H. Allen, 1893)

Ayto, John (ed.), *Brewer's Dictionary of Phrase and Fable*, 17th edn (Orion, 2005)

Balleine, G.R., *The Bailiwick of Jersey: The King's Channel Islands* (Hodder and Stoughton, 1951)

Baring, Anne & Cashford, Jules, *The Myth of the Goddess* (Penguin, 1991)

Bellamy, H.S., *Moons Myths and Man* (Faber & Faber, 1936)

Bellows, Tony, *Jersey Wonders* (ELSP, 2004)

Bender, Barbara & Caillaud, Robert, *Archaeology of Brittany, Normandy & Channel Islands* (Faber, 1986)

Bission, Sidney, *Jersey, Our Island* (Batchworth Press, 1950)

Blackstone, Chris & Le Quesne, Katie, *St Martin: The Story of an Island Parish* (Phillimore, 1999)

Bois, G.J.C., *Jersey Superstitions in Etching and Poetry* (Bois, 1981)

Bord, Janet & Colin, *Earth Rites: Fertility Practices in Pre-Industrial Britain* (Paladin, 1982)

—— *Ancient Mysteries of Britain* (Grafton, 1986)

Briggs, Katherine, *The Anatomy of Puck* (Routledge and Kegan Paul, 1959)

—— *The Vanishing People, A Study of Traditional Fairy Beliefs* (Batsford, 1978)

—— *British Folk Tales and Legends: A Sampler* (Granada, 1977)

Bulkeley, James, *La Hougue Bie de Hambie* (Whittaker, 1837)

Bullfinch, Thomas, *Bullfinch's Mythology* (Avenel, 1978)

Burl, Aubrey, *Prehistoric Avebury* (Yale University Press, 1979)

—— *Rites of the Gods* (Dent, 1981)

Cabot, Laurie & Tom Cowan, *Power of the Witch* (Arkana, 1990)

Carey, Edith F., *The Channel Islands* (A & C Black, 1930)

Carré, Albert L., *English–Jersey Language Vocabulary* (Don Balleine Trust, 1972)

Cashford, Jules, *The Moon: Myth and Image* (Cassell, 2003)

Channel Islands, Black's Guide Books (Black, 1927)

Channel Islands Anthology, The, no. 1 (Toucan Press, 1972)

Channel Islands Anthology, The, no. 2 (Toucan Press, 1975)

Cirlot, J.E., *A Dictionary of Symbols* (RKP, 1976)

Clark, Leonard, *Sark Discovered* (Dent, 1956)

Clarke, David L., *A Guide to Britain's Pagan Heritage* (Hale, 1995)

Cles-Reden, Sibylle von, *The Realm of the Great Goddess* (Thames & Hudson, 1961)

Cliff, W.H., *History, Flora, Fauna and Guide to the Island of Jethou* (The Guernsey Press, 1960)

Collum, V.C.C., *The Re-Excavation of the Dehus Chambered Mound at Paradis, Vale, Guernsey* (1933)

Cooper, J.C., *Fairy Tales: Allegories of the Inner Life* (The Aquarian Press, 1983)

—— *Symbolism:The Universal Language* (The Aquarian Press, 1982)

Cope, Julian, *The Modern Antiquarian* (Thorson, 1998)

Coutanche, Henry, Coutanche, Sheila & Feuvre, Suzanne (eds), *St Lawrence, Jersey* (The Parish of St Lawrence Publications, 1999)

Cox, J. Stevens, *Prehistoric Monuments of Guernsey and Associated Folklore* (Toucan Press, 1976)

—— *Guernsey Folklore*, Guernsey Historical Monograph 12 (Toucan Press, 1971)

Coysh, Victor, *Alderney* (David & Charles, 1974)

Cunliffe, Barry, *Jersey in Prehistory: A Centre or a Periphery?* (Société Jersiaise, 1995)

Davidson, H.R. Ellis, *Gods and Myths of Northern Europe* (Pelican, 1964)

Davies, R.T., *Medieval English Lyrics: A Critical Anthology* (Faber, 1963)

Dean, Tony & Shaw, Tony, *The Folklore of Cornwall* (Batsford, 1975)

De Garis, Marie, *Folklore of Guernsey* (The Guernsey Press, 1986)

Devereaux, Paul & Thomson, Ian, *The Ley Hunter's Companion* (Thames and Hudson, 1979)

Dewar, H.S.L., *Witchcraft and the Evil Eye in Guernsey* (Toucan Press, 1968)

Durand, Ralph, *Guernsey: Present and Past* (The Guernsey Press, 1933)

Edwards, Gillian, *Hobgoblins & Sweet Puck* (Geoffrey Bles, 1974)

Eliot, T.S., *The Complete Poems and Plays* (Faber, 1969)

Elliot, Blanche B., *Jersey: An Isle of Romance* (T. Fisher Unwin, 1923)

Fitch, Eric L., *In Search of Herne the Hunter* (Capall Bann Publishing, 1994)

Fordham, Frieda, *An Introduction to Jung's Psychology* (Pelican Books, 1986)

Forest of Vazon: *A Guernsey Legend of the Eighth Century, The* (Harrison & Sons, 1889)

Fraser, Anna, 'Blackthorn' (www.the-tree.org.uk)

Frazer, Sir James, *The Golden Bough* (Macmillan, 1963)

Gaster, Theodor H., *Myth Legend and Custom in the Old Testament* (Harper & Row, 1975)

Gimbutas, Marija, *The Gods and Goddesses of Old Europe 7000–3500 BC* (Thames and Hudson, 1974)

—— *The Language of the Goddess* (Harper Collins, 1991)

—— *The Living Goddesses* (University of California, 1999)

Glendinning, Alex, *Eye on the Past Yearbook 1992* (Island Eye, Channel Islands, 1992)

Graves, Robert, *The Greek Myths* (Penguin, 1992)

—— *The White Goddess* (Faber, 1948)

Grimal, Pierre, *The Dictionary of Classical Mythology* (Blackwell, 1987)

Harrison, Jane, *Ancient Art and Ritual* (Moonraker Press, 1978)

Harte, Jeremy, *Alternative Approaches to Folklore:* A Bibliography 1969–1996 (Jeremy Harte, 1998)

Hawkes, Jacquetta, *The Archaeology of the Channel Islands, vol. 2: Jersey* (Société Jersiaise, 1937)

—— *Dawn of the* Gods (Chatto and Windus, 1968)

—— *Early Britain* (Collins, 1945)

—— *Man on Earth* (The Cresset Press, 1954)

—— *Man and the Sun* (Readers Union, 1963)

Hawkes, Ken, *Sark* (David & Charles, 1992)

Heselton, Phillip, *Earth Mysteries* (Element Books, 1991)

Hickman, Trevor, *Neolithic Tombs of Guernsey and Their Subsequent Use* (Wymondham, 1988)

Hillsdon, Sonia, *Jersey: Witches, Ghosts and Traditions* (Seaflower Books, 1984)

—— *Jersey* (Landmark, 2001)

Hitching, Francis, *Earth Magic* (Cassell, 1976)

Hole, Christina, *Saints in Folklore* (Bell, 1966)

Holland, Clive, *Things Seen in the Channel Islands* (Seeley, Service, 1929)

House, John, *Renoir 1841–1919: Artists in Guernsey* (Guernsey Museum & Art Gallery, 1988)

Howard, Michael, *Earth Mysteries* (Hale, 1990)

Hughes, Pennethorn, *Witchcraft* (Pelican, 1965)

Hunt, Peter, *The Dolmens of Jersey* (Société Jersiaise, 1998)

Hutton, Ronald, *The Pagan Religions of the Ancient British Isles* (Blackwell, 1991)

James, E.O., *Prehistoric Religion* (Thames and Hudson, 1957)

Johnston, David E., *The Channel Islands: An Archaeological Guide* (Phillimore, 1981)

Johnston, Peter (ed.), *The Archaeology of the Channel Islands* (Phillimore, 1986)

Jones, David E., *An Instinct for Dragons* (Routledge, 2002)

Jones, Kathy, *The Ancient British Goddess* (Ariadne, 2001)

Kalamis, Catherine, *Hidden Treasures of Herm Island* (Wood,1996)

Kendrick, T.D., *The Archaeology of the Channel Islands, vol. 1: Guernsey* (Methuen, 1928)

Kipling, Rudyard (ed. Sarah Wintle) *Puck of Pook's Hill* (Penguin, 1987)

Kinnes, Ian & Hibbs, James, *The Dolmens of Jersey* (Aris and Phillips, 1988)

Kollerstrom, Nick, *Gardening and Planting by the Moon 2005* (Quantum, 2004)

Lake, Chris, *These Haunted Isles* (Redberry Press, 1986)

L'Amy, John, *Jersey Folk Lore* (La Haule Books, 1983)

Lane-Clarke, Louisa, *Folklore of Guernsey and Sark* (Le Lievre, 1880)

Leek, Sybil, *A Ring of Magic Islands* (American Photographic, 1976)

Lemprière, Raoul, *Customs, Ceremonies and Traditions of the Channel Islands* (Hale, 1976)

—— *History of the Channel Islands* (Hale, 1974)

—— *Buildings and Memorials of the Channel Islands* (Hale, 1980)

McCormack, John, *Channel Islands Churches* (Phillimore, 1986)

McCulloch, Edgar, *Guernsey Folklore* (Elliot Stock, 1903)

McEwan, Graham J., *Mystery Animals of Britain and Ireland* (Hale, 1986)

McGregor, Eadie, Peter & Fionnuala *Channel Islands Blue Guide* (A&C Black, 1998)

Mackenzie, D.A., *Myths of Crete and Pre-Hellenic Europe* (Gresham, 1917)

Mallet, John, *Discovering Jersey: 30 Circular Walks* (John Mallet, 2004)

Malmesbury, William of, *Gesta Regum Angelorum* [Deeds of the English Kings], 1125 (OUP, 1999)

Man, Myth & Magic: An Illustrated Encyclopedia of the Supernatural, vols 1–7 (Purnell, 1970)

Marshall, Michael, *Herm: Its Mysteries and its Charm* (The Guernsey Press, 1958)

Maugham, R.C.F., *The Island of Jersey Today* (Madison, 1938)

Meaden, George Terence, *The Goddess of the Stones: The Language of the Megaliths* (Souvenir Press, 1988)

Mohen Jean-Pierre, *Standing Stones* (Thames and Hudson, 1999)

Molyneaux, Brian Leigh, *The Sacred Earth* (Macmillan, 1995)

Moorey, Teresa, *Paganism: A Beginner's Guide* (Hodder & Stoughton, 1997)

Murray, Margaret, *The God of the Witches* (Faber, 1931)

—— *The Witch-Cult in Western Europe* (Oxford Paperbacks, 1921)

Newton, Sam, *The Origins of Beowulf* (Brewer, 1999)

Nilsson, Martin, *Greek Folk Religion* (University of Pennsylvania Press, Philadelphia, 1972)

Ogier, Darryl, 'Night Revels and Werewolfery in Calvinist Guernsey' (*Folklore*, 1998)

Parker, Robert, *Miasma: Pollution and Purification in Early Greek Religion* (Clarendon Press, 1983)

Parlett David (ed.), *Selections from the Carmina Burana* (Penguin, 1986)

Partridge, Eric, *Origins: A Short Etymological Dictionary* (Routledge & Kegan Paul, 1958)

Patton, Mark, *Jersey in Prehistory* (Le Haule Books, Jersey, 1987)

—— 'Stone Axes on the Channel Islands: Neolithic exchange in an insular context' (*Oxford Journal of Archaeology* 10 (1), 33–44, 1991)

Patton, Mark, Rodwell, Warwick and Finch, Ogla, *La Hogue Bie Jersey* (Société Jersiaise, 1999)

Pennick, Nigel & Devereux, Paul, *Lines on the Landscape: Leys & Other Linear Enigmas* (Hale, 1989)

Pepper, Elizabeth & Wilcock, John, *Magical & Mystical Sites: Europe & British Isles* (Harper & Row, 1977)

Pollack, Rachel, *The Body of the Goddess* (Element, 1997)

Poole, Keith B., *Unfamiliar Spirits: Ghosts of the British Isles* (Hale, 1989)

Poynder, Michael, *Pi in the Sky: A Revelation of the Ancient Celtic Wisdom Tradition* (Collins, 1992)

Price, Simon & Kearns, Emily (eds), *The Oxford Dictionary of Classical Myth and Religion* (OUP, 2003)

'Quarterly Review of the Guernsey Society' (1969–1973)

'Quarterly Review of the Guernsey Society' (1974–1978)

Raglan, Lord, *The Hero* (Methuen, 1936)

Renouf, John & Urry, James (eds), 'The First Farmers in the Channel Islands' (Committee Jersey, 1976)

Review of the Guernsey Society, summer 1992, vol. XLVIII, no.2

Rodwell, Warwick, *Les Écréhous* (Société Jersiaise, 1996)

—— *The Fishermen's Chapel* (Société Jersiaise, 1990)

Rooke, Octavius, *The Channel Islands, Pictorial, Legendary and Descriptive* (L. Booth, 1858)

Rugg-Gunn, Andrew, *Osiris and Odin: the Origin of Kingship* (H.K. Lewis, 1940)

Russell, Jeffrey B., *A History of Witchcraft, Sorcerers, Heretics and Pagans* (Thames and Hudson, 1980)

Sebire, Heather, *The Archaeology and Early History of the Channel Islands* (Tempus, 2005)

Sharkey John, *Celtic Mysteries: The Ancient Religion* (Thames & Hudson, 1991)

Shayer, David, *Swinburne the Poet Visits Guernsey and Sark 1876* (Toucan Press, 1980)

Société Jersiaise Newsletter No. 10, Spring 1989

Sheldon, Lady Diana & Apsley, Lady *To Whom the Goddess* (Hutchinson, 1932)

Sinel J., *Prehistoric Times and Men of the Channel Islands* (J.T. Bigwood, 1923)

Spencer, A.J., *Death in Ancient Egypt* (Penguin, 1982)

Stead, J., *A Picture of Jersey or Stranger's Companion through that Island* (J. Stead, 1809)

Stevens, Anthony, *Ariadne's Clue: A Guide to the Symbols of Humankind* (Penguin, 1998)

Stevens, Charles, Arthur Jean & Stevens Joan, *Jersey Place Names* (Société Jersiaise, 1986)

Stevens, Joan, *Jersey in Granite* (Royal Trust Company of Canada, 1977)

Straffon, Cheryl, *The Earth Goddess* (Blandford, 1997)

Streep, Peg, *Sanctuaries of the Goddess: The Secret Landscapes and Objects* (Bulfinch, 1994)

Sullivan, Danny, *Ley Lines* (Piatkus, 1999)

Syvret, Margeurite & Stevens, Joan, *Balleine's History of Jersey* (Phillimore, 1981)

Thorpe, Lewis (trans.), Geoffrey of Monmouth, *The History of the Kings of Britain* (Penguin, 1966)

Toms, Carel, *Times Past in Guernsey, Alderney, Sark and Herm* (The Guernsey Press, 1985)

Trees in Jersey (Jersey Association of the Men of the Trees, 1997)

Uttley, John, *The Story of the Channel Islands* (Faber, 1966)

Valiente, Doreen, *An ABC of Witchcraft Past and Present* (Hale, 1984)

Well, James A., *The Nature of Jersey* (Amanuensis Books, 1989)

Whitlock, Ralph, *In Search of Lost Gods* (Phaidon Press, 1979)

Wolley, Freda, *Guernsey Legends* (The Guernsey Press, 1986)

Wood, John Edwin, *Sun, Moon & Standing Stones* (Oxford University Press, 1978)

Wooton, Patrick Alwen, *Lihou: The Holy Island* (The Guernsey Press, *c.* 1965)

Wunderlich, H.G., *The Secret of Crete* (Souvenir Press, 1974)

Yearsley, Macleod, *The Folklore of Fairy Tales* (Watts, 1924)

Index